Camelot and the Vision of Albion

BOOKS BY

GEOFFREY ASHE

King Arthur's Avalon
Land to the West
Gandhi
The Quest for Arthur's Britain
King Arthur in Fact and Legend
Camelot and the Vision of Albion

CAMELOT AND
THE VISION OF ALBION

Geoffrey Ashe

ST. MARTIN'S PRESS
NEW YORK

AFFILIATED PUBLISHERS:
Macmillan & Company, Limited, London—
also at Bombay, Calcutta, Madras and Melbourne —
The Macmillan Company of Canada, Limited, Toronto

CONTENTS

Prologue: Unanswered Questions   1

Part One: The Making of a Myth

  1 An Atlantic Realm   19
  2 The Age of the Druids   39
  3 The Irrepressible Celt   56
  4 A Prince of the Fifth Century   70
  5 The British Myth   94

Part Two: The Glory and the Enemy

  6 *Plus ça Change* . . .   109
  7 The Anatomy of Compulsion   120
  8 The Undercurrent   134

Part Three: The Succession

  9 Albion in Transition   147
 10 The Immortal City   168
 11 The Dissentient Radicals   186
Epilogue: The Return of Arthur   210
Bibliographical Note   221
Index   223

Prologue

Unanswered Questions

1

The hill, of course, is far more than a hill. It is a presence, an enchantment, a challenge; and it eludes, though not for ever. When we first met, Cadbury Castle and myself, I walked three-quarters of the way round under its earthwork defences, wondering where there was a path that went up. At last I found a path and it went up. But this hill, which has so long maintained its claim to be Camelot, has subtler gestures of evasion.

If you stand on its crest, looking out from the ghostly walls of King Arthur's palace, you can see Glastonbury Tor rising far away above Avalon like a misplaced Mexican pyramid. Yet if you traverse the space between and stand on the Tor, looking back over the same Somerset levels, Cadbury Castle will escape you. It is there, but from that angle it blends expertly into the hills behind it. To start out from Camelot to Avalon – the way, perhaps, of Arthur's passing – is no more than following your eye. To start out from Avalon to Camelot – the way (one presumes) of his return – is an act of faith. Going in that direction, you will only see Cadbury Castle clear in front of you at the end of a long zigzag through country that tells you nothing.

And when you arrive, the Cadbury people may tell you something else. According to a local report, King Arthur has been there all along in any case. He may indeed have gone to the Somerset Avalon for burial, or to a remoter isle of the same name for healing and immortality. But then again, he may lie in a cave in Cadbury hill itself, sleeping under the roots of his buried city: a cave housing a hoard of treasure, closed in by gates of wrought iron or gold.

I

Cadbury, in fact, splits up the legend of its own hero with ambiguities. That is its quality. It presents images that do not always cohere. Even its weather can be discontinuous. An observer on the hilltop in sun or cloud is apt to see quite different weather rolling in from the distance, or sweeping across the nearby lowland from which the murmur of humanity floats up to him. Where Glastonbury is weird with a weirdness that is still single, Cadbury is fragmented. One aspect of it does not lead smoothly into another.

Its ancient ramparts are huge and daunting, yet the centuries have blurred them with a dense growth of trees that defeats the entire logic of the citadel. I have reconnoitred this hill with one of the ablest photographers in England, and he could not photograph it. All he ever got was unmeaning disconnected detail, a tree, a bank, a stretch of grass. Cadbury Castle can be taken in as a whole from the air, and from vantage-points on neighbouring hills. Otherwise, visually, it frustrates. Yet it also fascinates. At night I caught it once in silhouette from a road, and it retorted by sprouting an impossible floodlit tower on top – a half-moon, as I soon realized, climbing in the dark sky behind.

Its montage of themes and shapes is disjointed, dissociated, a vast anagram. The letters of the anagram glide beautifully before you and can be enjoyed for their own sake. To decipher the message, you must reach out and handle them yourself. The hill communicates, but it communicates coolly. Even if you accept that it really is Camelot, you must still decide for yourself what you mean by that.

2

The questions which it raises go far outside, like the questions raised by Glastonbury, its more fiercely magical companion. To a large extent they are facets of the same multiple problem. But behind all the tricks of vision, the camouflage, the concealing mists that come and go, there is a stubborn, solid reality.

South Cadbury Castle, to give the place its full name, is a hillfort of the Iron Age before the Roman conquest. Its ditches were dug and its banks heaped up by the Celtic people popularly lumped together as Ancient Britons, who (it may be as well to stress at once) were not blue-painted savages, and did not build Stonehenge.

There has never been a castle here, in the medieval architectural sense. The hill is an isolated mass of limestone five hundred feet high, near the Somerset-Dorset border. Human labour has surrounded it with four defensive perimeters, one inside and above another, beginning near the base. The banks and ditches are now much flattened by crumbling and silting, but in places they remain formidable. They slope at an average angle of thirty-five degrees to the horizontal, and sometimes much more. The thick overgrowth of trees extends most of the way up, for fully half the way round. Paths run through along the ditches, though not reliably. In spring these woods are colourful with bluebells and primroses. At night they are opaquely disturbing. This is a Tolkien forest rather than a Malory forest. Nettles abound; the normally-accompanying dock-leaf does not.

The modern path leads up from South Cadbury village at the north-east of the hill. It climbs steeply through breaks in the ramparts, and leads out into the enclosed eighteen acres of grass which cover the top. The path can confuse visitors by being murderously difficult after a shower yet safe after a downpour, because light rain makes the mud slippery, whereas heavy rain washes it downhill and uncovers the stones underneath. Access was formerly by another path at the opposite point, now poorly defined, which comes up from Sutton Montis and enters through a wider gap. There are traces of a third entrance on the east.

The huge enclosure on top, where the ancient inhabitants lived, is by no means flat. It goes on rising above the highest and innermost rampart, to a summit ridge. A plateau stretches along the ridge: the western portion of it was called 'King Arthur's Palace' long before anyone dug it up to see. From here you have the best view of Glastonbury Tor, twelve miles away north-west over central Somerset. If you turn and walk to the rampart in the other direction, you can look down into the valley where South Cadbury lies, and across it to an arc of hills that spread off into Dorset.

Before the Roman Conquest, Cadbury's people belonged to the same cultural realm as the famous Glastonbury lake villages. Their stronghold abutted on the lands of the Durotriges, and they may have been part of that Celtic tribe themselves. No one knows what they called their hill. The name 'Cadbury' occurs elsewhere, within Somerset and outside. The 'bury' is Saxon. The 'Cad' may be Saxon or it may not. There was a Celtic word *cad* meaning 'battle',

3

and we come across personal names beginning with it, such as Cadwallader. A hero named Cadwy figures in the lore of the West Country. He is even mentioned as a joint ruler with Arthur, though in a different part of Somerset, and he may be the original of a 'Duke Cador' in Arthurian legend. Is Cadbury 'Cadwy's fort'? But if so, it must have had an older name too.

Within easy walking distance is the river Cam, with the village of Queen Camel beside it. The 'Queen' was added in the Middle Ages, for much the same reason as the 'Regis' was added to Bognor. Previously the village was simply Camel. The first known linkage of those evocative syllables with Cadbury Castle is in the *Itinerary* of John Leland, an author attached to the court of Henry VIII. Leland travelled widely through England noting down what he saw and heard, and in 1542 he had this to say, in his rather erratic spelling:

> At South Cadbyri standith Camallate, sumtyme a famose toun or castelle. The people can tell nothing thar but that they have hard say that Arture much resortid to Camalat.

The most interesting thing about Leland is his matter-of-fact curtness. He does not discuss whether the hill-fort beside the village is or is not Camelot. That is its name, and there is no more to be said. For him the question is how much anybody still knows about it. As he indicates, his gleanings on the spot were meagre. It seems that he heard of a silver horseshoe being found, and of Roman coins turned up by the plough, in the fields below and on top also. The villagers used to carry off 'dusky blew stone' which was not the predominant substance of the hill.

Other antiquarian writers copied from Leland. In 1724 William Stukeley made the further statement that the hill bore traces of Roman occupation – pavements, hypocausts, the ruins of arches, with camp utensils and slingstones. But Stukeley is somewhat less than reliable. He is one of the major culprits, for instance, in the growth of fantasy round Stonehenge. Whatever may have been visible in his own time, nothing Roman was showing above ground by the end of the nineteenth century, when archaeologists began to take note. If the Roman lore of the hill remained hazy for them, so did the Arthurian lore. The local legend of Arthur's cave, almost certainly dating from far back, was still potent. When one archaeological party toured the Castle, an old man anxiously asked

4

them if they had come to dig up the King. But neither he nor any-body knew where the cave was.

In the 1880s the rector of South Cadbury actually tried digging, in search of evidences of habitation. He happened to uncover what looked like a flagstone. The instant reaction of the workman helping him was that they had found the entrance to Arthur's cave. Unfortunately, the lifting of the big flat slab disclosed nothing under it but another big flat slab.

To this day, folk of the neighbourhood will come to you with suggestions as to where the cave is, or where it used to be, since it may have got silted up. There are patches of soft earth, where a stick can be thrust in for several feet without hitting anything that stops it. Indeed the cave story is only one aspect of a belief, geologically credible, that the hill is not solid all the way through, but contains pockets of hollowness. At two places in its defensive ditches, water is found. King Arthur's Well is on the left of the path from South Cadbury, Queen Anne's Well is a long way round to the right. Allegedly, if you slam down a cover on the mouth of either of these, a listener at the other can hear. (I know of only one actual attempt to do this; it was unsuccessful.)

Of course the legends of Camelot include ghosts. On St John's Eve at midsummer – or perhaps at Christmas – the ground rings with hoofbeats as Arthur and his knights ride down the older track, to water their horses in Sutton Montis. More substantial, possibly, are the dead of Camlann, Arthur's last battle, where he and Modred fell. The Somerset Cam is one of the conjectured scenes of this battle. In a field near the west side of Cadbury Castle, farm labourers once unearthed a number of skeletons, lying together in close and careless disorder as if the corpses had been bundled into a mass grave.

Bones, however, seldom come to us labelled. Until lately the only clear historical fact belonged to yet another phase of the British past. From about A.D. 1010 to 1016, in the reign of Ethelred the Unready, Cadbury was the site of an Anglo-Saxon mint. This could be inferred from the existence of coins naming it as their place of origin. A well-preserved specimen has the King's head on one side, with the inscription EDELREDREXANGLORU.X, 'Ethelred king of the English', and on the other a small ornamental device with the inscription GODONCADANBYRIM, construed as meaning that the royal coiner signed himself 'God at Cadbury':

a mint mark which must surely have inspired confidence in the currency. Ethelred's purpose in resettling this out-of-the-way citadel was doubtless to keep his mint from the clutches of Danish raiders. But the stronger Canute who reigned afterwards had other ideas. The Cadbury coinage peters out.

The first proper excavation was done on a small scale in 1913 by St George Gray, best known for his work on the Glastonbury lake villages. At Cadbury he found stone implements, the remains of a piece of wall, and pottery and other things which reminded him of his Glastonbury material, and might be assigned to the last years before the Roman conquest. Nothing turned up to connect the place with Arthur. Arthur flourished, if he did flourish, round about A.D. 500, between the Roman withdrawal from Britain and the final Anglo-Saxon advance. In other words he belongs to the British dark age. (Archaeologists today are rightly rebelling against that phrase, but no alternative has yet been agreed on.)

It was only in the 1950s that the Camelot claim began to be taken seriously, outside the neighbourhood, by more than a handful of enthusiasts. A large area of the hilltop had been ploughed. Rain washed the loosened earth downhill, as it had been doing for centuries on and off, and the topsoil left behind was shallow and jumbled. Over it there presently strolled two Somerset archaeologists, Mrs Mary Harfield and Mr J. Stevens Cox, not once but many times. Mrs Harfield in particular liked to take her dog Caesar there for walks. While Caesar wandered, she prodded the soil with an umbrella, and patiently collected a medley of objects that came to light. Among the finds of this period were bits of dark-age pottery – imported ware, of a kind already known at Tintagel – which supported the belief that some British noble had lived there at the right time to be Arthur.

Gradually the mists of legend began to solidify into a more sober, but more interesting reality. To discuss whether this hill-fort 'was' Camelot, as more were now willing to do, required a careful understanding as to what such an identification would mean.

It could not mean that a splendid city lay concealed under the grass, complete with Round Table, tilting-ground, and knights in armour. Camelot in that sense is an invention of the romancers who worked up the Arthurian Legend in the Middle Ages. Chrétien de Troyes may have been the first to mention it, somewhere about 1170. In the ensuing three centuries of story-telling the city flits

6

about England, usually in the south, occasionally in the north. The location at Winchester which we find in Malory is far from unanimous, and even Malory does not stick to it. Camelot strictly so-called, the Camelot of romance, has lost touch with history and geography. It is a symbol, conjuring up a golden age in chivalric terms.

But Cadbury Castle could have been the original Camelot in another sense, as the real Arthur's headquarters. This would, mean, roughly, that it was reoccupied and perhaps refortified by a great British leader of the dark age; by a warrior known to posterity as Arthur, who gained the victories over the Saxon invader which (as most historians think) were the nucleus of the Legend.

With the dawn of that cloudy possibility during the late 1950s, the issue of excavation arose in earnest. The Camelot Research Committee was formed in 1965. Some purists jibbed at its name as prejudging the case. But the long-standing tradition – noted by the Ordnance Survey – was enough to justify it, whether or not the excavation turned out in favour. Careful warnings accompanied the Committee's first public announcements, as in *The Guardian* of 28 May 1966, which contained the admonition: 'Any suggestion that we are going to dig up a nice round wooden table, or the Holy Grail, is pure nonsense.'

Whatever might emerge at the dark-age level, it was certain that the hill had a vast amount to tell about other periods. Thus the project could appeal to archaeologists and the lay public alike. With Sir Mortimer Wheeler as President, Dr Ralegh Radford as Chairman, and Mr Leslie Alcock as Director of Excavations, the Committee, in the summer of 1966, began digging.

3

As for me, I was secretary.

I am not an archaeologist. According to my archaeological colleagues, our five seasons of excavation do suggest that Cadbury Castle may be Camelot as defined. All honour to them. It is for them, not me, to interpret that result in detail, together with a great many more. I cannot write the Book of the Dig, and this is not it. Still, anyone who has been so close has the right to try a personal stocktaking. Mine is an outcome not only of the project itself, but of much more that has led up to it and accompanied it, over the past quarter-century.

When I say 'personal' I stress the word. My reflections are not routine supplementary remarks, such as the Committee's only non-archaeological officer might have been expected to add. They are strictly my own; I hardly suppose that anybody else would reflect in just this way or in just this order. But out of them, I would like to hope, something of more than personal interest may come.

The question which for me has hung over it all is: why?

Where did so much enthusiasm spring from? Every public allusion to the Cadbury project brought in inquiries, contributions, orders for literature, offers to help – dozens, hundreds of them, from both sides of the Atlantic. Cadbury Castle is far from easy to climb, yet during each six-week season of excavation, over five thousand visitors climbed it. They not only toiled up the muddy path and up the slope to the summit, they trudged bravely all over the enclosure, necessitating a permanent guide service. Thousands of excavation reports were sold to them, and also by mail. Thousands of pounds streamed in from a variety of sources. This went on happening although it was clear at an early stage that while some of the finds were indeed Arthurian, most were not.

From the start, admittedly, there was always enough dark-age stuff to evoke the spell. But why the spell anyhow – not only for natives of Britain, but for Americans and others? Why is there a ready-made public, young and old, for the cycle of legend which the Middle Ages called 'the Matter of Britain': for Arthurian fiction, for non-fiction, for Broadway musicals? Why do the authors of Arthurian books receive so many readers' letters? Why is Glastonbury so disturbingly magical that most of those who touch it seem to go mad? Why the persistent feeling that that Arthurian shrine will be the scene of some vivid rebirth – a feeling which once inspired a Glastonbury Festival supported by Shaw, G. K. Chesterton and Laurence Housman, and today attracts the junior mystics of post-hippiedom? Why the persistent feeling that the prophecy of the return of Arthur himself – his awakening in the cave, or his homecoming from Avalon – has a valid, if uncertain, meaning? Why do intelligent people still keep speculating about the whereabouts of the Holy Grail (and even, alas, finding it)?

The spell is a fact. It has proved itself in terms of hard cash, hard work, and immense consequent benefits to the archaeology of Britain. To call it a load of rubbish, a waste of time, is not to exorcize it but to make it a more intriguing riddle. The reasons for the power of the Arthurian Legend are not at all obvious. Not when we find that it can dispense with its heraldic splendours, move into the archaeologists' underworld of post-holes and dirty pottery chips and crude tumbledown walls, and still be powerful. One of the most amazing things about the Cadbury dig was that so few visitors expressed any disappointment at what they saw.

For myself, the fascination was borne in upon me long before these excavations. Yet I have no remembrance of being much enthralled, as a child, by the stock romance of 'King Arthur and his Knights'. A few images linger, such as a coloured picture of Sir Galahad kneeling before the Grail. But I also recall a story in a boys' weekly about a time-machine, where the inventor suggested going back to find out if there really was a King Arthur, and with this I recall that his proposition didn't excite me in the least. Likewise I recollect reading a fair amount of Tennyson and Malory, as a student; and the impression which this memory carries with it is an impression of *not* being hooked.

The legends never worked alone. What did finally begin to engage me was the attitude of one or two modern authors who took the legends seriously without taking them literally, and considered what lay behind them. Glastonbury was the first Arthurian theme to take hold. I am almost sure that it reached me through Chesterton's *Short History of England*, about 1945. As for the problem of the post-Roman dark age and the historical Arthur, it started to attract me about 1948 when I read *The Battle for Britain in the Fifth Century*. This book was written by Trelawney Dayrell Reed, a friend of Augustus John's whose creative spirit employed a different medium.

Neither Chesterton nor Reed can be reckoned among historians in the formal sense. Perhaps ungratefully, I have left them out of the bibliographies of my own books. Yet the approach I am describing, under the stimulus of minds that overlapped art and poetry as well as scholarship, was more fruitful than a purely academic approach could ever have been. One of the lessons of open-minded research is that there is a wrongness which leads to rightness more effectively than rightness itself. Schliemann, who found

Troy because he believed in the literal truth of Homer, illustrates
that ironic truth with a force which the years have not diminished;
and, with all respect to exact scholars and professional archaeologists, I think some of them know quite well that the Cadbury
project would not have started when it did, if it had been left to
them.

Whatever the case may be with others, I would probably never
have been drawn to the Matter of Britain by exact scholarship,
whether of the archaeological sort (which had not gone far at the
time I am speaking of) or the literary (which then studied the
legends without looking behind them) or the historical (which
usually preferred to leave the dark age extremely dark). Nor was I
a nostalgic retreater into the past. I read H. G. Wells long before I
read Malory or Tennyson, I was aware of Gandhi long before I was
aware of Arthur.

The best way of putting it is that the Matter of Britain began
coming to life for me when it began fitting in with one of my few
settled certainties. I think I must call this patriotism, however un-
fashionable the word may be. It never had anything to do with the
loyalist patriotism of my parents, the spirit of 1914, so to speak. I
was and am unexcited by the Union Jack and stately homes and the
triumphs of British capitalism. As for the Empire, my first distinct
thought about it was that Britain would never go right till it was
got rid of. A long time ago I lost any inclination to contend
strongly that Britain – or more precisely, England – was better
than other countries, and ceased to feel that it was even a relevant
question whether I liked living there. Whatever it was that I cared
about might lie below the surface of English reality, might be at
odds with its officially revered aspects, but was none the less absolute for me. From about the age of twenty I have known, quite
simply, that I could not live anywhere else.

In retrospect it is hard to be sure about such things; but my
belief is that the Matter of Britain, when it captured me at last,
did so because of a dimly perceived harmony with this conviction.
King Arthur's supposed realm with its royalty, pageantry, wealth,
and so forth, failed to inspire me in itself. So did the England of my
schooldays, with its jubilee of George V and its coronation of
George VI. The Matter of Britain first appealed when it acquired a
new dimension, when I first saw it as national in a profounder, more
authentic sense. Behind its familiar surface I began to detect a

mysterious offbeat quality, a transfiguring Otherness, far down in its almost hidden depths. Seemingly the real Arthur was not a king at all, and his story hinted at events which defied the history textbooks, yet must surely have had some intense validity or the Legend would never have taken shape . . . That is not so much an argument as an attempt to reconstitute a feeling. Chesterton – whose own style of patriotism affected mine – felt the same, much earlier. So did another poet, Charles Williams, and his friend C. S. Lewis, whose novel *That Hideous Strength* has a similar theme.

I started exploring the mysteries in earnest because of Glastonbury. My motive in attacking that perilous topic was not to re-tell the story of something dead and finished, but to re-awaken something that was, to me, manifestly alive, though suspended: a dormant power.

The place persuaded me of its magic without explaining it. My hope after that could be summed up as the restoration of Glastonbury with all it implied. I would find out what it did imply as I went along. Solution in practice, the *solvitur ambulando* technique, has always come naturally to me. Some of my early interpretations leaned too far to the Christian side, and laid too much stress on Glastonbury Abbey. That part of it is important but insufficient. Any rebirth must be a larger and subtler event than any purely ecclesiastical measure like rebuilding the Abbey. The trail from Glastonbury through its hero Arthur, and onward, has turned out to wind in many directions.

A unifying phrase which seems helpful is 'collective mystique'. The Arthurian enchantment in all its forms can be so described. But so can other myths, hero-cults, and mass obsessions. It was by a logical if roundabout progress that I found myself led back to some of my earlier admirations, such as Gandhi, a national hero who was the focus of a collective mystique in the twentieth century.

But the results of writing books, first on the Matter of Britain and then on topics not part of it, reinforced my impression about the former. The power of this particular theme prompted me to produce books about it; the response to the books was further proof of its power. I refer, not to sales, but to readers' letters. Arthurian topics brought them to me plentifully, others did not. There was indeed a ready-made public for the Matter of Britain, with positive ideas and interests. I was touching a nerve. The eruption of zeal over Cadbury only confirmed what my overstuffed file of correspondence had been attesting for years.

After the opening phases of excavation, a belief grew that I could now state a little better what the whole business was about. In the course of contributing to a book entitled *The Quest for Arthur's Britain*, published in 1968, I felt able to write this:

> To live with the Arthurian theme for long is to feel that the prophecy of Arthur's Return means something, though it may be hard to say what. An answer, possibly, has now begun to take shape. As the exploration of national roots goes on, there are signs in Britain of a new disposition to ask, 'What are we, how did we come to be so, where are we meant to go from here?' Inquiry in depth is injecting a fresh element into the national scene, an element of reappraisal. From this a new and acceptable patriotism, a new sense of national vocation may surely come. The quest for Arthur's Britain cannot be the only factor in such a renewal, but it can be – indeed, it already is – a stimulus. One day we may discover that the Fact has been more truly potent than the Legend, and that King Arthur has returned, after all, by abdication.

It was imprecise, it was potentially dangerous. One could hardly forget the loathsome nationalist myths of the Hitler era. Yet it was not so very remote from what I concluded the career of Gandhi had been partly about, not only for his own country but for another. To quote myself again:

> Because of him Britain learned as important a lesson as any country has ever learnt. It was not a lesson given entirely from outside, but one that Britain evolved out of her own better conscience, which unwittingly made Gandhi its agent . . . After 1930 the better conscience spoke up again . . . In response to Gandhi Britain resigned a world mission which had outlived whatever rightness it had, and turned back to a humbler and saner quest for self-realization. The quest has yet to reach its term, but the movement is no longer the wrong way.

Always I had been sure that Avalon and Camelot looked forwards as well as backwards. They were keys. The real problem was to identify the locks. With the Cadbury project finished, I believe the results can help us to think along the right lines. We can inquire more hopefully into the nature of the Arthurian spell. Furthermore, we can go on to a deeper understanding of collective mystiques, British and otherwise; we can build a bridge from mythology to contemporary fact, pass from shadows to truth, and – perhaps – apply our conclusions.

4

The first of all the lessons of the Somerset Camelot is that we can only see Arthur in correct focus by seeing a great deal more. Romantic visitors during the digging were sometimes distressed by the fact that many diggers took little interest in him, or in his period. This distress was not confined to visitors. There were romantic volunteer helpers too, who had come for the dark age only, and wrote off the finds from other periods with contemptuous malediction.

In the early stage, while never sharing their resentment, I was close enough to their state of mind to sympathize. But readjustment came swiftly. It was soon manifest that the broad spread of interest among the diggers was entirely proper, even in Arthurian terms. The logic of their discoveries guided me (and ought to have guided everyone) towards a truer perspective. The brilliant season of 1967, which established Cadbury as the citadel of an 'Arthur-type figure', also established that his presence was simply a chapter in a long story. Cadbury Castle is a British Troy. Human settlement stretches from Neolithic to medieval times. Some layers are far richer and more informative than the dark-age layer. Yet they are not unrelated to it.

Archaeology lends an odd, backhanded credit to that outrageous person Geoffrey of Monmouth. The legend of King Arthur took literary shape when it did because of the wildly inventive *History of the Kings of Britain* which Geoffrey concocted in the 1130s. The nature of this *History* is often forgotten, because most of the subsequent romancers confined their attention to King Arthur himself, with his supposed contemporaries and near-contemporaries. But Geoffrey makes him only the most splendid in a long line of British monarchs, which descends from 'Brutus' well before 1000 B.C., and maintains continuity even through Roman times.

Some other bits of the *History* did find their way into literature: King Lear and Cymbeline are the major instances. However, the millennial sweep of the fancied British kingdom was lost. Geoffrey is remembered now almost solely for his inflated Arthur. Which is unfair. While he will never regain his lost prestige as an historian, he has an intuitive sense of the way Arthur should be looked at. If the romancers had drawn on him more widely and less selectively, their modern devotees might have less trouble adjusting themselves to the realities of Cadbury. They would be predisposed to take an interest in thousands of years instead of a few decades.

This ghostly rightness of Geoffrey of Monmouth leads on to the more profound rightness of a greater genius. It would be claiming too much for William Blake to say that he absorbed Geoffrey's rightness without his wrongness. But he came nearer to doing so than anyone else. In 1809 he published a Descriptive Catalogue containing notes for an exhibition of his own paintings. One of these was entitled 'The Ancient Britons'. In the notes to this, he introduced Arthur and also a symbolic figure, the giant Albion, whose name is the ancient name of Britain. With two oracular sentences, Blake places Arthur against a background of oceanic antiquity:

> The giant Albion, was Patriarch of the Atlantic; he is the Atlas of the Greeks, one of those the Greeks called Titans. The stories of Arthur are the acts of Albion, applied to a Prince of the fifth century.

That saying haunted me long before the Cadbury project. It was plainly a deep prophetic utterance, yet hard to invest with a precise meaning. But now, knowing more of Arthur than Blake did, we have reached a point where we can test it as a serious clue. Dozens of commentators have toiled to elucidate Blake, and show how he built up his weird, disquieting, difficult mythology, with its feet of Christ walking on England's mountains, its transplanted Jerusalem, its Druids and giants. But the Arthurian unfolding has opened the way to a traffic in the reverse direction. A great poet and myth-maker may surely elucidate other poetry and myth. My impression, pursuing that line of thought, has been that through Blake's intuitions a whole series of themes can be seen to link up illuminatingly with the mystique of Camelot.

This book, I must repeat, is not the Book of the Dig, though it includes enough about the results to supply an informal introduction. Besides not being the Book of the Dig, it is not a scholarly treatise on prehistory, anthropology, or mythology. Specialists in those fields, if any read it, will doubtless find plenty to complain of. I do not care very much. This is a meditation or quest, a pursuit of topics which Cadbury points towards. It is my own small *Golden*

Bough. Its success or failure will be its success or failure in accounting for the Arthurian spell; in defining an acceptable meaning for such motifs as 'the return of Arthur'; in showing how these stubborn data of the imagination can be related to the life of society, past and present.

The thread running through the first part of the inquiry is this. What images of past Britain does Cadbury evoke? Can we detect among them – as Blake would imply we can – some sort of archetype or motif underlying the stories of Arthur; some sense in which the stories appear as a superimposition of older, deeper-seated patterns on a Christian British chief of the dark age? Is Arthur the shadow of a veritable Albion? And if so, does it explain his spell, and do we go anywhere from there?

The archaeologists and historians have been speaking for some time. Now let the poets speak as well. I have mentioned a few whom we shall not lose sight of. Here is a passage where one of them, Chesterton, salutes another. I propose it as a motto for much that follows:

> There is something personal about England . . . I will not be so daring as to define what William Blake meant by The Giant Albion; but we may agree that if the country called by poets Albion could be conceived as a single figure, it would be a giant . . . Perhaps if we were caught up by that eagle that whirled away [Chaucer] to the gates of The House of Fame, we might begin to see spread out beneath us titanic outlines of such a prehistoric or primordial Anak or Adam, with our native hills for his bones and our native forests for his beard; and see for an instant a single figure outlined against the sea and a great face staring at the sky.

PART ONE

The Making of a Myth

I

An Atlantic Realm

1

Cadbury's generations of hill-dwellers looked out over a changing landscape. To the north-west in particular, a speeded-up film would show patches of bluish water spreading and shrinking in the middle distance, and vegetation varying with it. When Arthur flourished, the 'Isle of Avalon', surmounted by Glastonbury Tor, sometimes actually was an island or nearly so. There had been a time previously when all the surrounding country was dry and forested, and a time before that when the same country was totally submerged. During the Roman heyday and the Arthurian age it was neither. It lay under shifting complexities of river and lagoon and marshland, with a sea-route leading up from the Bristol Channel, and wide variations from tide to tide, season to season, and year to year. In succeeding centuries, the marshes dried up enough each summer for neighbouring peasants to bring their animals down from the high ground for pasture; hence, according to one view, the name 'Somerset' – the place of the summer people. Later still, the Glastonbury monks and their tenants carried out reclamation schemes. But even in the eighteenth century a lake covered the Meare district.

It is against a background of crumbling shores, doubtful paths, fickle islands, and spectral marshlights, that much of the Arthur lore must be seen. Not that it is all based on Somerset; but Somerset exemplifies an aspect of early Britain and near-by lands, which impressed itself on legend as well as life.

Well within the career of *Homo sapiens* in the shape we know, the present British archipelago was part of the European land-mass.

A river with an estuary close to Norway traversed what is now the bed of the North Sea. Another flowed into the Atlantic from what is now the bed of the English Channel. In the course of ages the ocean encroached. Ireland and the Scottish isles became separate. The two huge rivers spread wider. But human beings had already entered this region, and they went on exploring it. They settled the plateau that became the Dogger Bank. They crossed the future Channel on foot. For a long time Britain remained joined to the mainland by an isthmus at the Straits of Dover, which did not break till after 6000 B.C. Many centuries later, when parts of Asia were civilized, it was still far easier to cross into Britain than Julius Caesar was to find it.

The creeping change did not halt because human tribes were multiplying. The Dogger Bank disappeared under the surface, with the implements of its stone-age settlers. So, after 1500 B.C., did the inhabited floor of Mount's Bay in Cornwall. The single 'Isle of Scilly' mentioned by a Roman writer split up into the present cluster, with human works on the sea-bottom between them. The collapse of Dunwich is (geologically speaking) a thing of yesterday. Here and there, the land has counter-attacked, with or without men's aid. Glastonbury is no longer hemmed in by lakes, nor is Ely.

Some of the senior legendary themes of these islands are rooted in the instability of the map and the ubiquity of water. Such are the stories of sunken regions like Tristram's Lyonesse, the Lost Cantref in Wales, and the vanished land between Wales and Ireland, which is mentioned in the *Mabinogion*. The Druids of Roman Gaul had traditions of immigration from 'outlying islands' overwhelmed by the sea, and the British-descended Bretons have their lost city of Ker-Is. Besides these stories of outright inundations – which are unlike most of the Deluge legends, because the water stays where it is and never recedes – there are proliferating fantasies of minor islands that come and go, mysterious voyages, communities cut off by the ocean. The tales of the Irish are more imaginatively spacious than those of the Britons, but the same motifs occur in both countries. They are apt to carry with them a sense of loss or estrangement – of ancient glories swallowed up; of separation by alien watery barriers; of unearthly sunset partings. The Passing of Arthur in Malory and Tennyson has a long, long ancestry.

Over those widening watercourses and the ridges and swamps, a whole series of peoples wandered into early Britain.' Scattered colonies of cavemen were supplanted by Neolithic tribes late in the fourth millennium B.C. They domesticated animals, tilled the earth, made pottery, and mined flint for farm tools and weapons. They lived in 'camps' on high ground, avoiding the dense forest and heavy soil below. More than a thousand years later, implements of copper and then bronze came into Britain with fresh invasions from the Netherlands and the Rhineland. For much more than another thousand years, the British Bronze Age continued.

Cadbury Castle began its career as an inhabited place about 3000 B.C., when the Somerset lowland was less waterlogged. This first, Neolithic occupation lasted perhaps a full millennium. But its traces on the summit plateau, like the traces of other periods, are difficult to sort out.

Over the plateau, and for some way down the slope, an endless washing of soil downhill has left only a shallow layer of earth between the turf and the limestone bedrock. All the relics of occupation are mixed up together, on much the same level. The bedrock itself is heavily marked. As an archaeologist has observed, few things are harder to destroy than a hole in the ground. Wherever some early Cadbury-dweller scooped out a socket for a post supporting a house-wall or fence, and packed the post round to hold it upright, the hole in the bedrock has remained with its filling, even though the post has rotted away. When the topsoil is removed, you see a tell-tale patch of different colour and texture from the yellowish-brown rock. By finding patterns of post-holes, foundation trenches, and so forth, the plans of vanished buildings can be recovered. But here, where dozens of generations have lived, the bedrock is a palimpsest and the plans overlap each other in daunting confusion.

Larger discoloured patches reveal storage pits. The people on the hill would scoop out a pit to hold (for example) grain, in a wicker basket. After long use the basket would become foul. It would then be burnt and replaced. But beyond a certain point the fouling would preclude further use of the hole, which became a cesspit or rubbish dump. Centuries of habitation have produced the same result as the centuries of building: innumerable pits in the rock. The grass, today, covers a wilderness of dustbins. Their

21

contents have the same sort of interest as a modern dustbin has for a market-research investigator. They contain the debris of household goods, tools, bones, and the rest of the impedimenta of living.

The Neolithic settlers were perhaps few at any one time, and did not leave much behind. Still, fragments of early pottery, flint arrow-heads, and polished stone axes, taken in conjunction with pottery and flints of a later type, prove a long presence. Remains of a human skull were found, and traces of primitive agriculture, and of a rough building or enclosure. While the ramparts encircling the hill are later work, a stratum of clay and stones over Neolithic oddments at the base of the top rampart may indicate a low bank on the boundary of the Neolithic camp.

After this remote occupation comes a gap. The next finds on the hill give a glimpse of a Britain around and after 1000 B.C., where the Bronze Age has long since replaced the Stone Age. Again the settlement seems thin. But it must have been a settlement, even if it was only a single farm. Ploughing occurred, and pottery and loom-weights are objects which roaming hunters would have been unlikely to drop. Knives, a razor, a spear-head, a piece of a bucket, are products of late Bronze Age workmanship. So is a little bronze pin with a double-spiral head like a ram's horns. The design is oriental, with parallels in Mediterranean lands during the ninth and eighth centuries B.C.

2

Whether or not anybody was living at Cadbury between the first known occupation and the second, this dimly visible scene of stone-workers followed by bronze-workers delimits a Britain that already has definite Arthurian bearings. It underlies one of the strangest legends in Geoffrey of Monmouth, his narrative of Stonehenge.

According to Geoffrey's *History*, the fifth-century British king Aurelius Ambrosius decided to raise a monument on Salisbury Plain over the graves of some British nobles murdered by Saxons. He consulted the wizard Merlin, who proposed to bring over a circle of standing stones from a hill in Ireland. The circle was called the Giants' Ring, or Dance, and was built of stones imported from Africa by giants who once lived in the British Isles. Merlin sailed to

Ireland with a party of Britons led by Uther, Aurelius's brother (afterwards the father of Arthur). The wizard dismantled the circle by his magic; the stones were loaded on ships and conveyed to Britain. There Merlin plied his arts again to re-erect them over the nobles' graves in the same pattern. The site was used later for the burial of Aurelius, Uther, and Arthur's successor Constantine. 'Stonehenge,' Geoffrey explains, is the English name for this monument.

Like much else that has been written about Stonehenge, this is nearly pure fantasy . . . but not quite. The British Isles of the stone-bronze overlap harboured secrets that still escape us. Between 2500 and 2000 B.C. the megalith-builders were arriving. They were a trading people from the Mediterranean. Their local cultures stretched back through Brittany and Iberia to Malta, Gozo, and Libya. Apart from trade, the chief bond among the megalith-builders seems to have been a religious one: a cult of the Mother Goddess who reigned also in Crete and farther east, though in the Crete of the high Minoan era she grew into a far more sophisticated deity. Closely related to this they had a cult of the dead. They put up standing stones, and piled immense mounds, hundreds of feet long, over small but elaborate passage-graves.

Stonehenge itself is not a temple of these original megalith-builders but of a more martial stock, who adopted some megalithic techniques, but added cults and practices of their own. Most of Stonehenge was built for Wessex chieftains who must have had substantial resources. Salisbury Plain was then the main centre of population in Britain. The bluestones of the older and smaller circle were transported all the way from Prescelly in Pembrokeshire, doubtless by sea up the Bristol Channel.

As Professor Atkinson has observed, Geoffrey of Monmouth not only speaks of the stones as brought by sea, he has them come from the right direction. Seemingly a tradition may have been handed down through three thousand years and attached (falsely) to Merlin.

The taller sarsen stones, with their implication of great engineering skill, were hauled overland from the Marlborough area – it is presumed, on rollers. The 'Stonehenge IIIa' which they compose is unique among northern megalithic monuments. Its stones are carefully dressed over their entire surface, and the structure is truly architectural. Objects found in the neighbourhood, and a carving on one of the stones, show that there were trade relations (direct or indirect) between Wessex and the civilization of the Aegean in the fifteenth century B.C., the Bronze Age civilization of Mycenae, deriving from Minoan Crete. At one stage it was suggested that the builders of Stonehenge IIIa employed Greek technicians. A review of carbon-datings appears to have ruled this out. While Stonehenge was certainly flourishing in the Bronze Age, it is earlier than Mycenae. Parts of it are contemporary with the first Cadbury settlement. Britain must have developed advanced skills without Mycenean aid.

In spite of all the nonsense about Stonehenge, the instinct that first scented a mystery in it was sound. The hardy theory of a Druid temple was broached in detail by William Stukeley in 1740. The role of that notion in the mythology of Blake will emerge in due course. More recently Dr Gerald S. Hawkins has interpreted Stonehenge as an astronomical computer. Certainly it hints at celestial observations, views on the gods, and technological expertise, which would have commanded the respect of a Greek; especially when the whole concentric edifice was still towering intact over the heads of visitors.

A likelihood exists (and, as we shall see, is relevant) that rumours of Britain and its temple did trickle through to that Aegean society where the stuff of classical mythology was being prepared. But Britain afterwards receded from sight, and survived in Greek consciousness, if at all, as a legend only. The commerce dwindled away, the high Aegean culture declined. For several centuries the Phoenicians and their Carthaginian kinsfolk monopolized westward seafaring. Britain had to be rediscovered and connected with the Mediterranean for a second time.

3

Cadbury Castle leads us backward from Arthur into a British past reaching far behind him. Yet this past is physically linked with him and his legend in the mosaic of the hill's bedrock. The linkage is in keeping, not only with Geoffrey's tale of Stonehenge, but also with Blake's cryptic statement about the stories of Arthur reflecting the acts of Albion, who was Patriarch of the Atlantic, otherwise Atlas and one of those whom the Greeks called Titans. If his statement has any factual meaning, it means that Arthurian legend stands in a long continuity. It has been shaped by things immensely older.

Seen thus, Arthur's hauntingness may begin to awaken echoes. We might suspect that it is like the hauntingness of the classical myths, amply attested by Freud and Jung and unnumbered poets. Could Arthur's story actually be such a myth, transposed and disguised, but traceable to the same matrix – the Minoan-Mycenean world with which Britain was temporarily in contact? It is not like any classical myth that comes to mind readily. Blake himself, however, plainly had ideas on the subject. The contents of his poetic Albion are too vast to unpack all at once. But the bare definition of his terms, in this one passage on Arthur, will carry us a surprising distance.

To begin with, 'Albion' is the oldest recorded name for the island of Britain. The Greek explorer Pytheas quite probably knew it, about 330 B.C. Even before him, there is a Carthaginian captain's report which refers (if a later paraphrase can be trusted) to 'the island of the Albiones'. A text ascribed to Pytheas's contemporary Aristotle, though in fact somewhat later, speaks of the two large 'Bretannic' islands in the outer ocean, Albion and Ierne. Ierne of course is Ireland. Afterwards 'Britannia' moves gradually into favour as a name for the bigger of the two. The meaning of 'Albion' is unknown; the etymology that looks to the word *albus*, 'white', with an allusion to the cliffs of Dover, is unconvincing.

Geoffrey of Monmouth makes it an early name for Britain, and no more. So does Blake in his early verse. After a while, however, he introduces the giant Albion as a symbol looming ever more tremendous and complex. The giant is not Blake's invention. He has a pedigree, which goes back through Milton and the Tudor chronicler Holinshed. For both of these Albion is a person, in the same equivocal sense as the characters of Greek myth. What Blake catches hold of, drifting down to him through a series of minds under mixed influences, is the idea of a primordial Atlantic world including Britain under its old name – a name derived from someone called Albion. He thinks of this Atlantic world as an abode of the colossi known to Greek myth as Titans, and makes Albion one of them.

Blake's England was much addicted to antiquarian guesswork. The question is whether this particular notion could be anything more. Who in fact were the Titans, and how did the Greeks think of them? Did mythology locate any of them – Atlas, for instance – in the direction of Britain? If so, was Greek imagination merely projecting its own dreams, or was it working on an acquaintance (however remote, however confused) with the real Britain and its people and cults? Is there any sign of an ancient 'Albion' with whom Arthur can be significantly connected?

The Titans were the gods of a supplanted order. When Hellenic tribes conquered Greece during the second millennium B.C., inaugurating the greatness of Mycenae and other cities, they brought in their sky-god Zeus (the same as the Roman Jupiter) and his celestial court. The deities of the conquered people suffered various fates. An important group centred on Cronus, whom the Romans were to equate with the Italian god Saturn. These were the Titans. When the victors' myth-makers had sorted out what we now know as Greek mythology – a long process, involved with further invasions and social changes – the Titans survived in it as objects of a curious love-hate, relegated to hazy distances on the edge of the world.

They were the offspring of Heaven and Earth. Cronus had formerly ruled all things; this ancient supremacy of his was never denied, even by his overthrowers. Cronus's divine relatives included Hyperion, the first sun-god, and Iapetus, together with Atlas, Prometheus and Epimetheus, usually said to have been Iapetus's sons. Through Prometheus and his own son Deucalion, who survived the Flood, Iapetus is the ancestor of mankind. Ocean, dwelling outside the rim of the inhabited land-mass and pouring his waters round it, was also a Titan. Cronus's consort Rhea was a form of the Great Goddess venerated in Minoan Crete. At the Minoan capital, Cnossus, she shared a temple with the rest of the Titans. The Goddess, however, had many cults and guises. In megalithic Gozo she presented herself as Calypso, Atlas's daughter. Aphrodite, another of her forms, was born – according to the earliest version – out of sea-foam during this Titan era. Even Athene may have originally been an aspect of the Goddess.

Cronus was portrayed holding a huge sickle or scimitar, with which he had castrated his father. Also, he was said to have been worshipped with human sacrifice, and to have devoured most of his children for fear of their dethroning him. Under that sinister aspect, the Greeks thought, he might be the same as the Phoenician

Moloch, to whom the children of Syria and Israel were offered up. Certainly a host of giants, Cyclopes, and other monstrous half-human beings, belonged to Cronus's vanished scheme of things.

Imaginatively speaking at least, the Titan world was the world of the megalith-builders and the societies that immediately followed them. It receded into dim centuries before the advent of Zeus's worshippers, and these expressed their awe at the works of their predecessors with tales of beings who were not as themselves. 'Cyclopean architecture' is a recognized term. Likewise, in the Arthurian context, we have Geoffrey's tale of Stonehenge as the Giants', Ring; and the stones are brought in the first place from Africa, where some of the early megalith-builders flourished. The Hebrews told stories of the Nephilim, Anakim and Rephaim, partly to account for the city-architecture of Canaan. (*Genesis* vi: 4; *Numbers* xiii: 28, 32–33; *Deuteronomy* ii: 20–21, iii: 11. Moffatt translates 'Rephaim' as 'Titans', though with an implication of stature rather than deity.) Also of course the Hebrews had their long-lived patriarchs before the Flood. One of the latter was Noah's youngest son Japheth, who survived the Flood and helped to repopulate the earth. He was actually the same person as the Titan Iapetus. His descendants in *Genesis* x: 2–5 are – roughly – the nations known to the early Greeks, and supposed by them to be Iapetus's progeny.

But there was more to these Titans and giants than their anarchic, sometimes horrible energy. The Zeus-worshippers never regarded their own god's gradual triumph as glorious, a casting of Lucifer from Heaven. It was less clear-cut. They identified their Zeus with a Cretan god, Rhea's son by Cronus, and told how he had eluded attempts to kill him. Zeus finally ousted Cronus in a ten-year war, assumed cosmic authority, and shared it among his own brothers and near relations. After Zeus himself, the chief figure of the new Olympian pantheon was his brother the sea-god Poseidon, the Romans' Neptune. Under their regime Cronus kept a few temples. But he dwindled into a patron deity of slaves – the conquered and dispossessed earlier people? – and an absentee deity at that. All the Titans with their allies had gone into banishment or bondage, some underground (the Cyclopes in the bowels of Etna), some on the borders of the inhabited world, and some of the greatest among the latter in the remote west. Here we may begin to suspect that Blake knew what he was talking about.

Atlas, who had commanded the Titans' army against Zeus, was condemned to stand in Morocco disguised as a mountain, holding up the sky on his shoulder; though he retained some sort of jurisdiction over the nearby tract of Ocean, which therefore kept the name Atlantic.

Cronus himself was believed to live farther away still with his court-in-exile, a divine Old Pretender over the water. The early form of the story, told in Hesiod's *Theogony*, places his enforced home in a sunless gulf beyond Atlas, recalling the Cimmerians' country which Homer puts somewhere outside Gibraltar. Much later, Greek geographers use the name 'Cronian Sea' for the dark and icy northern Atlantic. But in course of time the myth-makers relented. They moved the deposed king to brighter regions, and allowed him a consolation kingdom preserved from the shipwreck of his dominions. This was in a warm paradise away to the westward, also spoken of by Homer: in a fruitful Isle of the Blest, or on the sunlit plain of Elysium where there was no rain or snow, and a few favoured heroes enjoyed a carefree immortality denied to the rest of mankind. In Elysium lived red-haired Rhadamanthus, brother of Minos of Crete, where Cronus's family had been worshipped.

Purely Greek myth does not take us much farther. Its Titans are best summed up (I revert again to the surprising insights of Chesterton, who wrote acutely on such topics) as *the gods before the gods*. This is a weighty, widespread, yet elusive concept. It often happens – not only in Greece – that the gods now reigning over the world are thought of as successors, even usurpers, like Zeus. Sometimes it also happens that the present gods are inferior. The gods-before-the-gods are associated with a lost age of happiness in a distant past. And so it is with the Titans. They loom in the shadows as violent, amoral colossi. Yet in literature they acquire a halo.

Hesiod's poem *The Works and Days* sketches five ages of the world. These are the ages of gold, silver, and bronze; the age of heroes; and the age of iron, which is ours. There is an overall though irregular decline. The last three have a factual basis which archaeology admits. Hesiod's silver age, apparently matriarchal, was ignorant and godless but fairly peaceful. It was ended by Zeus, who made a clean sweep of its society and started afresh. Farther back again stretched the golden age . . . and this was the time when

Cronus reigned. Strictly speaking, the time when he reigned un-
challenged, because his final ousting did not come till after the
advent of bronze.

The golden age was an epoch of idyllic equality. Men lived
effortlessly on the fruits of the earth. They laughed and danced
and never grew old. Death had no terrors for them. They thought
of it as merely falling asleep; with an assurance, one gathers, of
waking up. Certainly their spirits still linger on earth as rustic
genii, givers of good luck, and unseen champions of justice. Iron
Age humanity under Zeus is far baser.

Greeks generally concurred with Hesiod. 'Life under Cronus'
was proverbial for a happy time. The same sense of loss through the
change of gods, rather than progress, appears in the Prometheus
myth. Prometheus (his name means 'forethought') was the one
Titan who realized that Zeus was the coming god, and went over to
him. Besides helping Zeus into power, he helped mankind. According to Aeschylus it was he who kept alive the hopes – admittedly 'blind' hopes – which, for a while, still held the fear of death
at bay. He was the culture-hero and 'lover of men' who brought
fire to earth. Precisely for this, Zeus banished him to the Caucasus
and chained him to a rock for perpetual torture. The rising cosmic
despot also gave the woman Pandora to Prometheus's brother
Epimetheus. By opening the notorious box, she unleashed most
of the evils that plague humanity.

When Roman mythology digested Greek, and equated Cronus
with its own Saturn, it developed the same nostalgia for a vanished
Saturnian kingdom. The benign aura gathering round the arch-
Titan was doubtless a reason for the shift in his Atlantic exile from
the gloomy sub-arctic to a kindly Fortunate Isle farther south.

3

Cronus's sunset realm, and the westerly location of Atlas, both
point to another topic which explorers of British legend are apt to
find in their path. The obsessive notion of lost Atlantis, the Island
of Atlas, has a spell resembling Arthur's. Blake brings Atlantis also
into his symbolism, and implies that they are connected: not
directly, but through his Atlas-Albion and the Titan motif. Before
we can close in on Albion we must decide whether Atlantis really
does fit into any intelligible picture.

As such, it is a literary invention. Its inventor was Plato, who, like Geoffrey of Monmouth, obscures the nature of the materials he works with. His account of Atlantis is in the linked philosophical dialogues *Timaeus* and *Critias*. It purports to be based on a tradition learnt by the Athenian lawgiver Solon from an Egyptian priest, about 564 B.C. according to one calculation. There are two items of outside evidence that Solon did hear some such tradition, but none at all as to what it was before Plato took it up.

Nine thousand years ago, the Egyptian priest is alleged to have said, a huge island lay in the Ocean outside Gibraltar. It was as big as Libya and Asia – that is, Asia Minor – put together. From it you could reach other islands, and pass by way of them to 'the opposite continent encircling the Ocean'. Long before, when the gods divided up the world, Poseidon had received the main island. He begot ten sons on a mortal wife. The oldest was Atlas. The island and the nearby part of the Ocean were named after him. (This of course must have happened before Zeus and his brethren took sole command. Atlas's sky-upholding servitude still lay in the future. Plato, either altering family relationships like other mythographers, or adopting a change made by someone else, turns him from a cousin of Poseidon into a son.)

Atlantis became the centre of a 'great and wonderful empire', ruling over the neighbouring islands, parts of the trans-Atlantic continent, Europe as far as Italy, and Africa as far as the border of Egypt. It was governed by a confederacy of regional kings descended from Poseidon's sons. The line of Atlas was paramount. Atlantis had a mild climate, with two harvests a year, and abundant natural wealth. The nobles used gold and silver in quantity, decorating their palaces with golden statues. They had hot baths. Copper and tin were employed, and the copper alloy called orichalc, but not iron. In a fertile plain, the agricultural heart of the country, stood a citadel of circular form, with concentric channels round it where ships could dock. Within the citadel was Poseidon's temple. Bulls were sacrificed there.

After many generations of peaceful grandeur, the divine spark in the Atlantean dynasties faded away. The rulers became 'tainted with unrighteous ambition'. At the time which Solon's informant spoke of, 'nine thousand years ago', their armies pushed forward to attack Egypt and Greece. Zeus, mentioned here for the first time, resolved to punish them. Though most of their opponents collapsed, the newly founded republic of Athens defeated the invasion. Her warriors freed Atlantis's subjects in Europe and Libya. Then came a day of worldwide earthquake and flood. The Athenian army disappeared into the ground. Atlantis itself sank under the waves. Its place is marked by shoals, blocking the passage across the Ocean.

Plato's main purpose in this fable was to point a moral. *Timaeus* and *Critias* are sequels to his *Republic*, and he pretends that ancient Athens more or less realized his own Utopia. The Egyptian priest says to Solon: 'There formerly dwelt in your land the fairest and noblest race of men that ever lived, and you and your whole city are descended from a small seed or remnant of them which survived. . . . The city which now is Athens was first in war and in every way the best governed of all cities.' With much more, in both dialogues, about its ideal constitution. The message is that whereas empires decay, city-states have superior moral force, and a power of self-regeneration. Athens beat Atlantis; and the 'remnant', in course of time, created the revived Athens of Solon and Plato, which repeated the triumph by beating Persia.

Few of Plato's Greek commentators took Atlantis literally. The theory of Ignatius Donnelly and his followers, who have claimed that the lost land existed as described and that the Azores prove it, is a modern, geologically hopeless aberration. Yet the Platonic amalgam is not conjured out of a total void. If we emend the absurd 'nine thousand years' to 'nine hundred', some of the factors begin to be recognizable, and to link up with the rest of Atlas's world.

Atlantis has an advanced Bronze Age society. Its baths, bull sacrifices, and other features, suggest Minoan Crete. At the end of the affair Zeus is supreme over gods and men, as, during the last Minoan phase, he was – on the Greek mainland anyhow. Accounts of Crete might well have been handed down by Egyptian priests, and improved on by Greeks. Egypt knew the Minoan Cretans as the Keftiu. Plato's story has several touches hinting that he tapped a confused tradition of Minoan expansion and ensuing Mediterranean upheavals during the later Bronze Age; and the cataclysm may incorporate memories of natural disasters that struck Cnossus and the Minoan outpost of Thera (Santorin) during the fifteenth century B.C. – though the scale of these disasters has been disputed.

Today the Cretan theory is perhaps prevalent. The riddle, however, is why Plato or his source should have transferred the fallen empire to a remote west. Because Atlas was already there? But why bring him in at all? Plato's behaviour is the more intriguing because, while the Cretan case is strong on some grounds, there are also grounds for looking elsewhere.

No argument will remove the fact that Plato, who knew perfectly well where Crete was, places Atlantis in the Ocean outside Gibraltar. He may have got the direction wrong, but the difference between 'inside' and 'outside' the Mediterranean is surely fundamental. Furthermore it is outside, not inside, that we find the sort of legends we need as source material – stories of permanent inundations, as distinct from passing deluges. We find the stories, and, as we have seen, a basis for them. The Dogger Bank, the Straits of Dover, Mount's Bay, and so forth, supply better 'Atlantises' than the Mediterranean, and folk-memories of such encroachments have been preserved. The Aegean trade with Britain in the Minoan-Mycenean era, the breaking off of contact, the likely speculations and travellers' tales about a huge island in the outer Ocean which nobody heard of any more, and parts of which had been swallowed up by water – these considerations point to Britain rather than Crete.

We have one case-history of the way in which Greek fancy did romanticize Britain. Little doubt exists that Britain is the 'Hyperborean' land spoken of by Hecataeus of Abdera in the fourth century B.C.

Opposite to the coast of Celtic Gaul there is an island in the Ocean, not smaller than Sicily, lying to the north – which is inhabited by the Hyperboreans, who are so named because they dwell beyond the North Wind. This island is of a happy temperature, rich in soil and fruitful in everything, yielding its produce twice in the year . . . The inhabitants venerate Apollo more than any other god . . .

In this island, there is a magnificent precinct of Apollo, and a remarkable temple, of a round form, adorned with many consecrated gifts. There is also a city, sacred to the same God, most of the inhabitants of which are harpers, who continually play upon their harps in the temple . . . The Hyperboreans use a peculiar dialect, and have a remarkable attachment to the Greeks, especially to the Athenians and the Delians, deducing their friendship from remote periods. It is related that some Greeks formerly visited the Hyperboreans, with whom they left consecrated gifts of great value, and also that in ancient times Abaris, coming from the Hyperboreans into Greece, renewed their family intercourse with the Delians.

It is also said that in this island the moon appears very near to the earth, that certain eminences of a terrestrial form are plainly seen in it, that Apollo visits the island once in a course of nineteen years, in which period the stars complete their revolutions . . . The supreme authority in that city and the sacred precincts is vested in those who are called Boreadae, being the descendants of Boreas, and their governments have been uninterruptedly transmitted in that line.

Hecataeus's astronomical data have been cited in the debate on the Stonehenge computer theory. Whether or not he is thinking of Stonehenge, his 'round temple' and the double harvest, divinely-descended rulers, and so forth, all have an Atlantean air.

One further feature of Atlantis favours Britain against Crete. This is Plato's strangely pointless reference to islands beyond, forming a route to a continent across the Ocean. They have no bearing on his myth. Yet if we do invoke Britain as a source, they could embody some piece of seafaring hearsay about the northern route to America, the Viking route. A voyager can indeed go from Britain by way of islands beyond – the Orkneys, Shetlands, Faeroes, Iceland, Greenland – to the New World. As we shall see, this idea is less far-fetched than it sounds. The northern route, whether known or conjectured, does appear elsewhere in Greek literature.

Atlantis need not be a dilemma. A myth-making process can blend separated lands together into a single country of the imagination. We do not have to choose between Crete and Britain. Plato's artistry was fully capable of fusing them into a new creation, and this, in essence, is what he seems to have done. But we can do better. Both islands can be seen as parts of one thing, a common source of motifs trickling down from the second millennium B.C. To a certain extent the trade-routes united Bronze Age Britain with the Bronze Age Aegean. To a certain extent also, Crete and Britain were extremities of a network of cultures which was none other than the Titan world.

The linkage is chiefly through the megalithic societies that can be traced from the central Mediterranean to the British Isles, and shade into the Bronze Age at Stonehenge. They reveal a cultic kinship which has led one authority to speak of 'the realm of the Great Goddess'. The same Mother who becomes Cronus's wife in Crete, and Atlas's daughter in Gozo, has her temples and dedicated tombs in numerous other places including Britain. Clover-leaf and cellular precincts, symbolic of her womb, are found in Malta and northern Africa and Ireland. In the passage-graves under such mounds as those at Morbihan in Brittany, Newgrange in Ireland, her dead tranquilly awaited rebirth.

What society corresponded to her cults, in the Mediterranean and Iberia and Brittany and Cornwall, we know only sketchily. Yet Hesiod's golden-age people who had no fear of death, and his silver-age people who lived under their mothers' control and did not sacrifice to gods, may well be hints at her regime. Nor can we say precisely how she fitted in with the rest of the Titans. There are no particulars of the Cretan temple which, as Rhea, she shared with them. But they all belong to the same substratum of European civilization. The bond between the Aegean and Ocean regions in the person of the Titan Atlas is more than a fiction; and the Goddess, in one of her ever-shifting aspects, is Atlas's daughter.

Cronus too is a bond, with his oceanic Elysium. Atlantis is not the same place. It shows, however, the same gravitational pull, attracting motifs to a western centre, the abode of the Titans' exiled chief. Seen as an imaginative synthesis of the Titan world, combining Crete and Britain, Atlantis gilds reminiscences of both with the glow of the Cronian golden age, when its empire (presumably) was founded. Its earlier rulers, says Plato, 'were obedient to the laws, and well-affectioned towards the god, whose seed they were; for they possessed true and in every way great spirits, uniting gentleness with wisdom. . . . They despised everything but virtue.' Their wealth seemed only a burden to them.

Nor should we neglect, as most readers do, the Athenian side of the story. Athene's young city-state shows similar golden qualities even when Atlantis is careering downhill. There is a sort of equivalence between the fall of Atlantis and the fall of the Titans, Atlas being common to both. The first, like the second, is an act of Zeus, who is absent from the beginning of Atlantis's history but sovereign at the end. Under his blow the empire dies, and nothing remains but those cryptic lands farther over the Ocean, with access barred. Athens too is plunged into a dark age by the loss of her finest citizens in the moment of victory.

Psychologically this lost glory remains the chief content of Atlantis. Speculative writers from Donnelly onward have located all the Edens of mythology there, and credited their real Atlantis with a real master-civilization, of which Egypt, Mexico and Peru were mere offshoots. A single theory is made to embrace every major culture within credible range. They are all said to have been constructed out of salvage from the wreck of the same ship. By a highly charged logic, the continent drowned in sunset waters becomes symbolic of lost innocence, of a pristine and godlike human nature submerged by corruption.

To the Greeks, the Titans' fall seems to have been final. There is no clear notion that Cronus can ever hope to regain power. Aeschylus wrote a play portraying Zeus releasing some of his prisoners, and allowing Prometheus to be unbound. The latter event is related to an obscure prophecy about Zeus's own fall. But this never happens. So far as one can infer from the surviving fragments of text, Prometheus's unbinding is part of a pact that leaves Zeus in charge. It is not followed, as in Shelley's drama on the same theme, by an apocalypse. For astrologers Saturn is a sad planet associated with defeat.

5

The Britain that built Stonehenge belongs chronologically to the world of Titans and giants; and the legends amount to a fair case for a kind of spiritual membership. Albion in his mists could have been a Titan, lord of an Atlantic realm, whether or not he was Atlas under a different name. Behind Blake we can detect a prescientific consciousness of these things among English writers. Notions hover in the air prompted by Geoffrey of Monmouth. Speaking of the island of Albion in his *History*, Geoffrey says it was once peopled by a race of giants, like those who built Stonehenge on its Irish site. They died out, and settlers from fallen Troy moved in, led by Brutus. The Trojans drove the remnant of giants into caves in the mountains. The island was re-named Britain after Brutus. He fathered a line of kings, and the descendants of his Trojans became the Britons.

Albion as a person does not appear in Geoffrey. He is introduced by later authors to account for the pre-Trojan giants, and he has a most peculiar history. It begins not in Britain but in Provence, between Marseilles and Arles. Early Greek colonists noticed the Plaine de la Crau, a level area strewn with boulders. They explained its odd look by adding to the saga of Hercules. His tenth labour was to fetch the cattle of Geryon from an island off the coast of Spain. On the way home (it came to be related) his party was attacked by

Ligurians living around the mouth of the Rhône. The Greeks' arrows ran out. Hercules prayed to his father Zeus, who sent a shower of stones. Aeschylus alludes to this battle in *Prometheus Unbound*. Subsequent authors add details on the Ligurians' two leaders. They were sons of Poseidon, and one was named Ialebion or Alebion or – according to a single, dubious reading – Albion.

The curtain now falls for a long interval, and rises again on Elizabethan England. Raphael Holinshed, in his *Chronicle* which Shakespeare studied, makes the inevitable connection between legend and geography. After the Flood, he tells us, the land now called Britain was ruled by a dynasty descended from Japheth. Then 'Albion the giant', son of Neptune (Holinshed uses the Roman name), came from the Mediterranean with a company of his own giant race, descended from Noah's second son Ham. Albion conquered the island and gave his name to it. After a long reign he went over to Gaul to help his brother in the fight against Hercules, and was killed. The giants continued in the island for six centuries. In the end they became few, and gave the Trojans no trouble.

Spenser in *The Faerie Queene* (IV. xi. 16) makes out Albion to be, in some unexplained manner, an ancestor of the Britons. Perhaps the largest Trojans intermarried with the smallest giants. Albion himself remains colossal. He appears among the sea-gods and heroes at the wedding of Thames and Medway:

> Mightie Albion, father of the bold
> And warlike people, which the Britaine Islands hold.
> For Albion the sonne of Neptune was,
> Who for the proofe of his great puissance,
> Out of his Albion did on dry-foot pas
> Into old Gall, that now is cleeped France,
> To fight with Hercules, that did advance
> To vanquish all the world with matchlesse might,
> And there his mortall part by great mischance
> Was slaine: but that which is th' immortall spright
> Lives still: and to this feast with Neptunes seed was dight.

Milton sums up the Holinshed version in his own *History of Britain*. He scorns its dependence on 'late surmises', but he does give it.

The giant Albion in Blake seems to have begun as a conflation of Holinshed and Plato. Albion is allegedly Poseidon's son, and so is the Platonic Atlas . . . therefore Blake equates them. To make this guess, however, is no more than to disclose where an extraordinary myth-maker may have found raw material and a hint. Once the combined figure took shape in Blake's mind, it acquired a life of its own. He was clear that Albion-Atlas must belong to the primordial world before Zeus's rise to power. That being so, the parentage and exploits ascribed to him could and should be dropped, as false rationalizations by a later age. Quite fairly; such things have often happened. Thus Aphrodite, who actually came into the world before Zeus, was turned by Zeus-dominated afterthoughts into his daughter. Hesiod, the authority for her real birth, similarly implies that Poseidon's 'son' Atlas was, in origin, senior. Anyhow Blake wanted him to be so, and made him so, thereby establishing Britain in his mythology both as a Titanic domain and as a piece or aspect of the Atlantean empire.

But was it all just an academic-poetic game? We have arrived, independently, at an ancient Britain which some classical minds may have connected vaguely with Titans, may have romanticized into a kingdom of Atlas, may have invested with primeval Cronian glories. Britain is at least in the right general direction from Greece; the principal gods-before-the-gods did get planted in this sector of the world's rim. Tenuous links may be starting to appear between early Britain, Geoffrey's giants, Blake's Albion. But we have yet to unearth evidence that there is more here than fancy. Are there any signs that people in Britain, during the pre-Christian centuries, actually had a god or hero who could be identified with a male Titan? If so, can we trace any tradition of this Albion-figure, moulding the Arthur of legend?

Suppose, for instance, that a well-defined deity was worshipped at Stonehenge. Reports of his unique shrine might have drifted along the trade routes, coupled with a suggestion that he was the same as Atlas. Similar essays in would-be comparative mythology certainly occur later, as Greek knowledge reaches out into Asia. Gods as far off as India are equated with gods of Greece. Indians, we are informed, worship Zeus and Dionysus – meaning Indra and Siva. Was there, at the world's opposite end, a native god beside the Ocean whom Greeks saw as a Titan, and in whom we might discern something of what Blake's Albion is meant to express?

The pre-Roman remains at Cadbury put us in contact with a Britain where, if ever, he flourished and his memory lingered. In

37

sifting them further, we must ask whether the physical continuities under the topsoil are matched by continuities of tradition; whether the legendary Arthur does indeed look like a projection of some far earlier Albion. If he does, then a fresh clue to his spell may presently emerge.

2

The Age of the Druids

1

The break in communications which reduced Britain, in Greek eyes, to a ghost or a void, was due partly to events ushering in the Iron Age. Homer's heroes succumbed to cruder Dorian invaders with iron weapons. Barbarism engulfed Greece for several centuries. Meanwhile, Phoenicians and Carthaginians were the only civilized Mediterranean-dwellers who knew the outer ocean. They may have sailed to Cornwall for tin. But most of their maritime effort was directed into warmer zones. To deter rivals they spread reports (based on the Sargasso Sea and portions of the African coast) that navigation outside Gibraltar was difficult and dangerous. The shoals said to mark the site of Atlantis probably reflect rumours of this kind.

Western contacts were resumed by the nascent civilization of classical Hellas about 600 B.C., when Greek colonists founded Massilia, i.e. Marseilles. However, there was no rediscovery of Britain till the voyage of Pytheas more than two hundred years later.

In the meantime, Britain also had entered the Iron Age. The metal came in with new invaders whom it is permissible to call Celts. Celtic pioneers – enterprising, land-hungry peasants – settled in southern England during the eighth century B.C. Further waves followed them. It was the Celts who built the British hill-forts. The forts vary in size, but are all spacious, with enclosures ranging from six to eighty acres; Cadbury's eighteen is about normal. Today only grass-covered banks and ditches are visible. When the forts were occupied, there was liable to be an unmortared stone wall running round the topmost bank, with a timber

39

stockade. These earthwork 'castles' were not merely strongholds for an emergency, they were places of residence for dozens of families. The amount of labour that went into them was immense. They imply a disunited, warlike society, and also a fierce determination to live.

During the fourth century B.C., equipped by now with iron, the Celtic world was rising toward a zenith. Celts overspread not only Britain and Ireland but a large part of the continent, where most of them belonged to the stock known as Gauls. A Gaulish army sacked Rome in 390. Gauls took over the whole of what is now France and gave their name to it. So many planted themselves in northern Italy that the Romans called it Cisalpine Gaul. Related tribes dominated half Germany and Central Europe. They raided Greece, and seized part of Asia Minor, whence the name 'Galatia', the Gauls' Country.

Gaul itself from the third century B.C. onward was divided, not into Caesar's 'three parts', but into far more; and Britain likewise. Each tribe had its patch of living space and its chieftain, with nobility, priests and bards, and internal subdivisions. Phases of inter-tribal unity gave way to phases of conflict. The main wealth was agricultural – ploughland, flocks, herds. The Celts everywhere were hearty eaters, boiling pork in huge cauldrons, and drinking beer and mead. They lived in houses of wood or wattle-and-daub, using stone mainly for fortification.

Their characteristic culture was the La Tène type, a trading culture resulting from contact with the urban folk of Provence and Italy. Amber, furs, forest products and slaves flowed southward. Metal goods, wine and, more important, ideas and crafts went north. The La Tène culture possessed good wheelwrights, and fast horse-drawn chariots; its metal workers were skilful and imaginative; it originated Celtic art, with its genius for linear abstract design.

This culture was brought to Britain in the third century B.C. by Celts who crossed over from Armorican Gaul. It flourished (probably over older foundations) at the two Glastonbury lake villages of Godney and Meare, a few miles from Cadbury Castle. They were built on artificial islands, heaped up as places of safety. Godney grew to an irregular polygon of three acres. On the bed of the lagoon which then covered the district, logs were laid, cemented with clay, and held in by vertical piles. Access was along a causeway, with a drawbridge at the village gate. Inside were more than sixty wattle huts. Most were thatched and circular, ten to twenty feet across. The villagers paddled over the water in dugout canoes, fishing and fowling, and raised livestock on neighbouring dry ground. They used bronze for household items, such as needles and pins, and iron for tools, such as saws and sickles. Carpenters worked expertly with a kind of lathe. Potters made handsome bowls, patiently and slowly, without the wheel. Their terracotta ware was decorated with linear patterns. Traces of adornment and games – brooches, beads, dice – reveal a certain polish and leisure, and the proofs of overseas trade are incontestable.

Julius Caesar in 55 B.C. reconnoitred a Britain where these western centres were still prosperous, but where the centre of gravity had been shifted by a last Celtic infusion. The Belgae had overrun the Thames valley and the south-east, and set up a king-dom. Cunobelinus, whose capital was at Colchester, is the Cym-beline of Geoffrey of Monmouth and Shakespeare. He reigned from A.D. 9 to 42. By now several of the British tribes were issuing coinage imitated from Mediterranean models. This was the Britain which produced Caractacus and Boudicca, or Boadicea. Such Celtic rulers, in Britain and Gaul, now depended to some extent on a system of election, and on councils of elders. But they had not learnt to co-operate with each other.

The Roman conquest was begun by the Emperor Claudius in A.D. 43. After his return to Rome, most of the fighting fell to the Second Legion under Vespasian. According to Suetonius he marched westward, fought thirty battles, and took twenty towns – in other words, hill-forts. Cadbury Castle was one of them. The Durotriges who held Dorset may or may not have been in posses-sion of it. At any rate, Vespasian took it by storm about the year 44, and for more than three centuries it lay within the imperial frontier.

2

On all of Cadbury's career as an Iron Age citadel, excavation has shed a rewarding light. Archaeologically, this turned out to be the richest phase.

The transition to the pre-Roman Iron Age in Britain began toward 500 B.C., after the earliest Celtic immigrations. At Cadbury nothing shows where one metallurgical era stops and the next starts. No abrupt change or break marks the transition. The first Iron

Age inhabitants, if they were different at all, carried on in much the same style as their precursors. They may have adopted features of house design, notably the circular form.

Their goods, especially the remains of pottery, attest a growing population down to Vespasian's conquest, with no further interruptions. The many storage pits provided plentiful hauls, with objects that could often be dated by comparison with similar finds from the hill-fort of Maiden Castle in Dorset. Cadbury's earliest Iron Age pottery may belong to the sixth century B.C. It is coarse, but decorations made on the rims by the potters' finger-tips show that aesthetic feeling was not absent. Later comes far finer ware of Glastonbury lake-village type, with cross-hatched and curvilinear ornaments. The same period has yielded bronze pins and a corroded piece of a scabbard. In the final phase, just before the conquest, the Cadbury-dwellers were using jars thrown on the potter's wheel – as the Glastonbury ware is not – as well as spinning and weaving apparatus, querns, brooches, and Durotrigian coins.

The Britons' preparations for Vespasian's assault left some traces. Iron tools were found close to the topmost rampart, and stores of unexpended slingstones. All this effort was in vain. The last British pottery of all is heavily marked by fire – mute evidence, in all probability, of Roman sacking of the fort.

This Cadbury hill-top settlement must, in its later phases, have been fairly populous. In the bedrock there are many post-holes of various dates, and ring-shaped trenches, the foundations and drainage ditches of circular houses at least thirty feet across. Near some of them on the eastern part of the summit plateau, a plot of ground was uncovered containing hearths and fireplaces. Among these were scattered iron swords, daggers, scabbard fittings, and bronze shield bosses, one with an elaborate three-dimensional decoration. Here the armourers may have had their workshop.

A small oblong building, toward the west end of the same plateau, seems to have been a shrine. It is defined by several big post-holes marking a rectangle fifteen feet by twelve. Around it, in pits, complete skulls of oxen and horses came to light, carefully and deliberately laid in place – surely ritual offerings. Eastward, near the hypothetical workshop, there are foundations of a more sophisticated temple of the early first century A.D. This is also rectangular, with an outer vestibule and an inner sanctuary. Further animal bones nearby may be the remains of sacrificial victims.

The hill's enormous earthworks, which turned it into a 'castle', belong to this Iron Age occupation. In those days the hill was not wooded, and must have been a most formidable sight. The entrance was through the south-west gate, approached by a road coming up along the ditch and turning at a right angle to climb steeply into the fort.

By far the most interesting of the ramparts is the top one immediately surrounding the enclosure. Its whole perimeter is about 1,200 yards. When sliced through at several points, it turned out to have been rebuilt three or four times in the pre-Roman Iron Age alone – not to mention later reconstructions, of which more in due course.

The original bank, on top of the Neolithic layer, was stiffened with a mass of rubble and clay. Inside and outside were rows of posts, perhaps supporting timber fences. Beams over the top of the rubble apparently braced the structure and held it together.

Many years later, when the first rampart was silted and crumbling, a more advanced type of Celtic military engineering remodelled it. The second rampart, on top of the first, was faced with a drystone wall, expertly laid, made of slabs of imported lias. Again there were rows of posts, fitted into gaps in the stonework. Between, the main rampart was a mass of limestone blocks quarried from the hill. In due course this rampart also lost its shape, and again the hill-dwellers remodelled it. Their later work, constituting a third, a fourth, possibly a fifth rampart, is less well defined. It is clear, however, that a last attempt was made to refurbish the fortifications on the eve of the Roman attack.

Inside what is probably the last but one of their superimposed walls, a human skeleton was unearthed. A young man, short but sturdy, had been killed and buried. The body was folded up in a foetal posture, crammed into as tiny a space as possible. Priests, it seems, sacrificed this youth to the gods of the hill to obtain a blessing on the wall. They are known to have done likewise at Maiden Castle.

3

The skeleton and the temple were far apart, without visible connection, and they may not have been quite contemporary. Still, with every due warning against a stampede into madness, it is fair to count the sacrifice as a Druid sacrifice, and the temple as a Druid temple.

The word 'Druid' is thought to mean 'oak-knower' and to refer to a secret lore of trees. In Celtic Britain and Gaul (Ireland gave them a lower status) the Druids were custodians of learning, mythology, ritual, and magic. They constituted a powerful inter-tribal priesthood with judicial functions, alongside the bards and seers. It was recruited mainly from upper-class families. The neophytes were taken to secluded retreats in caves and forests, and launched on a course of instruction which could last as long as twenty years. One of their main tasks was to memorize vast quantities of oral lore in verse form. The Druids' ban on writing it down is the reason for the doubts that still envelop their cult.

Julius Caesar records a current belief that Druidism was systematized in Britain. In his own time, the more diligent Druids of Gaul went over to British colleges to study. When the Romans occupied Britain they took measures against the Druid order, as they had done already in conquered Gaul. One motive for the invasion itself may have been a suspicion that the British colleges were stirring up trouble through their continental graduates. Druidism was certainly seditious. However, a more open cause for Roman hostility was the Celtic practice of human sacrifice. Over this the Druids presided, in rough wooden shrines or gloomy forest-sanctuaries, with grotesque carved figures of gods. Victims were stabbed, shot to death with arrows, plunged head-first into water, or caged in colossal wicker images which were set alight. The Druids sacrificed animals too, as in a famous ceremony concerned with gathering mistletoe. But their ritual killing of human beings shocked the Romans, who had stopped doing it themselves, and were now champions of civilized conduct.

Together with their ugly customs, the Druids transmitted teachings of enduring interest. They had unusual astronomical learning. This is shown by an engraved plate called the Coligny Calendar, which appears to employ a nineteen-year cycle for reconciling the solar and lunar years. Hecataeus, in the passage already quoted, implies that it was known in Britain.

Druidism also taught what no other popular religion then did, west of the Levant – a positive doctrine of immortality. Greeks and Romans, oppressed by the dreary near-nothingness of their own afterlife, envied the Celts' faith. Some drew parallels with the

Pythagorean theory of reincarnation, and urged that the Druids must have been influenced by Pythagoras, or even that they influenced him, perhaps through the mysterious traveller Abaris whom Hecataeus mentions. Reincarnation does appear a few times in sagas of pagan Ireland. But it is doubtful whether the Druids of Britain ever taught it. The Celtic afterlife seems generally to have been another one like the present, though, if all went well, it would doubtless be happier. It was lived in an Otherworld – inside a hill, or on a far-away island, but still on earth. Favoured human beings might glimpse these places, and talk with the gods and mortal-immortals who peopled them. The Celts' belief was so confident that they could raise money on an IOU payable in the next life.

Lucan, the Roman epic poet of the first century A.D., addresses the Druids thus:

> You, ye Druids . . . you who dwell in deep woods in sequestered groves: your teaching is that the shades of the dead do not make their way to the silent abode of Erebus or the lightless realm of Dis below, but that the same soul animates the limbs in another sphere. If you sing of certainties, death is the centre of continuous life. Truly the peoples on whom the Pole Star looks down are happy in their error, for they are not harassed by the greatest of terrors, the fear of death. This gives the warrior his eagerness to rush upon the steel, a spirit ready to face death, and an indifference to save a life which will return.[1]

Lucan is doubtless trustworthy here. But even among classical authors there was a disposition to make too much of the Druids. They became mixed up with the 'Hyperboreans' whom Hecataeus located in Britain, a supposedly wise, happy race, living far from the Mediterranean and close observation. Like Rousseau, some Greeks and Romans yearned to discover an unspoilt country where Cronus's golden age lingered on. In the writings of a series of wishful thinkers – Polyhistor, Dio Chrysostom, Hippolytus, Diogenes Laertius – the Druids blossomed into philosopher-statesmen and masters of wisdom. This was the notion which Stukeley and his successors revived, in conjunction with the delusion that Stonehenge, and other megalithic structures, were Druid temples. It led to much wild pseudo-scholarship, and to 'bardic' eccentricities that go on to this day; also, to some of the bolder flights of Blake

[1] *Pharsalia*, I. 451–62. Translation quoted from Nora K. Chadwick, *The Druids*, pp. 53–4.

himself. When Blake went wrong about the Druids, he stood in a ready-made tradition of wrongness.

Yet it was one of those peculiar wrongnesses which should not be cavalierly dismissed. Underneath the fancies, it reflected a feeling about Britain which was, and is, inseparable from the feeling evoked by Stonehenge. The longevity of the notion that the Druids built Stonehenge, or used it, is a fact of history in itself. Again and again, people who have peered into British antiquity have felt themselves to be glimpsing something offbeat, original, eerie: a land that is in Europe yet not quite of it, with gifts and secrets of its own. Albion may be a Titan, and a citizen of the classical world, but he is also Patriarch of the Atlantic. Nor is this intuition baseless. If we have not yet found Albion at home in his own island, we have already found a Britain which is part of an oceanic realm linked with the Mediterranean yet separate. Distinctively, creatively separate. In the Bronze Age, Britain has its unparalleled temple. In the Iron Age, it has its Druid schools.

There are early witnesses for British belief in haunted offshore islands, otherworldly journeys by water, and ghostly phenomena alien to southern experience. The classical authors who glorified the Druids, as Magi with a secret wisdom, were not building on sheer illusion where Britain was concerned. Even the golden-age fantasies had a basis: the Druids' doctrine of immortality. The British schools inspired an equanimity in the face of death which Hesiod assigned to the age of Cronus alone, and which, many authorities prove, was lost afterwards in non-Celtic countries.

4

When Plato speaks of the islands beyond Atlantis, which were stepping-stones to a farther continent, he introduces a motif which can derive only from Britain if it derives from anywhere. In the Iron Age at least, the ability of Britons to look beyond their own land – not merely to Ireland, but clear across the Atlantic to the far side – can be documented. Embedded in the documentation, moreover, is the sought-for figure of the native Titan himself, the authentic Albion.

It was in 330 B.C. or thereabouts, not long after Plato wrote, that Pytheas took his ship out into the Atlantic. He was a merchant from the Greek colony of Marseilles. He sailed up to Britain and all round, and ventured farther northward still. His account of the voyage survives only in extracts quoted by authors who are none too friendly. However, some of the fragments are convincing. Among other matters he speaks of Britons as telling him about a place called Thule, which they already knew of, and as showing it to him. It appears that he may have gone there with British pilots. Thule was six days' sail from northern Britain. Its summer night lasted only two or three hours. From somewhere in it or near it, you could see the midnight sun. Around Thule the land, sea and air were mingled; a reference, one supposes, to snow and fog. A day's sail beyond, the sea was frozen.

Past interpreters of this passage have given themselves undue trouble by trying to square it with another, where, it used to be thought, Pytheas described Thule as inhabited by people who kept bees and ate oats. Scholars now admit that the report may be garbled and that the bee-keepers and oat-eaters may have lived elsewhere. Thule in fact is probably Iceland. It is located in that general quarter by every west-European writer who comes afterwards – by Pliny in the first century A.D., by the Gothic historian Jordanes in the sixth, by the Spanish bishop Isidore in the seventh, by the Irish geographer Dicuil in the ninth, by the Icelandic chronicler Ari Frode in the twelfth. The last two accept its identity with Iceland as a matter of course.

Pytheas, therefore, attests an early British awareness of land beyond Britain, along the same northern route which Plato's detail can be construed as hinting at. About A.D. 75 we get a more surprising report, coming at a time when the Romans had conquered Britain, but Celtic traditions were still accessible.

Its transmitter is Plutarch, one of the most revered of all sources for the classical world. He brings it into an imaginary conversation in Plato's manner, on 'The Face in the Moon'. This blends astronomy with mythology, and includes a debate on whether the moon is inhabited. Among the speakers is a Carthaginian named Sextius Sylla, a real person whom Plutarch consulted for antiquarian lore. Sylla tells a strange tale of expeditions from Britain to a kind of college at a shrine across the Atlantic.

The voyagers start westward from Britain – from the north or south rather than the middle, because they apparently miss Ireland – and sail for five days to an island called Ogygia. (Homer has an island so called, ruled by Atlas's daughter Calypso, but it can

hardly be the same.) In the Ogygian area, there are more islands
where the summer night is only an hour long. The voyagers go on
in the autumn across a stretch of sea somewhat over five hundred
miles wide, with drifting debris, and perhaps ice. Aided by a prevailing wind they come to a gulf in the 'great continent' on the far
side of the Ocean. Vaguely in this region are three other islands. On
one of them is the shrine.

Part of Sylla's account is credited to British informants. These
may, indeed, be responsible for the whole of it. In another dialogue
on 'The Silence of Oracles', Plutarch quotes an official named
Demetrius who went to Britain. Demetrius heard much from the
natives about outlying islands, and gods and heroes associated with
them. One passage in Sylla's account echoes him exactly, and must
be of British provenance, whatever else is not. Demetrius quotes his
Britons as follows:

> There is, they said, an island where Cronus is imprisoned with
> Briareus keeping guard over him as he sleeps; for, as they put it,
> sleep is the bond forged for Cronus. They add that around him are
> many deities, his henchmen and attendants.

Sylla, after mentioning the three islands far west of Britain, goes
on to particularize about the shrine and its god:

> The natives have a story that in one of these Cronus has been
> confined by Zeus, but that he, having a son for gaoler, is left sovereign
> lord of those islands and of the sea, which they call the Gulf of
> Cronus . . .
> The natural beauty of the isle [of Cronus] is wonderful and the
> mildness of the environing air . . . Cronus himself sleeps within a
> deep cave resting on rock which looks like gold, this sleep being
> devised for him by Zeus in place of chains. Birds fly in at the topmost
> part of the rock, and bear him ambrosia, and the whole island is
> pervaded by the fragrance shed from the rock.

Sylla goes on to describe the Titan's court, composed of spirits
who attended him in the days of his power. Cronus's 'sovereign
lordship' is cryptic. But despite being asleep, he is not a mere inert
figurehead. He dreams, and his companions interpret the dreams.

> Many are the utterances which they give forth of their own
> prophetic power, but the greatest, and those about the greatest
> issues, they announce when they return as dreams of Cronus; for the
> things which Zeus premeditates, Cronus dreams.

In his dialogue, then, Plutarch presents a figure from the

Britons' mythology whom Greek inquirers could, and did, identify with a Titan. Before asking who this 'Cronus' was, and what he implies, it is worth considering how old he may be. Is he Celtic, or did the Celts annex him? Is there any hint that he does date from megalithic or Bronze Age Britain and the Titanic era? Was he already there when the traditions took shape that went into the tale of the Titans' exile, and – possibly – Atlantis? In the known prehistory of the Indo-European peoples, nothing (Professor Stuart Piggott assures us) precludes a religious concept coming down to these Britons from very much farther back, perhaps as far back as the second millennium B.C.

The expeditions described by Sylla are said to embark when Saturn, Cronus's planet, is in Taurus. This is a rare event. The requirement suggests that the exiled god, like many others, has a 'bull' aspect and must be approached under it. His identification with Cronus may have been effected partly or wholly by way of the so-called Phoenician Cronus, a Semitic god with a bull's head, who had a temple at Tartessus in Spain. Sylla's nationality hints as much, and so do one or two other details.

It is worth noting, with extreme caution, that there was also a hazy equation between the Phoenician Cronus and the deity Talus, worshipped in Crete. Besides sometimes taking the form of a bull, Talus was a colossus, a personification of Bronze Age technology, and a sun-god.[1] Such a god would also be appropriate to Stonehenge, that colossal master-work in a Bronze Age kingdom, with a solar orientation. Mythologists of the sort who decided that Talus was Cronus (in a late and strange guise) could have extended that identification to a British god resembling him. The god's departure would then correspond to the disuse of his main temple in the Celtic era, leaving only residual cults, as with Cronus in Greece; and the Celtic motif of the mysterious island retreat would be easily assimilated to Cronus's exile.

I make no apology for insisting again on Plato's odd, pointless touch about the island route. If he drew on any report from Britain when composing his fable, this detail was surely part of it. He says too little himself to warrant serious conjectures about the real northern route to America by way of Iceland and Greenland. But, passing into the Iron Age, we have found Britons talking fairly concretely of this very thing: a northern route. To judge from Pytheas

[1] See R. F. Willetts, *Cretan Cults and Festivals*, pp. 100–2.

they probably knew Iceland; and the story relayed by Plutarch is, explicitly, about a passage from Britain by way of islands – some of them evidently sub-arctic, because of the short night – to a trans-Atlantic continent.

These Celts may well have been transmitting older beliefs about islands, a continent, a god in exile. They may even have been re-calling actual crossings in the long seafaring era of the megalith-builders and Mycenean traders: crossings which, if they occurred, would strengthen the case for a factual and British-derived tradition behind Atlantis.

Plutarch's account has gleams of curious correctness. His Ogygia could be southern Greenland. Cape Farewell is almost due west of Cape Wrath. The five days' sail is too short. But, for some reason, a mis-location of Greenland at just about this distance from Europe is a recurrent error in early geographers, including Norse-men who might have been expected to know better; hence, the understatement is not fatal to credence.

Past Ogygia with its neighbouring islands (and Greenland has plenty), the further passage of five-hundred-miles-plus through drifting debris, the sailing before the wind, and the arrival in a large bay in the opposite continent, could be construed as going over the Davis Strait from the Frederikshaab area to Labrador, and coasting round into the Gulf of St Lawrence. Plutarch adds one remarkable detail. He places the mouth of his bay in approximately the same latitude as the north end of the Caspian Sea. The forty-seventh parallel, which crosses the north end of the Caspian, also crosses the larger outlet of the Gulf of St. Lawrence, between Cape Breton Island and Newfoundland.

On this showing, the three islands at the far end of the voyage could be picked from several candidates in the Gulf – Cape Breton, Grindstone, Anticosti, western Newfoundland. While the Gulf climate is far from mild in winter, memories of its summer and autumn could supply the agreeable atmosphere of the island of Cronus. I do not know of any caves in those parts which would fit the sketch of his oracular shrine. The Micmac Indians of Nova Scotia do have legends of a divine hero named Glooskap who vanished into a cave in Cape Breton Island, where he still is.

This is hardly the sort of thing one can stress without evidence. The vital fact is the repeated motif of 'islands beyond' leading to a continent across the Atlantic. It suggests that the British Titan discovered by Demetrius in the first century A.D. may have a long life behind him. His early cult may even have been contemporary with the Bronze Age sources of Atlantis. Plutarch's unhesitant assumption that this deity is Cronus might be taken as reflecting a British belief, noted by Demetrius but not spelt out in the text, that he once flourished nearer to home but went away. At all events, he has one feature which rules out any mere borrowing from the Greeks. Cronus, in classical mythology, does not lie sleeping. The Celtic Titan does. This motif of his sleep, with the dreams and consultations implying that he is not wholly finished or out of touch, gives him a dimension which the Cronus of the Mediterranean lacks.

Robert Graves has made a valiant attempt to identify him. He argues that 'Cronus' sounds like the Greek *corone*, a crow or raven. Some such bird is supposed to have accompanied the chief Titan. Now the Celtic legends of Britain, and Ireland too, tell of an important person named Bran . . . and Bran means The Raven. In the British legends that come down through medieval Wales, Bran is a gigantic monarch of ancient Britain. In Irish romance he is a hero who voyages west to enchanted islands, and eventually settles on one of them. The two Brans, though different, are both probably humanized versions of the same Celtic god. The leader of the Gauls who invaded Greece in 280 B.C. was named Brennus, and Livy gives the same name, though perhaps mistakenly, to the Gaulish chief who took Rome 110 years earlier. Farther back still in the wanderings of peoples and the dawn of mythology, Bran the Raven and Cronus were conceivably one. Or the Celts could have identified their own Bran with a pre-Celtic god, a god having Mediterranean affiliations. Anyhow we shall be meeting Bran again.

Meanwhile, the facts are interesting enough. In spite of Blake's Druidic illusions, here in the lore of the Britons with their Druid sages there is a Titan. Whatever his nature, he proves that some such concept existed in British imaginations. Blake's 'Albion' embodies a valid insight.

Admittedly Blake says, in the text we have been probing, that Albion was Atlas. On the face of it, he has the right idea but the wrong Titan. But to have vindicated his acumen even so far is to justify looking through his writings for what he says about Albion in other places. He says a great deal. The search soon discloses that his Albion is a figure with several aspects. Blake thought of him differently at different times.

Atlas is an acceptable name for him. As the lord of an Atlantic realm, associated with Atlantis, he is rightly so called. But when I began, myself, to explore those parts of Blake's work which (like many readers) I had shied away from, I was impressed to find that Albion had another aspect that did answer to the British Cronus. In the symbolic book *Jerusalem*, Blake portrays him falling into a deep sleep or deathlike trance, and lying on a rock in the sea. Albion's sleep corresponds to a cosmic decline. As the reign of Zeus is worse than the reign of Cronus, so the world of Albion's slumber is under a shadow, not to be dispelled till his awakening.

We shall return, as I did, to Albion as well as Bran, and make his acquaintance at more length. The immediate point is that Blake's symbol turns out to be very comprehensive and startling indeed. Albion is Atlas, but more than Atlas. Poetically he contains the whole Titan 'picture' in a British form. And by some rare intuition, Blake steers our thoughts toward an actual phenomenon in the history of British minds.

The Iron Age remodellers of the Cadbury earthwork – or if not demonstrably they themselves, at any rate fellow-Celts in the land of Cymbeline – believed in a 'Patriarch of the Atlantic' spanning the Ocean and its islands; asleep or in abeyance now, withdrawn to a cave in a blissful western isle of his own, yet not dead or finally irrelevant. Obviously the Arthur of Avalonian legend is beginning to glimmer on the horizon. The question which recurs is whether, by following the clue, we can unlock his secret.

5

One further matter. The Britain where Demetrius met his informants was fast being absorbed into the Roman system, though the informants themselves may have been born before the conquest. Rome possessed her laureate or official bard in the person of Virgil, Augustus's sovereign poet whom all educated men read; and Virgil had already made Cronus – in his Roman guise as Saturn – a newly significant person, with a non-Greek addition to his myth.

Virgil adapted the golden age to his own literary ends. According to Italian legend it had been most golden of all in Italy, where, for a while, the defeated Titan found a refuge, and ruled Latium till his final eviction. Afterwards, the same harsher time set in as elsewhere. But like many of the best minds of his day, Virgil was influenced by Stoic philosophy. This enlarged and altered the traditional cosmos. For Hesiod, the world sank from the Cronian age of gold to the age of iron, with nothing said about a final reversal. The Stoics, however, believed in cycles. Degeneration might happen, and doubtless would. But sooner or later the cycle would run its course, and then would come a fresh start.

The dawn of the Roman Empire inspired hopes that the fresh start might be imminent. Rome seemed to be fulfilling the Stoics' dream of the Cosmopolis, the City of Man, the world-civilization. Messianic longings were fed by Jewish and 'Sibylline' prophecies flowing into the common stock of ideas. Virgil, seeking an image for the reign of the Caesars, portrayed it as a cosmic renewal in the Stoic manner – and, poetically, as the return of Saturn. This was his innovation. The gods-before-the-gods would soon live again, through the reborn world-order of the *Pax Romana*.

In his Fourth Eclogue, written in 40 B.C., Virgil said:

> We have reached the last era in Sibylline song. Time has conceived and the great Sequence of the Ages starts afresh. Justice, the Virgin, comes back to dwell with us, and the rule of Saturn is restored . . . The Iron Race shall end and Golden Man shall inherit the world.

And so on, with much imagery from Hesiod, who was one of Virgil's poetic masters. In the *Aeneid*, composed after Augustus's rise to supremacy, the same thought is subtly altered:

> There in very truth is he whom you have often heard prophesied, Augustus Caesar, son of the Deified, and founder of golden centuries once more in Latium, in those same lands where once Saturn reigned.[1]

The first passage points not merely to the Titan's unextinguished vitality, as with the Britons, but to a concept of his reinstatement; spiritually, at all events. In the second passage, the Emperor fulfils the same hope. He is *Saturnus Redivivus*.

With the Celtic Titan in mind, it is arresting to realize that Virgil himself was born, technically, a Gaul. He may or may not have had Celtic blood. But his birthplace was near Mantua in Cisalpine Gaul, where his father was a peasant craftsman. Caesar

---

[1] Translations in Penguin Classics (*Eclogues*, E. V. Rieu; *Aeneid*, W. F. Jackson Knight).

did not come there as governor till the future poet was eleven; Roman citizenship was not granted to the people till later. The theory of a Celtic element in Virgil's poetry has had its upholders. Conceivably a return of the Titan was part of the Druids' lore, which Plutarch missed but Virgil, being closer, did not.

There is one tantalizing allusion besides Plutarch's to a Cronian cult among the Celts. Dionysius of Halicarnassus, in a work entitled *Roman Antiquities* (I. 36–38), deals with the story of the ancient Italian golden age. He enlarges on it at more length than Virgil. Having argued that the superiority of Italy to other lands, even after Cronus-Saturn's departure, explains Italian veneration for him, Dionysius goes on:

> It is said also that the ancients sacrificed human victims to Cronus, as was done at Carthage while that city stood and as is still done among the Gauls and certain other western nations.

The Greek word here translated 'Gauls' is *Keltoi*. Classical authors tend to make 'Gaul' and 'Celt' interchangeable terms, and treat the islanders as distinct. Hence Dionysius's 'other western nations' are probably in Britain and Ireland, the two countries besides Gaul where Druidic rites flourished. He implies a Cronus cult extending to the brink of the unknown Ocean.

The mention of the so-called Phoenician Cronus at Carthage suggests a loose mode of thinking apparent elsewhere. Cronus was worshipped with human sacrifice, therefore any god worshipped with human sacrifice is Cronus. This 'logic' may underlie the identification of the British Cronus in Plutarch. In either case or both, other features of the Phoenician Cronus may have helped the identification. But it is not out of the question that Dionysius heard something more interesting about the British god.

Drawing on these sources, the omniscient Milton tracks the Titan's banishment all the way. He refers (*Paradise Lost*, I. 519–21) to the fallen angels,

> Who with Saturn old
> Fled over Adria to th' Hesperian Fields,
> And ore the Celtic roam'd the utmost Isles . . .

'Adria' being the Adriatic Sea and 'Hesperia' Italy. Milton was one of Blake's favourite authors.

Whether Virgil got the return of Saturn from Celtic myth, or whether he thought of it for himself, the Romans brought it to Britain enshrined in his poems, as part of the classical syllabus to which the sons of the Celtic gentry were soon exposed. Even if a Second Coming from that sunset Elysium could not be envisaged in Britain before the country was Romanized, it assuredly could be afterwards.

3

The Irrepressible Celt

1

At Cadbury Castle the proved traces of Rome are scanty. Nothing corroborates the eighteenth-century tales of widespread ruins. During and soon after the actual conquest, the legionaries dropped a few oddments: worn coins of the Roman republic, a hinge from a cuirass, a silver harness-fitting, part of the binding of a shield. The Romans allowed the rampart to fall into disrepair. They had no use for it, and they did not want rebels to use it. On the slope north-east of the summit plateau, the foundations of two or three timber buildings, with field-ovens, suggest a guard post. The buildings were small. It does not appear likely that even they were in service long.

But this near-vacancy speaks loudly in itself; and the continuing eloquence of the hill extends outside the ramparts. Rome not only seized the British citadel but suppressed it and made it a solitude. To judge from a supplementary dig in the village, the conquerors uprooted the Celtic inhabitants and resettled them below, so that they could never make their old fort a stronghold in any rising. And so (more or less) matters were to stand for centuries, while Britannia remained firmly Roman.

The move had echoes in other places. Britain's absorption into the Roman Cosmopolis was not a smooth development out of its native culture. It was imposed. The Celtic order was broken and re-set whenever policy required that it should be. Roman education, city-building, centralization, and bureaucracy forced society into a new mould, except in the high country of Wales. The Romans not only presented the Britons with a new god in the shape

56

of the Emperor, they tried to attach the British gods to the imperial pantheon. To some extent the same was done everywhere, often on philosophic as well as political grounds. But whereas other provincial deities – Mithras, Osiris, Cybele – managed to preserve their own stubborn personalities, most of the gods of Britain became almost adjectival. Along Hadrian's Wall, for instance, a series of little local spirits dwindled into aspects of Mars with Latinized names, like Belatucadrus. Sul of Bath and a few of his divine colleagues kept a sort of identity. But as long as Rome was paramount, as long as the repression of the Druid order and tradition remained effective, Britain's religion crumbled into a miscellany of feeble cults.

About the same time as the discoveries at the foot of Cadbury hill, something was found on top which gave a clue to the beginnings of its reoccupation, after the Roman-dictated gap. This was a gilt bronze letter 'A', elongated and narrow. Failing a definite explanation, it was presumed to have come from a votive inscription in a temple, built on the hill in a late phase of the Roman Empire. A few morsels of appropriate building material (but, unfortunately, no further letters) supported this view.

The ghostly temple corresponded to a known trend. By the fourth century A.D. the central grasp on Britannia was weakening. The Celt was quietly reasserting himself. One result of the imperial crises which ended with the triumph of Constantine was a realization that Britain was not an inert dependency, but a place where things could happen. Carausius, an admiral, actually declared British independence and maintained it for several years. Constantine himself was proclaimed in York by the troops stationed there. Later, in 383, a pretender named Maximus was proclaimed in the same way, and held western Europe for a while with an army including British soldiers: an exploit which left such a deep impression that he passed into the island's folklore, reappearing as 'Macsen' in Welsh legend, and as 'Massen' in Cornish, centuries afterwards.

Economic changes contributed to a social one. The Empire's cities never fully recovered from the disasters of civil war in the third century. By the time of Constantine, the dominant unit of society in Gaul and Britain was the villa. The wealthy provincials, and some of the resident officials, lived on large farms with every amenity. Life there was more stable, the supply of necessities more

57

reliable, the dangers from currency fluctuation less. The villas were not associated with villages like medieval manor-houses. They were generally distinct from the peasant communities rooted in the land.

Among the Britons this rural emphasis aided a gradual resurgence of the Celtic spirit, which had never been urban in the first place. The south-east, and the Gloucestershire area, developed a villa civilization. The British landed proprietor was now more nearly self-sufficient than his immediate ancestors. He was a classically educated man with Roman citizenship and a large establishment – his family, his craftsmen, his farm-labourers, his slaves. These lived (or at least the more privileged ones lived) in a spacious centrally heated house, which might be built round three sides of a court, with a veranda or cloister, and as many as thirty or forty rooms. Adjacent workshops supplied many of the villa community's needs besides food. The mosaic floors expressed the owner's cultural tastes in soft colours. Some had mythological or religious motifs; but in some the abstract linear art of the Celt began to revive.

Thus the better-off British household tended more and more to be a self-contained unit, less subject to the vagaries of the bureaucrat or autocrat overseas. Britannia as a whole tended the same way. Under the early Empire the Romanized island had imported pottery from Gaul, oil and wine from Spain, metal goods from Italy. By the middle of the fourth century most of such imports could be dispensed with. British ceramic ware was manufactured on an impressive scale. The textile industry was growing. Coal-mining had begun on Tyneside. Tin-mining had resumed in the long-depressed promontory of Cornwall. Villa owners possessed table services made of British pewter. Britain exported hunting dogs, which were famous; cattle and iron and slaves; and – compulsorily – grain.

After the middle of the fourth century, with Rome ever more distant and distracted, the Celtic gods started to creep back. They still came in company with the gods of the Empire; but they came. It is to this phase that the final Cadbury temple must have belonged. Another was located and excavated some years ago in the bleaker hill-fort of Maiden Castle. The greatest and, perhaps, the trend-setter, was the temple at Lydney in the Forest of Dean, founded in the middle 360s. This too was inside Iron Age earthworks. The cults revived in the monuments of the heroic past.

The Lydney temple stands on a bluff near the Bristol Channel. It is a basilical structure with a guest-house and cubicles for pilgrims, who slept in them and awaited the god's messages in dreams. The god in question was Nodens, who seems to have been the same as an Irish god called Nuadu Argatlam, Nuadu of the Silver Hand. He was a hunter, a fisherman, a healer, and, like St Anthony, a finder of lost possessions. His worshippers, some of them people of social standing, left token offerings at the shrine – ornaments, coins, votive images. Cadbury's letter 'A' was taken as indicating a temple because of similar letters found at Lydney.

We do not know who the last gods of Cadbury were. To judge from Maiden Castle, the cult may have been more Romanized than at Lydney, less purely native. But Celtic resurgence could not now be assimilated any more, even to the extent that it had been assimilated in villa society. The time for that, if there had ever been a time, was past. However successful the villa owners might be in having the best of both worlds, their mode of life could never convert the British majority – the sort of humble folk who had been evicted from their homes in Cadbury Castle. The crude technology and unscientific farming of the Roman world left the peasant masses poor. The constant demands for taxes and army service drove them into alienation. Celtic ways – their ways – inevitably carried seeds of subversion.

When Christianity became the Empire's religion, many of the villa people turned Christian and preserved their still-cherished *Romanitas* in that form, which was in fact the most durable form, as Britons like St Patrick were soon to prove. But by doing so they increased the tension. The peasant majority remained pagan, a state of affairs that did not basically alter till after Britain split off from the Empire. It needed only a loss of grip by the Romanized gentry for Britain to slide toward a reshaping, an authentic Celtic rebirth: a rebirth (to revert to Blake's terms) of Albion and all he stood for, however camouflaged by changes of personnel.

The first break came in 367 when barbarians assailed Britain from three sides. Saxons in fleets of crazy boats rowed over the narrow seas into the south-east. Picts from Caledonia, aided by British malcontents, poured across Hadrian's Wall. Irishmen in big curraghs – structurally like the Britons' skin-covered coracles, but elongated into efficient and seaworthy craft – disembarked in Wales. The defensive forces collapsed. Many British soldiers deserted the eagles and joined the bands of barbarian plunderers. Theodosius, a Spanish general who afterwards became emperor, managed to pacify the country in a campaign which took more than a year. He only succeeded even then because the British city council of London remained loyal, and supplied him with a base. Elsewhere the balance of the system was gone. The same Romanized class remained on top, but its economic foundations were crumbling.

Many villas had been wrecked, or impoverished by looting. Some remained empty; squatters lit cooking fires on the rich mosaics. Others were left hopelessly understaffed, because the slaves had been killed or taken prisoner, or had run off of their own accord. At least one British industry, pottery, slid into almost total extinction. Villa society continued on a subdued scale, with advancing dilapidation, for decades longer. It helped to preserve imperial traditions and attitudes, the Latin language, the Christian faith, the idea that Britons were citizens of a world-civilization. But the Celtic rebirth shown in the hill temples was something else, which the decaying civilization could neither nourish nor digest. After centuries of eclipse the tribal mode of life began to recover, and the Celtic art-forms began to be practised again in earnest.

New energies developed in the higher country, notably Wales. Wales had always been the least Romanized area. Mostly it was a land of garrisons and military highways. Welsh as we know it, derived from the Celtic British language, is not rich in Latin words. Those which it has tend to relate to architecture, household appliances, and books. The oldest Welsh law codes are not based on Roman law but on Celtic custom. As the Western Empire waned, the free imagination of Cambria and the other borderlands reasserted Celtic mythology with much else, and interwove it with the imperial and Christian inheritance.

The results have reached us only in legendary versions, moulded, sometimes distorted, by many years of bardic transmission and Christian editing. Christianity, rejecting the pagan gods as gods, turns them into heroes or supernatural beings, or transfers their myths to historical characters. Yet we can still make out a context where Blake's dictum about the acts of Albion being 'applied' to Arthur begins to make sense in terms of present knowledge.

2

One of the best defined of the old gods is Nodens, of the Lydney temple. As we grope forward into medieval Welsh legend, we find that Nodens has a life beyond Lydney; only, with the Church in the ascendant, he undergoes changes. He becomes 'Nudd' and then 'Lludd Llew Ereint', and finally a British monarch in Geoffrey of Monmouth. As a humanized hero he is the original of King Lear, so far as anyone is.

Furthermore he has a son, Gwyn ap Nudd. Gwyn is king of the fairy-folk and lord of Annwn, the underworld. He has – or had – a home within sight of Cadbury Castle. The Life of St Collen relates how that hardy British saint climbed Glastonbury Tor, entered Gwyn's palace at the top, and, after thwarting some attempts to entrap him, banished the whole heathen structure with holy water. Gwyn has another home alongside the pre-Christian burial ground at Pembrey near Llanelly. He takes part in the Wild Hunt, careering through the clouds with a pack of red-eared hounds, summoning the souls of the dead. In this capacity, as we shall see, he is a comrade of Arthur. Every May Day he fights a duel with Gwythyr ap Greidawl for the lady Creiddylad, who eventually usurps his place as the old god's offspring, and becomes Cordelia.

Classical authors noted a god whom they called the Celtic Apollo, the young musician Maponus. He was the son of the Gaulish Matrona, the presiding deity of the Marne. His British temples were at Corbridge, Ribchester, and Castlesteads. A circle of standing stones on the north shore of the Solway Firth was called the Place of Maponus and afterwards Clochmabenstane. It is possible that Maponus was the 'Apollo' worshipped by Hecataeus's British Hyperboreans. In that case his 'round temple', if not wholly imaginary, is perhaps more likely to have been Clochmabenstane than Stonehenge. The Solway Firth circle became a centre of public assembly and continued as such into the Middle Ages. Long before then, however, story-tellers had turned its god into the hero Mabon son of Modron, with an adventurous career of his own.

In the *Mabinogion* and elsewhere we meet Beli son of Manogan, king of Britain, who is thought to be originally Belenus, a Druid god. He becomes an ancestor of Welsh royal houses and a brother-in-law of the Virgin Mary. A goddess of inspiration, the Celtic muse Ceridwen, declines into a witch. As such she is the mother of the sixth-century bard Taliesin.

Taliesin was not the only real person drawn into this vortex of alchemic imagination. The pretender Maximus, proclaimed emperor in Britain in 383, turns up in a Cornish miracle-play and as the hero of *The Dream of Prince Macsen*, one of the best of the *Mabinogion* romances. It tells how he won the beautiful British princess Elen. The real Maximus may well have married a British wife. But this legendary Elen is a strange composite. She embodies a vague tradition of the Empress Helena, the canonized mother of Constantine the Great. Also she is Elen Luyddog, Helen-of-the-Hosts, a kind of patron saint of the roads where the legions marched. The road from Caernarvon southward is Sarn Helen, Helen's Causeway. In this last role she may have taken over the functions of some tutelary spirit. Elen and Maximus, like Beli, occur in Welsh royal pedigrees – as separate ancestors, not as husband and wife. In her antecedents she is a distinct figure, quite possibly divine.

Another pretender besides Maximus, the Constantine III who was proclaimed in Britain and took away the last legions in 407, also passed into legend. He is Custennin Gorneu, Constantine the Cornishman, and Bendigeit Custennin, Blessed Constantine, perhaps because he had close ties with the Church. Geoffrey of Monmouth presents him as King Constantine, reigning over all Britain in the fifth century. Arthur is his grandson.

After 410 Britain was still part of the Empire in name, but virtually independent. All these phantasms, divine and human, were beginning to move over the landscape in a shadowy dance. They, and many more, became the heroes and heroines of the Island of Britain. Passing from Celtic bard to bard, their sagas spread and intersected and branched out. Christianity, now slowly taking hold of the people, was reducing pagan religion to mythology, and there was no Druid order to fight back; but the mythology kept some of the features of the religion.

For one thing, it was less close-knit and coherent than the mythology of Greece and Rome. The old gods had never formed an organized pantheon. Celtic unity, it would appear, had lain chiefly in the Druid order itself. Once that was gone, the British and Irish Celts were left with only a scattered crowd of numinous ghosts. The spirit of a forest might be unrelated to the spirit of a near-by river. Both of them might be quite different from the spirits of the river and forest on the far side of a range of hills.

Moreover, these beings were not sharply divided into angels and devils, as in the Hebrew cosmos. They were more varied. Some of them were Christianized by being counted as demons. Others did not lend themselves to that treatment; they came to be explained by a new myth about neutral angels, who had fought for neither God nor Lucifer, and now had an intermediate status. This uncanonical theme of neutral angels found its way from Celtic legend into medieval romance. It occurs in a version of the Grail story, and figures briefly in Dante.

The Druidic concern with the soul's wanderings, and with Otherworlds which were not exactly heaven or hell, continued to haunt the Britons and their Irish neighbours in the dark ages. Hills, islands, stretches of water, and (of course) burial mounds, were haunted territory – points of contact, points of transition, with hovering presences which might be the shades of the dead or might not. Journeys by boat or through caves could lead to strange fairylands: the Earthly Paradise, Tir-nan-Og, Gwyn's realm of Annwn, or an isle of Ablach or Avallach which became the apple-orchard of Avalon.

Procopius, the Emperor Justinian's court historian, writes in the sixth century about the country which he calls Brittia. He says that the coast-dwellers on the opposite side of the Channel actually perform ritual ferryings of the souls of the dead to a British rendezvous. This bizarre traffic was across the broader part of the Channel. The fishermen who carried it on were probably of British stock, the settlers in Armorican Gaul who gave it the name of Brittany. Colonization of the peninsula began in the last decades of the Western Empire and went on for centuries. But Armorica was also the last continental centre of Druid influence, and the custom described by Procopius may have existed long before the Britons arrived.

The folklore which enshrined the heroes and demigods had in fact an intensely topographical quality. Celtic imagination had a strong sense of place. It ranged over the seas and mountains, particularly the western gulfs of sunset; it speculated about lost lands such as Lyonesse, and regions over the horizon; it sought to identify the gateways of the underworld with known islands and known hills – with Gresholm, for example, and Lundy.

Gwyn and Mabon, Beli and Macsen, Ceridwen and Elen, all live against a landscape. It is a pagan-Christian, Christian-pagan landscape. It includes Arthur's Glastonbury. While we cannot document the Cadbury mythos till later, it is of a piece with the rest. The sleeping immortal Arthur belongs to the same world, and he is placed in a suitable context: a cave below the temples of the gods of his hill.

3

Much of this mythology comes down to us through Celtic monks, reshaped by their assumptions, mingled with the lore of their saints, but, thanks to their scribal zeal, preserved. Whatever else perished in post-Roman Britain, the Church did not. St Patrick, himself a western Briton, planted it among the cousinly tribes of Ireland. St Ninian evangelized the lowland Picts. The missionaries of Wales, St Illtud and St David and many more, made Christianity the faith of the people as well as the nobles. St Samson drew Brittany into the same system. Celtic Christianity was freer and less pyramidal than that of the continent. Its leaders were abbots rather than bishops, and it gave a higher place to women.

Moreover, it was crucially if accidentally different in its attitude to the old order. On the continent, Christians remembered persecution at the hands of a secular power abetted by a strong priesthood. Therefore the old gods, even the fairly gentle Olympians, were all regarded as diabolic. The whole pagan heritage was viewed with suspicion and held at arm's length as something 'other'. In Britain (and still more in Ireland) this was not so. The old Celtic cults had no stigma of active anti-Christianity. Even in Ireland, where a remnant of Druids opposed St Patrick, their enmity was feeble.

So while clerics blotted out Celtic paganism as a religion, they were not implacable against the mythology in which it lived on. The monks, especially in Ireland, recorded pagan tales with only slight Christian revisions or half-hearted interpolations; and their own Christianity was apt to be odd and offbeat. In their writings we can glimpse (with much else) a continued dark-age awareness of the ocean and its resident Titan. The documentation spreads through a long tract of time, and the themes cannot be dated with much precision. But precision of dating does not matter in this case. It is enough that the themes are there.

Embedded in British and Irish manuscripts is the hero Bran, the Raven. His British and Irish guises are separate, but both almost certainly derive from a Celtic god of the Druidical heyday, the same whom Robert Graves believes to be the Titan in the Atlantic island. There is every reason to think that Bran has at least annexed some of the Titan's attributes.

Among the Britons he becomes the giant Bran the Blessed (Bendigeidfran), grandson of Beli, and king of Britain in an undatable past. He reigns in London, Caer Lundein, but prefers Harlech. Near Land's End is Caer Bran, Bran's Fort. In the *Mabinogion* he is the brother of the princess Branwen and leads an expedition to Ireland. The account of the crossing embalms what may be a folk-memory of immense antiquity:

> Bendigeidfran and the host of which we spoke sailed towards Ireland, and in those days the deep water was not wide. He went by wading. There were but two rivers, the Lli and the Archan they were called, but thereafter the deep water grew wider when the deep overflowed the kingdoms.[1]

In Ireland Bran is killed by a wound in his foot from a poisoned spear. His severed head possesses magical powers, singing and prophesying. After more than eighty years his followers bury it on Tower Hill in London, where it serves as a talisman against plagues and invasions from overseas. Unfortunately it is no longer there, for a reason which will appear in due course, but the Tower ravens are perhaps not unconnected with Bran. A sadder time followed him. Not only did the sea sweep in between Wales and Ireland, but Britain became desolate through civil war. His title 'the Blessed' cannot originally have had a Christian meaning. It may suggest the same aura of a lost golden age that surrounds Cronus.

However, it is the Irish Bran who crosses the western ocean and is absent for ages in a magical archipelago – not sleeping like the Titan in Plutarch, but definitely under a spell. *The Voyage of Bran* is a romance composed toward the year 700, probably in the monastery of Bangor near Belfast Lough. The monk who tells

[1] For the Welsh traditions of the sea's encroachment between Wales and Ireland, see Rachel Bromwich, *Trioedd Ynys Prydein*, pp. xc-xci.

Bran's story portrays him as a pagan chieftain in a far distant past, but safeguards his Christian acceptability by making him the recipient of a prophecy of Christ. There are also allusions connecting him with Britain; the divorce of the two Brans was not complete.

Bran, we are told, was strolling along the western shore of Erin, when he heard delicious music and saw an apple-bough covered with white blossom. He took it to his hall, and soon a strangely garbed woman appeared, from no one knew where, to claim it. She sang a song of a region over the western horizon, a region of many islands – 'thrice fifty', larger than Erin – and of the joy without care to be found there.

> There is a distant isle
> Around which sea-horses glisten:
> A fair course against the white-swelling surge . . .
> A delight of the eyes, a glorious range,
> Is the plain on which the hosts hold games . . .
> There is nothing rough or harsh,
> But sweet music striking on the ear,
> Without grief, without sorrow, without death . . .
> The sea washes the wave against the land,
> Hair of crystal drops from its mane.
> Wealth, treasures of every hue,
> Are in Ciuin, a beauty of freshness,
> Listening to sweet music,
> Drinking the best of wine.
> Golden chariots in Mag Rein,
> Rising with the tide to the sun,
> Chariots of silver in Mag Mon,
> And of bronze without blemish.

When she had sung she went away, taking the branch with her. Bran could know no peace till he had gone in quest of the happy realms across the water. He launched three stout curraghs, each with a nine-man crew, and they rowed westward for two days and nights. The sea-god Manannan approached them over the waves in his chariot; he spoke to them in riddling language, but let them pass. At length they reached the Island of Joy, and then went on to another island ruled by women, where Bran lived with the queen for a year. Or so it seemed. When the voyagers set out for home they were warned not to go ashore in Erin. One of them who did crumbled to dust, for, in mortal time, centuries had slipped by. Bran departed west again and was seen no more.

Here we find Celtic imagination continuing to play round sunset Isles of the Blest and an equivalent of Cronus's kingdom. The hero, of course, has been demoted from divinity, and his adventures have acquired a romantic colouring. But the myth breaks through. It is coupled with the motif, always important among the island Celts, of an Otherworld Quest *by water* – a plunge, psychologically speaking, into depths, into a womb of rebirth. The Irish tale of Bran cannot be reconciled with the Welsh. However, the Welsh still gives him a westerly passing and a kind of immortality, though his immortality, or rather Other-Life, is the life of his enchanted head only.

Some of the same ideas pervade a Celtic sea-legend which is Christian and far more famous, the legend of St Brendan's Voyage. This is one of the best case-histories of the 'mythification' of a real person. Brendan was a sixth-century Irishman who founded monasteries at Ardfert near Tralee and at Clonfert in Galway. Like many Irish monks of the period he was a bold seafarer. 'Sea-pilgrims' after Brendan are known to have travelled in their curraghs to the Hebrides, the Orkneys, the Shetlands, the Faeroes, eventually Iceland and perhaps Greenland, seeking a counterpart of the eastern hermit's desert, or else freedom from lay rulers and raiders. How far Brendan himself went, nobody can now say. To Iona, certainly; to somewhat more remote regions, probably. But legend credits him with a vast exploration of the Atlantic in quest of the Earthly Paradise, or the 'Land Promised to the Saints'.

The most literary account of this, the *Navigatio Sancti Brendani*, is far more than a mere Christianization of the pagan ocean-mythos that appears in *The Voyage of Bran* and some other Irish romances, such as *Mael Duin*. But mythology is a factor in it. Brendan is inspired to set out by a report he hears from a visitor named Barinthus. Barinthus is a pagan sea-spirit, Finnbar, in clerical disguise. His own Atlantic crossing was direct; but when Brendan tries to imitate it, the search takes years, and he discovers many islands. This is the will of God, who is revealing to him 'the mysteries in this immense ocean'. At last, after penetrating a bank of fog, he and his crew reach a sunlit country where fruit-trees grow. They traverse it for forty days without coming to a farther shore. An angel tells them to return, since their mission is accomplished.

In the Middle Ages it was believed that St Brendan did make the voyage and attain a distant landfall. The belief influenced map-makers and Columbus himself. The *Navigatio* reflects a surprising knowledge of Atlantic geography. This is more likely to be due to its author, who wrote four hundred years later, than to information literally handed down by the seafaring saint. A surviving earlier version is far less map-like. However, the voyage supplies something else, fully as interesting in the present context. It occurs as an episode in the life of another Celtic saint, the Breton Machutus (that is, St Malo), who is said to have sailed with Brendan. The voyagers come to an island with a sleeping giant on it. He wakes up and tows their boat, but the cable parts and they lose sight of him. Here once again is a Celtic Titan sleeping in the midst of the sea. But he does something which Plutarch's Cronus does not – something apposite to Virgil before, and to Arthur and the Blakean Albion afterwards. He wakes up.

4

Thus a scrutiny of the Celts of the British Isles, first during the rise of Rome, then in the Roman twilight and aftermath, discloses a Titan myth with tolerably firm outlines. It can be related both to the Graeco-Roman tradition and to the Celtic sagas. Indeed, all the versions may have the same substratum. By collating them we can arrive at a generalized statement, roughly as follows.

There were gods before the gods who now reign. One, in particular, was the arch-Titan whom the Greeks called Cronus, the Romans Saturn. He was known among the Celts, and the Celtic Bran has acquired some of his attributes even if he is not the same. This Titan is now in an island Elysium over the western water, perhaps reigning among other immortals, perhaps asleep in a cave.

The benign aura that haloes him is significant. When he and his relatives (such as Atlas) governed our world, men enjoyed a golden age. The glory of Atlantis, and of the lost lands west of Britain, was part of it. But the world changed. Crueller powers and corrupt ways have taken over. Atlantis, or its equivalent, has sunk. The fallen Titan's happy domain is confined to the Farthest West where he has gone into indefinite retreat. There alone does the carefree life still prevail, the life of golden and godlike beings, unafraid of old age and death.

Yet he is not lost to mankind, nor is the glory surrounding him. He still watches over some of his former subjects, such as slaves. One day he may wake up. In the light of the Virgilian mystique it is conceivable that he will come back, sweep away the usurping powers, and resume his old majesty. Then the golden age will revive with him, and start afresh.

4

A Prince of the Fifth Century

1

Most of the Cadbury visitors came because of Arthur and the Camelot story. We looked after them in a large marquee which was put up inside the ramparts. Here they could buy excavation reports and non-alcoholic beverages. Those wishing to tour the site were entrusted to the care of guides, who gave them a few minutes' introductory talk in front of a map, and then led them round.

I did some guiding myself. Not all my colleagues on the job handled it in quite the same manner. But my own tactic, after briefly describing the hill, was to say: 'Now suppose we ask ourselves whether this hill-fort "was Camelot", as local tradition claims: what does this actually mean – as history, not as legend? What sort of finds would have a bearing on the idea, and confirm it or otherwise as the case may be?'

The nature of the distinction has already, I hope, become clear. In medieval romance, Camelot is King Arthur's best-loved city, where he reigned over all Britain (and other countries) before the Saxon conquest. It is hopelessly elusive. Those place-names with *cam* and *camel* in them occur near Cadbury. But such names occur elsewhere, in Cornwall for instance; and antiquarian guesswork has sometimes inclined thoughtfully toward Colchester, the Roman Camulodonum. Camelot does not appear in any early map, or in the oldest tales of Arthur, or in Geoffrey of Monmouth. The first allusion to it, in Chrétien de Troyes (and even this is disputable), furnishes no clue to its whereabouts.

Subsequent authors hint at several locations. The only point of interest is a repeated statement that Camelot is now deserted and derelict. A tale called *Palamedes*, written toward 1240, says that the evil Mark of Cornwall destroyed the place after Arthur's death. The fourteenth-century poet Fazio degli Uberti makes the tantalizing if untrustworthy claim that he has seen 'wasted, ruined Camelotto' with his own eyes. He does not tell us where.

In Malory, Camelot is the city where Arthur keeps the Round Table and assembles his knights. Sometimes Malory makes it out to be Winchester. Once at least, however, a reader gets the impression that it must be in Scotland, because some foreign envoys, on their way back to a Channel port, stop at Carlisle en route.

Manifestly the Camelot of literature is a phantasm above real geography. In Tennyson's *Idylls of the King* it is symbolic of 'the gradual growth of beliefs and institutions, and the spiritual development of man'. T. H. White's *The Once and Future King*, when converted into a musical, inevitably became *Camelot*. The presidency of John F. Kennedy was referred to (until the fate of his family grew too poignant for frivolity) as 'Camelot on the Potomac'.

This city of the imagination is a gorgeous image projected by the tradition of a real Arthur with a real headquarters. It owes its glamour to the way in which the real Arthur came to be thought of. The first step toward understanding it is to get behind the legend, and define the Arthurian Fact in which the legend is rooted. If we can grasp this and relate Cadbury to it, we can go on to ask why the image acquired the splendour it did, whether and how the myths of an older world contributed to it, and what the potency is that makes it linger.

Something undoubtedly happened in post-Roman Britain that happened nowhere else. The unique Arthurian Legend does go back to a unique train of events. Like the rest of the Western Empire, Britannia was assailed by Teutonic barbarians. In Gaul, Spain and Italy the attack came chiefly from Goths; in Britain, from the Angles, Saxons and Jutes across the North Sea, commonly lumped together as 'Saxons'. There was, however, a difference. The Goths were not such complete savages as the Saxons were. Gauls, Spaniards, even many Italians, did not care much whether they were overrun or not. Britons did. Britain's leaders in the fifth century still saw themselves as imperial citizens, the standard-bearers of civilization. They had no wish to succumb to gangs of pirates.

Geoffrey of Monmouth portrays fifth-century Britain as ruled by King Constantine. After him comes a usurper, Vortigern, who makes friends with the Saxons and lets them live in Kent. They revolt, and Vortigern is killed. Constantine's son Aurelius Ambrosius becomes king, and the Britons partly recover. Aurelius Ambrosius is succeeded by Uther Pendragon, and Uther by his own son, who is Arthur. King Arthur subdues the Saxons and reigns gloriously till 542.

While Geoffrey's dynastic story is false, two of these five names are certainly genuine, and two more almost certainly. The real Constantine, as we saw, was the last of the pretenders. He was proclaimed emperor by the British army in 407, but took most of the troops overseas and never returned. In 410 the British local councils revolted against him and, in effect, declared Britain independent.

With occasional but dwindling Roman aid, they put up a long fight against the Saxons. But the north was harassed by Picts also, and the combined enemies were too much. The Romanized aristocracy lost control to what might be called a Celtic Nationalist faction. Border chieftains in Wales and the Scottish lowlands had been built up by the declining Empire as frontier auxiliaries, and were now extending their influence. The Vortigern whom Geoffrey makes the arch-traitor was apparently one of them. By the 440s he was paramount over a large part of Britain. He took the risky step of enlisting Saxons as mercenaries to fight the Picts, and allowing them to settle in Britain. Vortigern was following Roman precedents, but without Roman resources. According to tradition his first allies of this kind were the Jutish brothers Hengist and Horsa, who planted themselves in Thanet with three shiploads of warriors. Many more probably disembarked at other places along the east coast. They drove back the Picts, but they also encouraged their fellow tribesmen to flock over into Britain. Vortigern failed to meet the colonists' increasing demands for payment. They mutinied, and plundered lowland Britain with lurid atrocities. The emigration that turned Armorica into Brittany began in earnest at this time, as a flood of refugees followed the few British pioneers who had settled there earlier.

Geoffrey's 'King Aurelius Ambrosius' is Ambrosius Aurelianus, an aristocrat who revived the pro-Roman party. By about 460 Vortigern was dead or discredited. Leadership of the national resistance reverted to those who still thought of themselves as citizens, talked Latin, and professed a Christianity explicitly loyal to Rome. Politically, Britain was breaking up into small states, each with its own ruling family: Strathclyde and Elmet in the north, Gwynedd and Dyfed in Wales, and several others. However, Ambrosius seems to have organized a widespread command, and to have contained the invasion.

Uther Pendragon, supposedly his brother, escapes us as a figure of history. But after Ambrosius's death or retirement, and many fluctuations of fortune, the Britons at last won a crushing victory at a mysterious 'Mount Badon'. This battle was fought between 490 and 520. It was followed by a long spell of prosperity and near-peace, with the Britons on top, the Saxons confined to settlements near the coast, the Church flourishing, and bardic literature at least beginning to flourish. Not till about 550 did the Teutonic people start to advance again, slowly transforming most of Britain into England – Angle-Land.

This rally of an ex-Roman province against the barbarian is the Arthurian Fact. From it came the tradition of a British heroic age round about 500 A.D. – a tradition which was handed on with gradual embellishment in the north, in Wales, in Cornwall and in Brittany, and supplied King Arthur with his setting.

As for Arthur himself, he is best defined as 'the British general who won the battle of Mount Badon'.[1] Obviously there must have been such a general. While the oldest document mentioning the battle does not name him, the victory is credited in other places to a commander called Arthur, and never to anybody else. The early *Annales Cambriae* date the event in 516 or '18, adding that twenty-one years later Arthur and Medraut (i.e. Modred) were slain at another battle, Camlann. 'Camlann' means 'the crooked bank' and has sometimes been identified with Camboglanna, a fort on Hadrian's Wall, but the Somerset Cam and several similarly named rivers are also candidates. In the decades following the date of this battle we find four minor Arthurs among the nobility of Britain, one as far north as Argyll. All were presumably named after a single hero of national renown.

For these and other reasons it is easier to believe that Arthur existed than that he did not. But the *Annales Cambriae* and similar early sources never describe him as a king. He sounds like a local prince or aristocrat, of vaguely Romanized stock ('Arthur' is a Celtic form of the Roman 'Artorius'): one who rose to be the Britons' commander-in-chief, and perhaps also to some sort of

[1] Cf. Sheppard Frere, *Britannia*, p. 382.

de facto power, but not to recognized kingship. That was added by story-tellers much later.

The fullest account of him occurs in a *History of the Britons* compiled by Nennius, a ninth-century Welsh monk. Nennius draws on an older poem or chronicle describing Arthur as the principal warleader, *dux bellorum*, who fought against the Saxons alongside the British kings. He won twelve victories culminating in Badon. The places are named, but the interpretation is doubtful. A river 'Glein' and a region 'Linnuis' could be Glen and Lindsey in Lincolnshire, where the Angles were certainly encroaching. A forest 'Celidon' points to the Scottish lowlands. Badon itself must have been in the south, because there were not yet enough Saxons anywhere else for a decisive battle affecting the whole invasion. One guess is that it was the hill-fort of Liddington Castle near Swindon, which has a village of Badbury at its foot.

Early Welsh literature has more to say about Arthur. But the Arthurian Fact as stated – the British resurgence and temporary triumph, with an outstanding leader active about 500 – gives all that is needed for attaching a meaning to 'the real Camelot'. Camelot would be the chief stronghold of the chief British warleader in the right period, the man known to tradition as Arthur. Archaeologically, the question at Cadbury Castle from the outset was whether there was any sign that the hill-fort had filled this role. The local Arthurian lore was not evidence in itself. Archaeological finds, however, could give it fresh weight and interest.

I didn't, of course, say all this to visitors on conducted tours. I compressed the message into two or three minutes. But it seemed vital to make the main point; and it is doubly vital to make it, if we are to evaluate Arthur's legend in depth, relating it to Celtic antiquity and explaining why one Camelot gave birth to the other.

2

On 25 January 1969 *The Times* published an article by Professor W. H. Thorpe, F.R.S. It began:

If we look through the list of recent Nobel prizewinners it becomes obvious that many, perhaps a large majority, achieve this by great leaps of imaginative insight; leaps which, at the time they were made, may have had very little experimental or observational basis. Almost at random one can think of.the concept of the double helix . . . of quantum mechanics . . . of complementarity. All these in their inception were far removed from the work of the laboratory. Yet they played their role as great scientific theories because, though imaginative constructions of a wide generality, they were also close enough to physical or biological reality to allow experimental verification.

That text could serve as a preamble to the modern quest for Arthur, and the Cadbury project in particular. In 1959 there appeared a magisterial work, *Arthurian Literature in the Middle Ages*, edited and partly written by the late R. S. Loomis. It brought together the Arthurian 'work of the laboratory' at its best, including a discussion of the historical Arthur. But its only mention of Cadbury Castle was a reference to the cave legend. Nothing about the Camelot story; nothing about the archaeology of the hill; not a hint that excavation might shed any light. These matters were already being publicly aired when Loomis wrote . . . but not by professional scholars. The fruitful convergence of Arthurian studies which has since begun, partly because of Cadbury itself, would not have been initiated by any one group of specialists. It required a 'leap of imaginative insight', which, happily, took place. Cadbury's Arthurian yield, though less than that of the long pre-Roman Iron Age, does amount to as good an 'experimental verification' as it was ever sensible to hope for, and better than the Committee's first announcements foreshadowed.

The first clue, before excavation, had come from the Tintagel-type pottery found by Mrs Harfield. This was imported ware, brought in at a time when the native industry was almost extinct. Big jars and smaller bowls were shipped over from the eastern Mediterranean. The jars probably contained oil or wine. The archaeological value of Tintagel ware lies in the fact that it is one of the few things that can be dated to the British dark age, round about the time of Arthur. When found on a site, it suggests not only occupation at that time, but the presence of a wealthy household, lay or monastic, capable of importing expensive goods over a long and troubled route.

At Cadbury Castle, more of it was dug up in the first weeks of excavation, together with a corroded dark-age knife. These 'Arthurian' objects were found in three widely separated spots. Three lucky hits out of three, in such a huge area, would be unlikely; hence the dark-age occupation must have been an extensive one. Later seasons added to the haul of pottery items. There were

75

further fragments of jars, and a dish marked with a Christian cross. An early Teutonic button-brooch, ornamented with a helmeted head, hinted at the possible presence of Saxon prisoners taken by the Britons.

However, the discovery that put Cadbury in a class by itself was made when the gaps were cut in the top rampart. In cross-section the Iron Age reconstructions were all visible, one on top of another. Above the last of them was a layer of soil, accumulated during the Roman phase. But on top of that again, there was another wall.

It was more than twenty feet thick, a chaotic stratum of piled stones. Diggers called it 'the Stony Bank'. At some points it had slid utterly out of shape. But on the east, from outside, three or four courses of unmortared stone could still be seen roughly in position. Further inspection revealed slots in the wall. Posts, six feet apart, had once upheld a wooden breastwork. Timbers ran horizontally backward holding the uprights against the rampart. Here and there the foundations of wooden towers could be made out. The wall apparently ran all round the enclosure, with a gateway at the south-west entrance.

The Stony Bank was a fortification of pre-Roman Celtic type. But it could not be pre-Roman. The rubbish embedded in it included Roman tiles and blocks of tufa, a porous stone used especially for vaulting. These could hardly have come from anything but the presumed temple, built during the second half of the fourth century A.D. The wall, therefore, was later than that. On the other hand it was not of Saxon design, and from about the middle of the seventh century, perhaps earlier, this part of Somerset was in Saxon hands. A piece of Tintagel pottery on the back of the wall pointed to a conclusion hard to resist: that somewhere about the year 500 a major British chieftain reoccupied the hill and refortified it.

Reoccupation can be paralleled, though on a smaller scale, in Cornwall and Wales. Refortification cannot. Cadbury Castle turns out to have been converted into a dark-age citadel, far larger than any other yet found, with a totally unparalleled bulwark three-quarters of a mile long. Clearly this was the work of a military overlord with impressive resources: in the phrase of Leslie Alcock, the Director of Excavations, an 'Arthur-type figure'.

Traces of his buildings inside the enclosure were not easy to sort out from the confusion of the bedrock. But on the summit plateau, close to the area known as King Arthur's Palace, the foundations of a hall came to light. Tintagel pottery, once again, provided a rough dating.

The site of this hall is precisely central. A watchman on its roof could have seen the south-west gate, the north-east gate (if it was then in use), and almost the whole perimeter. With a move of only a few yards in any direction, the curve of the hilltop would cut off a large part of this panorama. Hence the hall may have been placed strategically by the commander of the fort.

It was sixty feet by thirty. A feature that delayed the recovery of its ground plan was a straight and continuous foundation trench, which was at first assumed to mark the gable-end of the building. Actually it marked an internal partition. The rest had to be laboriously charted by picking out lines of post-holes in both directions. The hall, when it stood, was a timber structure and probably thatched. There are still one or two medieval barns, as at Harmondsworth in Middlesex, which show what it could have been like – something very far from a mere glorified hovel. The partition stretched across, twenty feet from one end. It divided the hall into two chambers, one twice the size of the other. The smaller was possibly a ladies' bower; or if the hall was used for feasting, the nobles may have sat in the small chamber and the retainers in the large one.

After five seasons of excavation, only a fraction of Cadbury Castle had been uncovered. For the moment, however, the Camelot Research Committee had finished its work. Further results relating to Ethelred and the late Saxon period – yet another wall on top of the rest, and the foundations of Saxon buildings–are important to archaeology and history, but lie outside the Arthurian field.

As to this, what has emerged? Nothing with Arthur's name on it. But in archaeology you are lucky if you get names. More to the point is the evidence of the Arthur-type figure. The lord of Cadbury towers over the known British chieftains of his time, with an immensely bigger establishment and an immensely more elaborate fortress. The Welsh citadel of Maelgwn of Gwynedd, the premier British king of the middle sixth century, has also been excavated, as have those of several approximate contemporaries. None are on anything remotely like the Cadbury scale.

Whether or not the lord of Cadbury was indeed the hill's legendary hero, he was surely the right sort of man: a *dux bellorum*.

He lived on a site traditionally said to be Arthur's home, in the traditional period, with resources on the traditional scale. He was, at the very least, a person whom the legends could have grown round. Nowhere else does Britain supply any archaeological traces of such a person. Until other excavations bring them to light, it is easier to believe that this man was Arthur than that he was not.

One more thing can be said about him. Many of those who have speculated on Arthur have pictured him as the last of the Romans – a follower-on of the revival of Britain's Romanized citizenry, led by Ambrosius Aurelianus. I was once disposed to think so myself. Cadbury, however, has caused me to modify that view. The dark-age rampart shows no Roman influence; it is neo-Celtic. Cadbury's *dux bellorum* may have had ideas about Roman civilization, but he was, in practice, a Briton. Even if Arthur was not he, Cadbury helps to prove that the resurgence which Arthur came to stand for was predominantly a British affair, carrying on from a long pre-Roman past. As Geoffrey of Monmouth always implied; and as Blake always implied.

3

So we do catch glimpses of somebody who could be Arthur, in the right setting: a 'prince of the fifth century', in Blake's phrase, though his *floruit* extended into the sixth. If we now assemble everything further that is said about Arthur before Geoffrey's literary take-over, two things happen. A credible human being does dimly take shape. At the same time we can see how this human being was 'mythified', with the reborn Celtic past that is implicit at Cadbury moulding and transforming his reputation.

The basic material has been reviewed many times. I do not propose to go over it again in detail. Besides the records already mentioned, we have the baffling text of the sixth-century monk Gildas, who testifies to the Arthurian Fact and the victory at Mount Badon, but without unequivocally naming Arthur. We have some early poetry, most of it composed in the British kingdom of Rheged, centred on what is now Cumberland. We have some grotesque but intriguing passages in the lives of Welsh saints; and one complete Welsh tale; and title-headings and summaries of many further tales now lost, which can nevertheless be eked out in various ways; and a medley of local legends like the Cadbury group. We also have an indirect witness to the course of events in the *Anglo-Saxon Chronicle*, and a fair amount of evidence from archaeology, place-names, and so forth, to show who was living where, at what time, and in what manner.

At the end of a careful survey the Arthurian Fact – the British rally – will be clearer than Arthur as a person. It is likely to remain so. Still, a tentative sketch of Arthur's life can be hazarded. The only controversial issue that must be raised by way of preface is the question of the 'northern' Arthur. A theory has been put forward that the historical hero was a chieftain who lived beyond the Humber, campaigning perhaps in the Scottish lowlands; and that although the battle of Badon was doubtless fought in the south, it was won by some other leader, and later attributed to Arthur as part of a process of literary inflation.

Eminent as a few of its spokesmen are, this theory relies on some odd arguments and some significant evasions. To construct an Arthur without Badon involves such an arbitrary re-writing of the scanty documents that it is hard to see any remaining point in discussing him at all. And surely you cannot fairly stop short at saying that the British commander at Badon was not Arthur; you must suggest an alternative leader, and show why he got no credit whatever, anywhere, for the crowning victory on which the entire saga of British glory depended. Again, I do not think any advocate of the northern school has explained why there is no important tradition or legend giving Arthur a northern home, whereas several give him a home in the West Country.

The solid fact underlying the northerners' case is simply that some of the oldest known allusions to Arthur are in poems by the bards of the Cumberland area, who deal with northern events. To this may be added a certain bias in the material presented by Nennius. But no poetic allusion makes Arthur plainly a northerner, and the claim that northern matter never mentions people from anywhere else is demonstrably false. It is enough to observe that Arthur may have campaigned in the north and been remembered there, just as Alexander was remembered in many places besides his country of origin. Meanwhile, the practical appeal is the simplest. Adherents of the traditional West Country Arthur can now produce Cadbury Castle, where those who took tradition seriously have been vindicated. When their critics can produce a northern citadel like it, the case for a recount will be reasonable.

My own biography of Arthur would run more as follows. (I have factual support of scme kind throughout, but do not insist, or pretend that support is proof.)

He was born early in the 470s in the West Country, perhaps Cornwall. His parents were Christians of the minor rustic nobility, bi-lingual, and still hazily Roman in sympathy – whence their son's name, Artorius. In his youth Arthur led a freebooting kind of life and attracted followers. They joined him in raiding and feuding expeditions. He had a touch of the highland chief, a touch of the frontiersman. I have compared him to Davy Crockett; and as a warning to sceptics who argue that anyone credited with giant-killing and dragon-slaying must be fictitious, I would point out that Crockett himself, a U.S. Congressman, became the hero of tall tales as far-fetched as any told of Arthur.

The scene of these apprentice adventures may have been in Cornwall still. A hill-fort near Padstow has been proposed as the 'Kelliwic' named in Welsh legend as a home of Arthur. But he pushed eastward. His flair for leadership and his growing war-band made him a useful friend to have, in the chaos of Britain during the long struggle with the Anglo-Saxons. He was at least known to the ageing Ambrosius, possibly employed by him, before that commander's death or retirement. Also he allied himself with the chieftain Cadwy who was powerful in Somerset. (Several strands of tradition link the two. The theory that Cadbury was 'Cadwy's Fort', though unconfirmed, suggests intriguingly how Arthur might have come into possession of it.)

His principal lieutenants, named in some of the earliest verses, were Cei and Bedwyr – Kay and Bedevere. Arthur himself, or some genius among his men, revolutionized British methods of fighting by study of the late imperial cavalry, still a major arm of Byzantium. Importing horses that were bigger than the native breed, he equipped them with home-made mail, and their riders with weapons and protective clothing to match. Lacking stirrups and other accoutrements of medieval knights, Arthur's horsemen were never so formidable. But their capacity for swift movement, long-distance travel, and surprise, gave them an advantage over all other warriors. The Teutonic barbarians, who did not ride at all, were thrown into panic by their charges.

Offering his services to the British kings without close commitment, Arthur made himself indispensable over a larger and larger stretch of country. Almost without meaning to, he became a national leader, possibly appointing himself to the lapsed Roman military office of *Comes Britanniarum*. He routed the Angles who were entering up the Wash and Humber. He fought against Picts and British outlaws in the north-west, pacifying an area much disturbed by the late Roman policy of planting British tribes beyond the Wall as frontier auxiliaries. Finally he crushed a Saxon offensive at Mount Badon – Liddington, let us say – and gave Britain a spell of peace. Many Saxons actually gave up and sought new land on the Continent; Arthur was the only defender of any part of the former Empire who ever drove the barbarians out. Unfortunately for the Britons, he never drove them all out.

As to the dates of these events, I think Arthur's major campaigns began toward 500 and culminated between 515 and 520. Some put his activities, and by inference his birth, a decade or two earlier. 'Around 500' is the safe phrase, and quite proper where all dates are inexact.

Even after his victories Arthur was never recognized as a king. There are one or two curious allusions to him as 'emperor'. This could bear its Latin meaning of 'commander-in-chief' or could refer to some belated attempt to proclaim him Emperor of the West, like Maximus and the last Constantine. As Maximus becomes 'King Massen' in Cornish legend, so Artorius Augustus might have become King Arthur.

With whatever authority he enjoyed, Arthur settled down at his main base, and I shall believe that this was Cadbury Castle till convinced otherwise. He held court after a fashion with his wife Gwenhwyvaer. His exploits had given him a widespread if equivocal fame. In the lands bordering the Irish Sea, where he had come as a deliverer from Picts and pirates, he was remembered with warmth. Hence his rapid renown among northern bards. With another class of Britons his standing was very different. Because he had requisitioned Church property to support his forces, the monks heartily disliked him. Therefore he was denied most of the credit he deserved in the writings of the only Britons who wrote, from Gildas onward.

Apart from any imperial title which he assumed or accepted, Arthur's Roman-ness was slight. He gave lip service to the idea of defending civilization against the barbarian; and he had a few Roman tastes, such as wine-drinking, with a smattering of classical education. But he was a Celtic Briton, and had only vague notions of the faded civilization he professed to defend. After his death, Gildas could still speak of the Britons as 'citizens' and of Latin as 'our language'. Arthur would perhaps have done neither without prompting.

However, he was Roman in his religion, which was sincere if scarcely exemplary. When he received his death-wound at Camlann – in a campaign bravely undertaken, as an old man, against the rebel Medraut – the survivors of his army bore him as a matter of course to the monastery of Glastonbury. There he was buried among the relics of the saints. And there he stayed till 1190, when the monks dug him up.

Whatever Arthur achieved in person, the Arthurian Fact is a part of English history, not merely a Celtic flash in the pan. Arthur had an effect. He may have had an enormous effect, though, as one of C. S. Lewis's characters remarks, we are never told what *would have happened* if something else hadn't. At any rate the barbarians who threatened to overrun Britain were driven back, and by the time they advanced again, they were ceasing to be barbarous. The Britons' defence began caving in during the 570s, and by 633 the collapse was irretrievable. But meanwhile the rulers of Kent, Wessex, Northumbria and the other Teutonic kingdoms, whose people made England into England, were opening their realms to Christian missions and the higher culture that went with them.

Nor did Christianity imply only the Roman influence that St Augustine brought. It also implied a rich contribution from the Celts themselves. The flourishing Church of Wales and, still more, Ireland, was a product of the Arthurian victories. Ireland became the most civilized country of western Europe, a home of learning and art and youthful-spirited fervour. The preservation of that Celtic Christian society, and its branching out to Iona and beyond, would probably not have happened if the heathen had swept across to the Welsh mountains and the Irish Sea.

While the missions founded by Augustine were working in Kent and (less effectively) in other Anglo-Saxon kingdoms, St Aidan's Scots were coming in from the north, and Irishmen from the west. In 658, when the West Saxons captured Glastonbury, the British monks were neither killed nor expelled. An inter-racial community was allowed to take shape; here, in a sense, the United Kingdom was born. It was now possible for Saxon and British royalties to marry, for Saxon laws to recognize British rights. Because of the extreme slowness of the conquest, England emerged at last as a creative fusion of peoples; and the gradual process by which the little kingdoms merged into a greater unity was a political education in itself, with endless consequences.

The British legend-makers of Wales and the north, Cornwall and Brittany, who made Arthur a pre-eminent person, were correct in their judgment. What we have to assess, however, is the way they expressed their view of him. Being short of literal facts, they exalted Arthur by investing him with attributes he never had.

Other traditions were grafted on to his. Independent heroes were turned into members of his corps or his household. The *Mabinogion* tale *Culhwch and Olwen* is earlier than Geoffrey of Monmouth. Yet its Arthur, though not undisputed ruler of Britain, is already a 'sovereign prince'. Dozens of legendary figures are at his court; dozens of legendary adventures have been revised so as to happen under his auspices. This enlargement seems to be typical of Welsh saga during the dark ages, not only in Wales itself but in the British enclaves of Strathclyde, Cumberland, Cornwall and Brittany. Arthur, their supreme champion, became a sun that captured planets.

Most of the actual stories are lost, but a good deal can be reconstructed from the Welsh triads. These are mnemonic summaries of popular themes. The bards marshalled their repertoire by grouping stories in sets of three. Often the headings have been preserved – the 'Three Great Treacheries', the 'Three Exalted Prisoners', and so forth – with notes on each item in the triad. Not only is Arthur the outstanding hero, occurring in more triads than anybody else, he is the only one so important that several triads are expanded to tetrads to fit him in. Thus, after the Three Exalted Prisoners, comes the addition. 'And there was another prisoner even more famous, and this was Arthur', with a sketch of some adventures in which he was captured and rescued.

These triadic stories and characters are all set in a glorified 'Island of Britain' before the final Saxon conquest. Chronology is blurred, but the intended effect is of a British golden age – a secondary golden age if not the original – centred on Arthur's lifetime. When Geoffrey of Monmouth made him monarch of Britain, head of a noble knighthood, and conqueror of lands overseas, he enlarged and personalized this golden-age motif. Arthur's Britain 'excelled all other kingdoms in its general affluence, the richness of its decorations, and the courteous behaviour of its inhabitants'. Geoffrey adds touches of his own. Thus, women of fashion 'scorned to give their love to any man who had not proved himself three times in battle. In this way the womenfolk became chaste and for their love the knights were ever more daring.'

The Arthurian mystique was in due course annexed by the *parvenu* Anglo-Norman monarchy, which needed a splendid pedigree to match the Charlemagne mythos. The Plantagenets claimed to be the rightful successors of Arthur. Most of the medieval cycle was created in the countries on both sides of the Channel where educated people spoke French. Camelot, as a city of romance, brings the Arthurian glory into focus after it has turned chivalric, lost touch with history and Wales, and become a psychological asset of the English crown. While the courtly Arthur enjoyed high favour among the medieval nobility, he was not a hero of the people, like Robin Hood. But there was a popular Arthur legend also, as at Cadbury, which overlapped the romantic one.

Behind all this growth of Arthur were two major steps in 'mythification' which had already been completed before the Anglo-Normans discovered him. The major fictitious themes added to the historical soldier are his national kingship and his immortality. The immortality can be observed taking shape slightly before the national kingship. It is best to look at them in that order.

4

Some years ago Dr Ralegh Radford, afterwards Chairman of the Camelot Research Committee, excavated Arthur's alleged grave at Glastonbury Abbey. He concluded that the monks of the twelfth century may well have told the truth about it. Whether they actually found him, or only claimed to have found him for prestige reasons, their search was prompted by reasons of state. Henry II suggested it after hearing a tradition of Arthur's burial from a Welsh bard.

Henry's desire to get his predecessor dug up was itself prompted by a rival tradition, and here the politics came in. Many of the Celts of Wales, Cornwall and Brittany insisted that Arthur was still alive and their true sovereign. He would return to lead them against the

Anglo-Norman overlords, and recover their lost land. King Henry had domains on both sides of the Channel; he encountered this hope often enough to find it an irritant. Hence his wish to have Arthur proved dead. Henry did not live to witness the exhumation in 1190. But Edward I, when he was trying to subdue the Welsh, thought it worth while to go to Glastonbury and exhibit Arthur's very dead bones.

Officially the tomb was accepted. Most of the romancers who worked up and transmuted the traditions of Arthur took little notice of the belief in his survival. It was a folk-legend rather than a literary legend. It was kept alive by anonymous imaginations almost unaided. But it was kept alive with amazing stubbornness, not only by the Welsh and Cornish but eventually by the English as well, right down to the Cadbury villagers of modern times. And in the end it triumphed. We all know today that the Return is of the essence. Even the Glastonbury grave cannot get rid of it. As a figure of the imagination Arthur is inescapably pictured as still living, in some sense or other, and destined to reappear when Britain needs him.

Perhaps because it is so very much a popular and oral idea, the Return cannot be documented in the earliest matter. But among some Welsh verses in the *Black Book of Carmarthen* is a 'Song of the Graves' listing various warriors with their places of burial. Arthur is the exception: his grave is a mystery, 'concealed till Doomsday', according to one rendering. There may have been a British conspiracy of silence about his death, with a view to exploiting the terror of his name for a few years longer, or protecting his grave from desecration. But the hint was irresistible. William of Malmesbury, who carried out researches at Glastonbury about 1125, says that because Arthur's grave is 'nowhere beheld', ancient songs foretell his return. How ancient, it is impossible to say. But a few years before William's inquiries, some French priests visiting Cornwall were startled at the confidence of the local people that 'King Arthur' still lived – a confidence so aggressive that when the Frenchmen smiled, a fight broke out. The writer who records this fracas notes that the same delusion flourished in Brittany.

In his *History* Geoffrey of Monmouth sidesteps the issue. After the fatal battle of Camlann, he says, Arthur was mortally wounded and carried off to the Isle of Avalon (unlocated) 'so that his wounds might be attended to'. We are told no more, apart from a prophecy of Merlin that Arthur's end would be shrouded in mystery. Wace, who published a chronicle-epic based on Geoffrey in 1155, speaks of Arthur's death as doubtful. A number of medieval authors, not only in England and France but as far off as Italy, mention the promise of the Return either non-committally or with scorn. Malory, about 1470, accepts the Glastonbury grave. Yet he feels bound to add: 'Some men say in many parts of England that King Arthur is not dead, but had by the will of our Lord Jesu into another place; and men say that he shall come again, and he shall win the Holy Cross.' This is an admission that the belief was too potent to suppress. The disasters of plague and war, perhaps, had made the English yearn for rescue. At all events they had taken over the deathless King of Britain, and generalized him far beyond the crudity of a mere Celtic *revanche*, into a royal saviour and triumphant crusader. As we shall see, the dream was specific enough to be exploited politically.

To revert to the beginnings, when Arthur's non-death emerges into daylight in Cornwall, it is already linked with a kingship of some kind. This too may have been a popular fancy, and its meaning is nebulous. His literary legend as King of All Britain, and conqueror of countries beyond, first comes out clearly in Geoffrey, who makes him rule not only over the British Isles but over large parts of Scandinavia and western Europe. Parallel with Geoffrey there is a doubtfully dated preface to the life of a Breton saint, which depicts Arthur 'the great king of the Britons' winning victories in Britain and Gaul, and being 'summoned', at the end of his career, 'from human activity'.

Arthur the immortal is inseparable from Arthur the King of Britain. They are two aspects of the same *tour de force* of myth-making. If we go on to look at the legends in detail, we shall soon see at least a general sort of truth in Blake's dictum about the acts of Albion being 'applied' to Arthur: Albion as the patriarchal spirit behind early Britain. The long continuity suggested by the Cadbury rampart is echoed in the stories of the hill's hero.

On Arthur, in fact, the entire British past has (if sketchily) descended. His birth is due to a magical contrivance by Merlin, who – in romance, not in Geoffrey's *History* – becomes the Grey Eminence of his early reign. We recall Merlin's apparent absorption of a Stonehenge tradition three thousand years old. The wizard himself is both Christian and pre-Christian, a son of the Devil

86

with preternatural gifts; he evokes the pagan past. Besides his connection with Stonehenge, his name appears as well as Arthur's in the list of megaliths and fancifully interpreted natural features transferred by folklore from antiquity to the post-Roman age: Arthur's Quoit, Arthur's Stone, Merlin's Rock, and so on. These are spread over a long stretch of territory from Cornwall to central Scotland. They are the bones of Albion reanimated by Arthur.

The same is true, partly, of Lyonesse. The inhabited land under Mount's Bay, lost in the second millennium B.C., is probably an ingredient of the legend of Sir Tristram's country. But Lyonesse has drawn in a later folk-memory of the single *Sylina Insula* which broke up to form the main group of the Scillies, and was still united in the fourth century A.D. From the Roman period also comes Arthur's title of 'emperor', and his wars in Gaul and march on Rome, which are imitated from those of the pretender Maximus.

Legendary Arthur has annexed pagan mythology. Several exploits of the King and his knights derive from ancient Celtic motifs. One of the triads mentions Arthur alongside Mabon, the god Maponus. The tale *Culhwch and Olwen* lists other such characters at his court. As a folklore figure, Arthur is a Wild Huntsman, galloping through the clouds with Gwyn ap Nudd; a version of the Hunt hovers over the landscape near Cadbury. In a tenth-century Welsh poem *The Spoils of Annwn* Arthur makes a perilous voyage to Gwyn's kingdom in search of a magic cauldron, watched over by nine maidens – an Otherworld Quest by water in true pagan style, foreshadowing the eerier aspects of the Quest of the Grail.

The theme of a mysterious voyage recalls Bran. If we turn to Arthur specifically as king and immortal, we find the Celtic past coming to rest on him more precisely. Like Bran, 'the Blessed', Arthur embodies the glory of the Island of Britain, and presides over a noble era which he is, so to speak, the spirit of. Like Bran, he leads British forces overseas; and his Annwn quest has likenesses to Bran's invasion of Ireland which are beyond coincidence. Like Bran, he is mortally wounded yet still mysteriously alive. Bran, through the burial of his head on Tower Hill, goes on protecting Britain; and a triad tells how Arthur explicitly took over this function from him by digging the head up, saying Britain should rely on valour alone. While Bran reigns, there is land between Wales and Ireland, and it sinks like Atlantis after he is gone; so also with Arthur and Lyonesse. Bran is The Raven; and according to a folklore belief, the ever-living Arthur revisits Britain in that guise. The story is mentioned, oddly enough, in *Don Quixote*. Not so enormously long ago, an old man at Marazion restrained someone from shooting at a raven because it might be Arthur.

To say that the literary legend develops Arthur's royalty more than his immortality is to say that it fastens on the aspect which corresponds to the British Bran rather than the Irish. Arthur's reign is like Bran's in being glorious while it lasts, but also in ending with civil war and the desolation of Britain. Even in the early triadic matter a sense of doom is present. There is far more about Camlann than there is about Arthur's victories. Geoffrey establishes the King's apogee briefly, and then goes on to his Roman war and fall. During the Middle Ages the reign is enlarged upon. Through the Round Table an Arthurian charisma works on the realm. Then Malory skilfully enhances the drama by building up both phases. He shifts the Roman war backward, and thus makes room for a long, prosperous reign with Arthur at the height of his powers and, in effect, emperor of half Europe. The golden age is more golden; the fall is more tragic. Tennyson follows Malory.

But if romancers cared more about a credible kingship, popular fable kept a firm grip on Arthur's survival. This aspect recalls Bran in his Irish guise, and places the King himself in the realms of sunset. Indeed Arthur suggests what Bran may well have been, before he split into a Briton and an Irishman.

Where and what was the Isle of Avalon? According to one account it is the same as Gwyn's fairy kingdom of Annwn. The older, more authentic form of its name is 'Avallach'. By the twelfth century at any rate, it was usually said to mean the 'place of apples', a Garden of the Hesperides. The name was equated with the Irish *ablach*, an epithet meaning 'rich in apples' that was applied to an Elysian island in Irish legend. (Bran is summoned by a woman with an apple bough.) This view has been contested as a misunderstanding, on the ground that the island was named after a Celtic hero, Avallach or Aballach. He is a known figure, of respectable antiquity. But he himself may have been an Otherworld denizen like Gwyn.

Nobody knows how the name attached itself to Glastonbury, though the area certainly was an island, or nearly so, in Arthur's time. With its bizarre hill and natural moats, Glastonbury was well qualified to be Celtic enchanted ground. But it may not have become Avalon till the twelfth century, and then because of nothing more definite than a nebulous uncanny aura, plus the Arthur associations. While it was the only exact location which Avalon ever acquired on any map, it was not the only place where Avalon was ever supposed to be.

Avalon is one expression of the Celtic belief in an Otherworld harbouring the dead or at least the departed – an Otherworld reached by water, and either in the British Isles or accessible from them. We have seen that this is a belief which can be documented as far back as Arthur's actual period. Here are the words of Procopius in his account of the spectral ferry service across the Channel.

They say, then, that the souls of men who die are always conveyed to this place ['Brittia'] . . . Along the coast of the ocean which lies opposite Brittia there are numerous villages. These are inhabited by men who fish with nets or till the soil or carry on a sea-trade with this island, being in other respects subject to the Franks, but never making them any payment of tribute, that burden having been remitted to them from ancient times on account, as they say, of a certain service . . .

The men of this place say that the conduct of souls is laid upon them in turn. So the men who on the following night must go to do this work relieving others in the service, as soon as darkness comes on, retire to their own houses and sleep, awaiting him who is to assemble them for the enterprise. And at a late hour of the night they are conscious of a knocking at their doors and hear an indistinct voice . . .

They see skiffs in readiness, with no man at all in them, not their own skiffs, however, but of a different kind, in which they embark and lay hold of the oars. And they are aware that the boats are burdened with a large number of passengers and are wet by the waves to the edge of the planks and the oar-locks, having not so much as one finger's breadth above the water; they themselves, however, see no one, but after rowing a single hour they put in at Brittia. And yet when they make the voyage in their own skiffs, not using sails but rowing, they with difficulty make this passage in a night and a day. Then when they have reached the island and have been relieved of their burden, they depart with all speed, their boats now becoming suddenly light and rising above the waves, for they sink no further in the water than the keel itself.

With sundry added particulars. Where these ghosts ultimately went from their British rendezvous, we have no means of determining. And of course they are dead, whereas Arthur and Bran pass into an Other-Life. Still, all this brings us within hailing distance of Bran's voyage, and the seafarers who glide out of the mortal world. Though Geoffrey's first version of the Passing of Arthur merely conveys the King to Avalon without explanation, he wrote another – in a poem entitled *The Life of Merlin* – that supplies details.

Here the bard Taliesin discourses of Atlantic geography. First he mentions the Gorgades or Gorgon Islands, and the Hesperides. These names come from Pliny's *Natural History*. Geoffrey is likely to have found them in later authors, who improve on Pliny and portray the two island-groups as far off 'in the most secret recesses of the sea'. The Gorgades may be Madeira and its neighbour Porto Santo, the Hesperides may be the Azores. It was among these semi-mythical archipelagoes, the classical counterpart of the western isles of Irish legend, that Geoffrey finally decided to place Avalon.

In the poem Taliesin speaks of it as 'the Isle of Apples which men call Fortunate', thereby linking Celtic and classical motifs. He adapts a description of the Fortunate Isles, and says Avalon is ruled by nine sister enchantresses, probably the same as the nine maidens who guard the cauldron sought for by Arthur in *The Spoils of Annwn*. They also remind us of the women in one of the islands visited by Bran. Taliesin continues, still talking of Avalon:

> Thither after the battle of Camlann we took the wounded Arthur, guided by Barinthus to whom the waters and the stars of heaven were well known.

Barinthus clinches the connection with the Irish Atlantic mythos. He is St Brendan's guide as well as Arthur's.

This Avalon is the realm of Cronus and Atlas once again. It embodies the same dream, classical as well as Celtic, of a blessed place over the sunset waters. The dethroned yet undying King who goes there is going to the same region, and to somewhat the same destiny, as the Irish Bran in the Voyage. However, Arthur's is not the same destiny precisely. Cadbury itself supplies one of the sharpest reminders of the other version of his immortality. There, he is said to lie asleep in a cave with his knights around him. Folklore locates the sleeping King, or his knights, or his treasure, in other caves too – near Caerleon, and at Marchlyn Mawr in Caernarvon, and beside Snowdon, and at Alderley Edge in Cheshire and The Sneep in Durham and in the Eildon Hills near Melrose. This version is more peculiarly Celtic than the story of Avalon. And it repeats the 'sleep' of Plutarch's British Titan in his own western island, which is not part of the classical Cronus myth.

5

The ambiguity of the King's retreat is its most significant feature, and a glance at the British Titan is enough to show why. Undying Arthur has been given two different, seemingly discrepant roles. Yet in fact they are the same. The key lies immensely further back in time.

Somehow the Cronus myth has attached itself to Arthur. Sir John Rhys and R. S. Loomis drew attention to the passage in Plutarch long ago, but I do not know of anyone who fully appreciates what has happened. Which is very remarkable indeed. The myth has come apart on the way. The absent British god was alive but asleep, in a cave, surrounded by former henchmen, in a western Fortunate Isle. Popular imagination fastened on the more Celtic part of this image, making the fallen Arthur sleep in a cave, accompanied by his knights. Educated imagination preferred the part with a classical affinity, and took Arthur to a western Fortunate Isle. In both guises the undying King remains a Cronus-figure, a Titan, and only fully intelligible as such.

But he is like Cronus, the classical Cronus-Saturn, in his royalty as well. He once reigned, before the inferior powers now prevailing. His reign was a golden age when the Island of Britain found fulfilment and grandeur. Then a decline set in, leading to a war with his own elusive and upstart son, as Modred becomes in legend. Overthrown, Arthur departed west to the mysterious Elsewhere. But like Saturn in Virgil he may return, sweep away the corruption of ages, and resume his lost glory.

So Blake is right even in detail. As a person and not simply a personification, his Albion stands for the Titan-nature as manifested in Britain; and the stories of Arthur do turn out to be acts of Albion in that sense, applied to a prince of the fifth century.

How? Arthur's transformation clearly began because the Welsh wanted vengeance on the Saxons. They cherished dreams of their departed champion coming back to reconquer the country, and to restore Celtic supremacy in the Island of Britain. For this hope they found, let us suppose, a precedent in the myth of some Celtic hero or deity who had, in past times, become assimilated to Cronus. Once Arthur began to acquire his attributes he went on acquiring them, and grew into a more general symbol, that others besides the Welsh could adopt.

The obvious choice for this prototype is Bran, and the best hope of an answer may lie in Graves's conjecture that the being whom Plutarch calls Cronus is the Celtic god of that name. It must be stressed, however, that the god is not known to us directly. Even by combining the British and Irish heroes who seem to be derived from him, we cannot completely bridge the gap. Still less can we show the process happening.

Another theory (not ruling out the first) might arise from the tendency of some classical minds to fix the name 'Cronus' on any god worshipped with human sacrifice. In Roman Britain a place where such sacrifices were remembered might have prompted talk about Cronus, and made the Titan myth locally familiar, ready to hand for British adaptation. Cadbury itself has its single human victim, with a parallel at Maiden Castle. But in the absence of any sign of a regular cult, little weight can be given to either.

Whatever the difficulties, there is no simple alternative to the Titan. I do not think the historical Arthur could have been expanded into the legendary Arthur in any other obvious way, whether by the internal logic of the conception, or by 'applying the acts' of someone else.[1] It is no use going to the fertility gods – Osiris, Attis, and the rest – who died and revived, or vanished underground and came up again, every year. Arthur is not cyclic. In a sense he is a Sacred King, but not from the *Golden Bough* milieu. The Sacred King also corresponds to a fairly brief cyclic process, and the whole point of him is that he does die, whereas King Arthur does not. For this reason among several, the Christ of orthodox faith also fails as a prototype. Avalon is not Golgotha. To say 'the stories of Arthur are the acts of Jesus Christ applied to a prince of the fifth century' would be patently absurd. It is only in the erudite allegory of Spenser that Arthur ever resembles Christ.

In Arthur then, because of the myth-making which Blake so

[1] That is, within reach. There are New World myths with a certain aptness. But Arthur can hardly be a form of Quetzalcoatl.

surprisingly discerned, we face the august theme of the Return of the King: the far-off, charismatic, but historical ruler, lord of a golden age, expelled by baser powers yet preternaturally alive through the centuries, and destined to come back as a Messiah with his old splendour rekindled. The special quality of the legend is to suggest that the Titan 'pattern' may have a meaning in terms of real human events and hopes, in the real world. The suggestion is of course poetic and fanciful, but that is its content.

Legends of secret immortality have, it is true, been attached to other heroes. Outside Britain there were medieval fancies about an 'emperor' who had lain asleep for centuries and would wake up to perform marvellous feats. One or two such tales, current as early as the First Crusade, probably took shape without any Arthurian influence. It was sometimes rumoured that Charlemagne himself would rise to lead the crusaders. But these were cruder and shallower notions. The Titan themes – the sleeper's association with a lost golden era which was *other*; his tragic supplanting and eclipse; and his future reinstatement – played no vital part in them.

Later came the German tale of the Emperor Frederick who would come again. He is now usually said to have been Frederick I (Barbarossa). In fact, however, he was a composite, and began his career as Frederick II. This synthetic Kaiser did become a little like Arthur, in some versions – but only after the British legend was well known overseas, and parallels had been explicitly drawn. Arthur is the original, Frederick is a carbon copy; considerably smudged.[1]

[1] See Norman Cohn, *The Pursuit of the Millennium* (1970 edition), pp. 72, 93, 113, 123, 143.

5

The British Myth

1

We can now picture Arthur as a real British leader born in the fifth century, more Celtic (as Cadbury hints) than Romanized, and therefore capable, when turned into a legend, of absorbing and symbolizing a long British past. Above all he absorbed the Titan theme in its Celtic form. But defining him is still not an answer to the initial question. Even when we grasp that he emerges from an older world carrying overtones, we are still far from explaining his perennial spell, and showing why he can capture imaginations.

Cadbury itself gives no further help. Its Saxon phase is important but of no concern here. However, one more step is possible. We can turn again from Cadbury to the hill in the distance: to Glastonbury lying north-westward across the Somerset lowland. Alongside the Return of Arthur there are other dreams – the Finding of the Holy Grail, and the related if less famous dream of a resurrection of Glastonbury, as in John Cowper Powys's novel. Does this second Arthurian place reveal more fully what the spell is about?

The vast complex of Glastonbury legends is centred on the ruined Abbey. This is supposed to have been the oldest Christian foundation in Britain, and a repository of pre-Christian mysteries. Glastonbury's saga has gone on growing and proliferating into modern times. The full-blown story asserts that Glastonbury is the true Isle of Avalon, a place of religious awe to the pagan Celts; that Joseph of Arimathea, the rich man who buried Christ, came bringing the Holy Grail and built a wattle chapel afterwards known as the Old Church; that Christian hermits were on the spot in the

94

fifth century, and St Patrick organized them and gave them a monastic rule; that the foremost saints of the Celtic Church also visited the community; that Arthur was brought to it mortally wounded and buried in the monks' graveyard. The story has many ramifications. Later additions are the Holy Thorn, which supposedly grew from Joseph's staff; the visit paid by Jesus himself as a boy; the ritual maze said to be traceable on the Tor; and the giant zodiacal figures said to be visible from the air in the neighbourhood.

The questions raised by these beliefs are too complex to pursue here.[1] Most of them undoubtedly did grow round the monastery, and, in particular, the Old Church. This was an actual wattle structure, on the site now filled by the Lady Chapel. It was already standing when the Saxons overran central Somerset in 658, and the British monks, even then, seem to have been vague as to its beginnings. The earliest accounts of it declare that it was planted there miraculously, or built by 'disciples of Christ himself', and in due course – not at first – the name of Joseph of Arimathea is given.

Sceptical scholarship is prepared to allow that the Christian advent may indeed have been very early, and that there was a Celtic monastery on the site by the sixth century. Excavation has also revealed a small dark-age citadel on the Tor, which fits in well with one of the subsidiary tales, about Arthur's clash with a 'King Melwas'. The later life of the monastery as a joint Saxon-Celtic community, as a focus of convergent traditions, as the headquarters of the post-Danish revival under St Dunstan, and as the most splendid of English medieval abbeys, is a matter of history. Whatever the truth about the legends, there is a sixth-century Glastonbury Fact underlying them, as there is an Arthurian Fact. It is the status of the monastery as a centre of the Celtic Church, with a continuity of some sort extending backward and forward. A Welsh triad names the three great British monasteries as Glastonbury, Amesbury and Llantwit Major. Each had a 'perpetual choir' chanting the liturgy round the clock in relays. As Amesbury was destroyed by the Saxons in the 550s, the period implied for the greatness of British Glastonbury is before that.

In considering this mythology beside the Arthur mythology, two essentials must be grasped. One is that Glastonbury was a place where things began, a place of dawn, not decline. Well before the

[1] I have attempted a summary in an article on Glastonbury in the encyclopaedia *Man, Myth and Magic* (B.P.C., 1970).

twelfth century it was regarded as a starting-point, if not *the* starting-point, of British Christianity, and from its monastery many influences radiated. The second point to grasp is that the Christianity of this dark-age shrine was idiosyncratic. Glastonbury was a centre, not simply of the Church, but of that highly individual Celtic Church which Arthur's victories helped so much. The Grail cycle which is linked with Arthur and, obscurely, with Glastonbury itself, has a background in Celtic Christendom.

The upper-class Christianization which produced such Britons as St Patrick was extended to the people during the late fifth and early sixth centuries. David and the other saints remembered at Glastonbury were only a select few in a wave of apostles, chiefly Welsh, who presided over the wide flowering in Britain and Ireland. The Ireland that preserved legends of Bran and Brendan was the most cultured land of the dark-age west – the only one where any appreciable number knew Greek – and owed a vast debt to the saints from Britain.

This Celtic Church of the British Isles, which counted Glastonbury among its major communities, was Catholic in doctrine. But it was different. The first Saxon onrush in the 450s had almost cut it off from the Christianity of the continent. It was based on monasteries rather than dioceses; its ruling ecclesiastics were abbots rather than bishops; and the monks and·hermits, not the secular clergy, set the tone. They were freer than their brethren abroad. Many undertook wandering missions by land and water. Their lives often had a questing, exploratory air.

The monks had a more democratic outlook than the clerics of Gaul and Italy. Women were held in higher esteem, because the importance of monks made nuns important as well. We have noted how the absence of a strong pagan priesthood helped mythology to survive with a change of form rather than a complete censorship. But there was more to it than that. In the milieu of a less embattled religion, the Celts could possess books and pursue studies which the continental hierarchy frowned upon. Semi-pagan ideas, semi-pagan speculations, lived on in Celtic Christianity with a special vigour. The writings of the monks contain weird angelologies and formulae for converse with the spirit world. St Bridget, the namesake of an Irish goddess, is spoken of in pre-Christian terms as a reincarnation of the Virgin Mary, and, in some uncanonical sense, a priestess.

Though Celtic Christianity was never strictly heretical, it did convey an odd flavour, a 'Sense of Something Else' as it has been called. Most of the Cel.s were drawn into full conformity with Rome by the Synod of Whitby in 663. By that time their missionaries had influenced the Anglo-Saxons themselves. The debate at Whitby had a violence which the facts do not really explain, and concentrated on small points of discipline which seem to have been battle-cries rather than the true issues. Both parties flung the word 'heretic' back and forth. Both parties hinted at curious traditions descending from Simon Magus and the apostle John. The papalist Christians scented a heterodoxy which they never managed to pin down. They felt the presence of something elusive and baffling. Such was the Celtic Church, in which the main corpus of Glastonbury and Grail legend is rooted.

2

If the Glastonbury story of Arthur's passing is right, the others are wrong. The two conceptions of Avalon clash; the tomb in the Abbey rules out the cave. Loomis remarked on the irony that Cadbury villagers clung to their immortal king within sight of the place where his dead bones were so ostentatiously found. Clearly, if Arthur was buried in the Abbey, his return can only be figurative at most. What is striking is that although Glastonbury contradicts that part of his legend, the mythology produced by its own lore shows the same psychological impulse at work.

When Arthurian romance took shape, the 'other' Christianity, the Celtic 'Something Else', lingered as an afterglow in the west. The Grail cycle was a religious counterpart to the process that evolved King Arthur out of the *dux bellorum*. The official Church mistrusted the Grail, and with reason. It sprang from a fusion of motifs: an unsatisfactory fusion, performed by men who never quite mastered the materials they worked with.

At the earliest known stage there is a dimly discerned magical vessel that has nothing to do with Christ. It may have been a cauldron of inspiration and enlightenment kept by a Celtic goddess, or by a synod of goddesses. The quest motif emerges in the tenth-century poem *The Spoils of Annwn*, where the wonder-working cauldron is in the custody of nine Avalonian maidens. To reach it, Arthur and his warriors have to cross water and pierce the defences of fairyland. Only seven return alive.

When the Grail appears as such, it tends to keep an Avalonian context, though the meaning of 'Avalon' varies. A long poem entitled the *Conte du Graal*, by Chrétien de Troyes and others, portrays an enchanted vessel so called. This is not simply the cauldron under a new name. Though its origin is never explained, it now has Christian associations. A Host is carried in it.

In the 1190s come two verse narratives by Robert de Borron. Through some much-debated transition, Christianity of a kind has taken over. The Grail is said to be the vessel of the Last Supper. It fell into the hands of Joseph of Arimathea, and was brought to Britain and to the 'Vales of Avalon' by wandering Christians under his direction. The reference is to the low-lying country of central Somerset. An 'isle' of Avalon might be elsewhere, but no 'vales' ever were.

Joseph himself remains enigmatic. If he was already claimed as the founder of Christian Glastonbury, we can at least say where the romancer got hold of him. But there is no proof that he was. The source may have been in a book on the symbolism of the Mass, by Honorius of Autun. The priest laying the paten on the chalice is said to represent Joseph closing the tomb of Christ with a stone. Possibly someone's imagination took a hint, and linked Joseph with Christ's original chalice. However the linkage happened, the Grail became 'holy', drawing in a medley of speculations about the Mass, and the doctrine of the Real Presence on which it centres – yet still with a trail of pre-Christian imagery and ideas.

The results (at least in the earlier, more creative romances) are bewildering. The Grail stands for a Christian mystery entrusted only to Britain. It is a token of the friendship of God, the vehicle of a special sacrament. Strange rituals are built round it. Secret words are spoken. Visions of Christ and the Blessed Virgin are vouchsafed to those who approach the Grail in the right spirit. Not everyone sees them. The Grail sometimes has the air of a *speculum* like the crystal-gazer's ball, a channel for the scrying gift which some people possess (whatever the source of the images they see) and others do not.

By King Arthur's time, it is explained, the Grail has been lost. It is still in Britain, but in a mysterious castle surrounded by a waste land, and behind a watery barrier. The custodian of the Grail is the 'Fisher King', who lies wounded and immobile, neither living nor dead. The land became wasted when he sustained his wound. If the questing knight reaches the castle, and its occupants show the Grail, he is expected to ask a certain question. Should he do so without prompting, the Fisher King will be healed and the waste land will revive. A few knights attain a partial vision, and Galahad a complete one, but Galahad dies and the Grail recedes again.

The magical themes blend with the Christian in varying proportions. They are all adapted to the ends of Christian allegory, but they remain highly suspect. Jessie Weston, whose study of the problem inspired Eliot's *Waste Land*, maintained that the romancers were transmitting glimpses of an initiation ritual blending Christian and pagan ideas, which was actually performed by an occult sect.

To achieve the Grail completely, as Galahad's virtues enable him to do, is to undergo an experience which the writers never describe. Charles Williams compared it to the close of the *Divine Comedy*. Dante imagines a mystical insight into the nature of the Trinity and the Incarnation. As Dante is given this insight through the intercession of Mary, so there are hints that Mary replaced the pagan goddess behind the enchanted vessel, and that the Grail stories are influenced by some esoteric mode of devotion to her. If so, the cult of the Virgin at Glastonbury may be significant; the Old Church was her senior shrine north of the Alps.

It is more certain that the offbeat religion of the earlier Grail romances retains Celtic touches. The secret words spoken over the Grail, the question which is asked or not asked, belong to a spiritual tradition which evoked responses among the Celts. The actual question is usually stated as 'Whom does the Grail serve?' Apparently it unlocks some mystery of divine action in the world. Such an approach is out of keeping with Roman orthodoxy, as is the whole atmosphere of quest.

However, parallels can be found in apocryphal early Christian books. One, *The Questions of Bartholomew*, contains possible hints at the Grail theme. It is not known whether this book was among those which Celtic Christians continued to read after their banning elsewhere. But an undoubted apocryphal source of Grail romance, *The Acts of Pilate*, was available in Ireland. The motif of a questing Christianity recurs in St Brendan's Voyage. Recently Dr Valerie

Lagorio has shown that the account of Joseph of Arimathea and his followers, and their British descendants, is moulded throughout by Celtic ideas of sainthood and saintly families.

Behind the Christian complexities are the half-digested pagan ones, in which, as with King Arthur, a medieval legend absorbs fragments of an immemorial past. The Holy Grail is still, intermittently, a pre-Christian magical vessel. It is a source of life, not only spiritual but physical. Its apparition produces a literal banquet. This happens even in Malory's version: it floats through the hall at Camelot, and each knight receives, out of nowhere, the meat and drink of his choice. The waste land which the seeker must restore to fruitfulness, the strange female attendants who accompany the Grail, the nature of the Grail-keeper's wound (which in the franker versions is a form of castration), belong to a fairly palpable realm of fertility magic. Much the same could be said of the 'hallows' or ritual objects that sometimes go with the Grail, carrying blatant sexual symbolism. Non-Christian imagery has been pressed into Christian service.

Embedded in this tangle of cryptic themes are some which take us into the same background as Arthur. We find not only 'Avalon' but also the old alternative form 'Avallach', alleged to have been the name of the island's overlord. In the Grail stories the name is applied to a person, Evalake. Avallach's name has been corrupted, and he has been shifted to a different setting. The theme has evidently travelled a long way, and become disjointed and obscured.

More arresting still, indeed crucial, is the rebirth of the ubiquitous Bran in a new guise. When the Grail is Christianized, a character called Bron or Brons, certainly the same as the Celtic hero, enters the tale as Joseph's brother-in-law. He is the Grail's custodian after Joseph himself, and the original Fisher King, though others succeed him in that role. To realize this presence of Bran is to see clues to several of the riddles. Thus the wounding of the Fisher King, and the desolation of the land, may echo the wounding of Bran and the wasting of Britain that ensues. Some of the stories introduce a dish with a severed head on it, which is reminiscent of Bran's famous head. Bran is even associated with a magic cauldron, though its bearing on the Grail is doubtful. The assimilation of Bran to this legend of the first Christians in Britain was vaguely realized long before scholarship pieced it out. A Welsh tradition which may not be very ancient, but is more than a modern fancy, moves Bran into apostolic times and makes him preach Christianity in Britain.

The royal Grail-keeper, entranced in his fastness across a barrier of water, takes us back into the realm of Cronus and Bran and Arthur's passing, the Otherworld harbouring the immortal king. The sunset island has become a secret retreat in Britain, but the hero reappears. So does the motif of loss and return, embodied in the Grail itself. The author of one of the romances, *Perlesvaus*, puts in a strange seafaring episode. It seems to make little sense. But a comparison with the voyage legends of dark-age Ireland – those of Bran himself, and Brendan, and kindred adventurers – shows what the episode is based on. This is a country of the mind which the author knows to be relevant to the Grail.

Defining this common substratum of the Grail legend and the Arthur legend is more than a literary conclusion. The Grail confronts us, not merely with a few similar details, but with the same pattern of imagination. It is not often that occultists shed much light; in this case, however, one of them does. A. E. Waite, who belonged to the equivocal circle that included W. B. Yeats and Aleister Crowley, produced two books on the Grail. In one of these the clouds are rent by a flash of insight. Esoterically, says Waite, the manifestation which will finally restore the lost Grail and revive the waste land is cognate with the return of Arthur. They are two sides of the same coin.

The point of the Grail in its developed Christian form is that it is lost, yet may be found again. Once, the holy mystery was established in Britain openly. Its recovery, like Arthur's prophesied second advent, would be the reinstatement of a long-lost glory; or at any rate, of a long-lost promise. The dormant Grail-keeper would come back to life, the afflicted country would blossom with a new spring, the vanished vision would be recovered. Both legends express the same idea, that the lost is not lost. Modern hopes for a rebirth of Glastonbury, where Arthur and the Grail converge, can be understood as rationalized variations on the theme. The assorted projects for an English Bayreuth, for a rebuilt monastery, for a pre-fabricated millennial city, and so on, have all been inspired by the feeling of a magical presence, which the fall of the Abbey drove underground but could not kill.

3

Virgil saluted Augustus and his Empire as restoring the reign of Saturn. This was to proclaim the reinstatement of long-lost glory, the Titan glory, as a political fact. The equivalent did once happen in England. Arthur's second reign was once, after a fashion, proclaimed. A sign that we are close to penetrating his spell is that there is a phase of history when it can be seen influencing public affairs, precisely through an alleged reinstatement.

To follow the 'Matter of Britain' beyond the pioneers is to notice a change. Most of the authors wrote in French or in deference to French literary models. Theirs was the troubadour world. They and their readers were interested in knightly exploits, and courtly love, and the Grail quest, and magicians and monsters. Apart from the Plantagenets, who valued the mystique of the British monarchy, there was not much interest in Arthur's regime as such, or even in its head. The visionary kingdom was taken for granted as having flourished before the Saxon conquest. Britain had enjoyed her Saturnian age. But as far as the romancers were concerned, the historical picture contrived by Geoffrey receded into near-imperceptibility. Arthur himself dwindled into a sort of chairman.

Outside England this process went on till the subject became exhausted. In France the writing of Arthurian tales dried up. In Italy the chivalric apparatus was transferred from Arthur to Charlemagne, who was even given a round table of his own. In England, however, after what looked like a similar demise, Arthur's kingdom was rediscovered in the middle fifteenth century by Malory.

The single-volume *Morte d'Arthur* is a product of Caxton's editorial hand. Malory himself composed a series of romances in English; most of them were based on French originals, but through his rehandling the disintegration was reversed. He approached his subject with a seriousness and moral concern foreign to his predecessors, and an attitude not unlike Shakespeare's in the history plays. He restored a time-scheme and a sense of internal logic. Starting from Merlin and making him the prime sponsor of the regime, Malory traced Arthur's fortunes from his dubious birth at Tintagel through the sword-in-the-stone test, the setting up of the Round Table at Camelot, the triumphs, the Grail quest, the tragedy of Guinevere and Lancelot, the conflict with Modred, the throwing away of Excalibur, and the ambiguous Passing. Malory's sequence of events not only fixed the Legend, it gave the Arthurian age a shape and substance for English readers which it had lost everywhere else.

At the end Malory consigned Arthur to his Glastonbury grave, yet felt bound to note the widespread belief that he would come back. Caxton printed his tightened-up edition in 1485, describing it in the preface as a request performance. Arthur's fame still flourished. As for his return, the Welsh and Breton dream of a Messianic counter-blow against alien rulers had long since dissolved. Arthur was firmly annexed to the monarchy of England, and his return would involve the entire realm. Doubtless few educated men could believe that he would literally emerge from a cave, or sail homeward from Avalon. But his return might happen symbolically, as a rebirth of his kingdom, a reawakening of the majesty of his Britain. In the nightmare of the Wars of the Roses, with England's French domain lost and rival kings committing atrocities against each other, it was an event to be hoped for.

Within a few weeks of Caxton's publication of Malory, Henry Tudor overthrew Richard III at Bosworth. Though far from being a full-blooded Welshman, Henry reckoned himself as Welsh. He marched from Wales against Richard under the standard of the Red Dragon, which Geoffrey of Monmouth had made a British emblem opposed to the White Dragon of Anglo-Saxondom. As Henry VII he married the Yorkist heiress, and created a monarchy strong enough to stamp out further rebellion. A skilful propagandist, Henry promoted a Tudor myth composed of two connected ideas.

The first was that his marriage had united the warring Roses, and put a providential end to a long disorder caused by wickedness in high places. (This is the view of England's troubles and peace which Shakespeare adopted.) The second idea was that through his grandfather Owen Tudor, Henry had a claim to the throne which was prior to both the Roses. It went back through Cadwallader, a late 'British' king, to the family of Arthur himself. By the royal Welshman's accession, Arthur actually had returned to save his country. The Tudor regime was 'Britain' restored after an epoch of confusion. The visionary kingdom was real again. The long-lost glory was reinstated.

In that spirit Henry named his first son Arthur and had him baptized at Winchester, then the favourite site for Camelot. The prince died young and the reign of Arthur II never materialized. But Henry VIII did his best to take over the mystique. Interest in Geoffrey of Monmouth revived, with hot disputes over his historical truth. One of his more responsible defenders was John Leland, the same who made the first known allusion to Cadbury Castle as Camelot.

The Tudor resurrection of Arthur was bogus yet curiously effective. Under Elizabeth I, it grew more so rather than less. The Queen was said to have been foretold by Cadwallader in person. English claims in North America were buttressed by theories about an Arthurian discovery. Shakespeare, though he avoided Arthur, used Geoffrey's stories of Lear and Cymbeline. An aristocratic 'Society of Archers' studied Leland and held an annual celebration of Arthur's memory. One of the group was Lord Grey, the Governor of Ireland, who had Edmund Spenser as his secretary, and another was Sir Henry Sidney, whose incomparable son Philip probably gave Spenser the idea for *The Faerie Queene*. At all events Spenser planned his masterpiece as a vast elaboration of the Tudor myth at several levels of meaning and chronology.

Gloriana, the Queen, stands (more or less) for Elizabeth. Arthur as a young prince, deeply devoted to her, enters the story from time to time and shares the adventures of her knights. In a letter to Raleigh outlining his intentions, Spenser explains that he is portraying Arthur's education, and will go on to a sequel showing his public virtues when he was king. Less than half of this immense plan was completed. But in the fragment Spenser introduces Merlin, Tristram, and other Malory characters; paraphrases a large part of Geoffrey of Monmouth; presents the Tudor dynasty in plain terms as the glorious kingdom of the Britons restored, with a suitable pedigree for Elizabeth; and weaves an allegorical linkage between the events and personages of the two periods.

Such was the grandeur of the mystique that haloed Elizabethan England, in the eyes of its greatest narrative poet. After 1603 James I tried to annex Arthur with the rest of his royal inheritance. He called his double domain 'Great Britain', and found poets willing to flatter him in the right language. However, his British claim became entangled with the theory of Divine Right. Parliamentary lawyers retorted by exploding Geoffrey of Monmouth, none too soon, and rehabilitating the Saxons. When Milton contemplated an Arthur epic and decided against it, his Roundhead sympathies played their part.

Yet the Arthurian mystique of the Tudors lingered on with stubborn vitality. As late as 1757 it reappears in Thomas Gray's poem *The Bard*. Gray makes a medieval Welsh prophet foretell Henry VII's accession as a proxy rebirth of 'long-lost Arthur', bringing a renaissance under 'genuine kings, Britannia's issue' – a renaissance destined to inspire not only Spenser but Shakespeare and Milton, and 'distant warblings' farther on still.

4

In the light of the Tudors and all the rest, and what these things imply about the working of minds, let us try to define the archetype which is constant throughout, the active ingredient in the spell.

The stories vary, but they always tend the same way. There were gods before the gods, kings before the kings; Titans before Olympians, Britons before English; and their reign was a golden age. Or in Christian terms, there was a profounder Christianity in the wave-encircled realms of the Celtic West, before the Church as we know it. Then the glory faded. Injustice and tyranny flowed in. Zeus usurped the throne of heaven. Prometheus was bound. The sea encroached. The Round Table broke up. Arthur succumbed to Modred. The Saxons conquered Britain. Or the Grail was lost and the land became waste.

Behind most of these variants is an oceanic sense, a notion of the disaster as an estranging plunge into depths. Hence the island to which the lost king goes, in the sunset recesses of the Atlantic. But the depths are formative. Ocean is not only an engulfer but an all-engendering womb. If Arthur is not hidden in the midst of the sea, he is hidden in a hollow cave; and the Titan, his prototype, is in both at once. The place of apparent death is the place of life, Atlantis itself is the true Eden. Whatever the form taken by the myth, *the glory which was once real has never actually died.* Somewhere, somehow, Cronus or Arthur is still living, enchanted or asleep through the ages. The Grail is still in safe keeping. The visionary kingdom is still invisibly 'there', latent.

Nor is it all over. As Virgil darkly foreshadowed, the being who incarnates the mystery will return, from the island, from the cavern, from wherever he is: will return in the flesh or in the spirit. Or the visionary realm will be reinstated: Albion, Britain, or (as in Charles Williams's Arthurian cycle) 'Logres'. The Grail will be found. Glastonbury will be restored with all it implies. A symbolic Atlantis will rise again from the waves.

This is the British myth, of which at least a large part can be shown to descend from remote antiquity. I know of no fully-developed parallel myth anywhere else. Even the classical parts of it did not come to fruition in the classical context. Nobody today would be likely to take any of its variants literally, whole and entire. Yet the Arthurian spell seems to me to be rooted in it. The shape of the enduring interest is, to a great extent, like this – a haunting sense that something of sovereign and magical importance is lost-yet-not-lost.

Much of the amateur archaeological zeal has focused not so much on serious evidence as on a daydream of digging up some buried splendour, and restoring it to the light of day. The recurrent questions of the more naïve Cadbury inquirers concerned the prospect of finding, below the topsoil, precisely the two objects that symbolize Britain's ancient glory: the Holy Grail which was lost, the Round Table which was broken. And even among the majority who knew better, the atmosphere of the dig tended to have more of this quality than one would find, say, at a Roman villa.

Why people's minds should work like that, with such an insistent force, remains to be explained. But they do. Furthermore, once the pattern is perceived, something else is also perceived which confirms this diagnosis. The same pattern occurs in other settings. As a poetic statement, the British myth is indeed unique. But it is a statement of broader psychological fact. It reflects a human phenomenon, a mode of thought and behaviour, that can be traced through the world in a profusion of forms: one of the strongest constants in history, and one of the least recognized. Henry Tudor's political abuse of the myth was no freak, no mere *tour de force* of propaganda. Others have acted similarly with no reference to Arthur.

Let us see who they were and how they acted. What is the myth really about?

PART TWO

The Glory and the Enemy

6

Plus ça Change . . .

1

Though Carlyle's account of the French Revolution is out of fashion, I doubt if anybody has been more successful at evoking what it must have felt like. Here is an extract from his sketch of the anticipatory ardours:

> Behold the new morning glittering down the eastern steeps; fly, false Phantasms, from its shafts of light; let the Absurd fly utterly, forsaking this lower Earth for ever. It is Truth and *Astraea Redux* that (in the shape of Philosophism) henceforth reign. For what imaginable purpose was man made, if not to be 'happy'? By victorious Analysis and Progress of the Species, happiness enough now awaits him . . . Nay, who knows but, by sufficiently victorious Analysis, 'human life may be indefinitely lengthened,' and men get rid of Death, as they have already done of the Devil? We shall then be happy in spite of Death and the Devil. – So preaches magniloquent Philosophism her *Redeunt Saturnia regna*.

The Latin phrases are Virgil's, describing the return of Saturn. Carlyle uses them again farther on. Clearly they appeal to this forceful delineator of moods as apt expressions. Virgil coined them when Saturn's reign was part of an accepted mythical world-picture, a natural image. Their fitness for capturing the spirit of the 1780s is a deeper question.

The French Revolution, like the Tudor mastery of England, had its mystique as well as its logic; and, as with the Tudors, some of the antecedents were very ancient indeed. One of them happens to belong to a realm which a thoughtful poet, Charles Williams, saw as the polar opposite of Arthurian Britain. There is no need to exaggerate this factor. Simply as it stands, it is an oddly revealing preface to the Revolution itself; an odd disclosure of processes that nourished the roots of Reason, in a soil as alien to the British myth as it could well be.

Behind the French Revolution, behind the Enlightenment that led up to it, there was (among much else) an intellectual discovery of China. Confucian teachings were brought to Europe by Jesuits and had an instant appeal. Here, said Voltaire and others, was morality without dogma. Here was a doctrine of government by merit instead of birth. China became a potent weapon against the French Establishment; Confucius became what he has remained to some extent, the patriarch of all humanists who have pondered on society and how to improve it, without metaphysical concepts, without myths.

Very well. What *did* Confucius say?

2

He lived from about 551 to 479 B.C., and later Chinese thought, while it often perverted or disputed his teaching, usually took it as a point of departure. He was a cool and practical administrative consultant . . . and he based his doctrine on the Chinese equivalent of the Titans.

China, like Greece, emerges into our sight from an era during the second millennium B.C. which survives in history as a medley of myth and fact. From about 1100 B.C. the Chou dynasty became dominant, lasting more than eight hundred years. Its early phase became established in legend as China's golden age, formed by its traditional founders, and by certain 'Divine Sages' who ruled over earlier dynasties and left their mark.

Confucius accepted this. He regarded the early Chou epoch as the heyday of wise government and social co-operation. Succeeding generations had slowly declined. Confucius's main innovation was to sum up the ancient rightness of society as *Tao*, the Way: that is, the Way of the Former Kings. His aim was to restore the *Tao*. There was nothing superhuman about it. The men of old were governed by moral force instead of physical force; they practised the golden rule, in its restrained negative form, 'Don't do to others what you wouldn't like them to do to you'; they were ceremonious and cultured. Under these conditions the quality known as *jen* – the highest goodness of human nature – could flourish, as it does no longer.

While Confucius was unhopeful about actually seeing the Way restored, he took a temperate view of the requirements. A new saviour-king might arise, and was perhaps due after such a long interval, but he was not strictly necessary. There was no difference in kind between the Divine Sages and the men of Confucius's day, only a difference of knowledge and will. Confucius denied that he was a Divine Sage himself, and disclaimed special inspiration (except that the founder of the Chou dynasty appeared to him in dreams). Nevertheless he believed that if some ruler would give him a free hand, he could bring about the vital changes, because his study of the ancients supplied all he needed.

His programme was educational. It consisted in forming an elite of 'gentlemen', not unlike their English counterparts before 1914. Given enough gentlemen fully instructed in the Way, and given their presence at the top level, society could come right again. Confucius was by no means an agnostic. He stressed the ritual of Chinese religion, and the need to restore it to its ancient correctness. But he was profoundly unfanatical, in no sense a prophet or Messiah. His insistence on reinstating a long-lost glory is therefore all the more interesting.

Most Chinese thinkers preserved his reverence for history and the models it was said to provide. They looked for whole cycles of loss and restoration, and bent the facts accordingly. After various changes a philosophy based on Confucius prevailed. China produced only one durable school of thought to compete with it, the Taoism claiming Lao Tzu as its founder. This was a mystical anarchism in which *Tao* had a more elusive meaning. The Taoists reacted against almost everything in Confucius, equating civilized virtue with decadence. The one thing they did not react against was the concept of reinstating a golden age. Taoists put their own long-lost glory farther back, in a naïve Eden before good and evil. But they believed in it, and in the corruption which had obscured it. Their ideal sage was a poetic dropout, who recaptured the primal innocence in his own person. Even in this conscious antithesis to Confucius and all he stood for, the same mystique of the Chinese *Saturnia regna* most ironically appeared.

No social philosophy with Confucius's human bias took hold in the West till the eighteenth century. Platonists and Jews, Stoics and Christians, were all more preoccupied than the Chinese teacher with heaven as well as earth. The Greek school which did detach itself from the gods, Epicurus's, also detached itself from public affairs. Europe was not ready for Confucius till the eighteenth century: and so to France again. Here, it might seem, was an age when ancient myths really were irrelevant, because the *philosophes* led by Voltaire either emancipated themselves completely, or made up myths of their own. Carlyle's Virgilian tags are flourishes without deep meaning.

But are they? Voltaire, after all, did not make the Revolution or even live to see it. His brand of Enlightenment, satiric and sceptical, had its limits. Apart from its influence on one or two benevolent despots (and rulers like Frederick the Great were not, in the upshot, very benevolent), it was mainly destructive. No mass energies grew from it till its powers were harnessed to something different, by a theorist of a different stamp. Jean-Jacques Rousseau, not Voltaire, created the revolutionary movement; and it is he whose mystique must be looked into.

Jean-Jacques's scheme of renovation was the most potently radical ever to arise in Europe. Whether or not he understood the message of China, his own was a more spectacular version of it, with both Confucianist and Taoist touches. The heart of it was the idea that society had slid downward from a happy state, but that by sweeping away the age-old corruption, the essentials of this lost paradise could be restored for a fresh start. The point about sweeping away corruption gave Rousseau his practical impact on the bourgeoisie and, indirectly, the peasants. The Revolution broke out because they wanted various things swept away – the financial incompetence of the Crown, the privileges of the nobles, the wealth of the Church, the fetters on enterprise, the feudal exactions. Voltaire had broken the spell, but Rousseau sounded the call to action. In the name of love and brotherhood he unleashed a tempest of hate. But the guillotine, however frightful a shadow it casts, is only part of the story, and for anatomizers of myth the rest is worth getting into focus.

Rousseau was a French-speaking native of Geneva. A good deal of his system is patently personal in origin. This is one reason for its interest – that it is so plainly the outgrowth of a human personality, and of human obsessions. Outwardly Rousseau was affected by his upbringing in a small republic. His character was infantile and unendearing. He had a mother-fixation, a dread of responsibility, and, for much of his life, a persecution mania.

After a shiftless youth, he looked back with nostalgia on rustic idylls that seem to have been largely imaginary. Success as an author gave him an entry to cultivated circles. He quarrelled with everybody, notably Voltaire, and made futile efforts to return to the rural peace which he supposed himself to have once enjoyed. To call his doctrine a self-sublimation would be partially just. But he happened to be the man who could self-sublimate in a way that struck fire among the discontented.

In effect he took up the myth of Eden, and added a sequel altering its implications. The lost golden age which he affirmed was the most fundamental of all in the dreaming of mankind. Christianity depicted unfallen Man in the garden of God, and his exile through sin. Rousseau re-stated this dogma in purely human terms, and with one transfiguring amendment: that the primal innocence was natural, and its loss was a social process not subject to any divine decree . . . so Man might recover it. Potentially Eden lay ahead as well as behind. The Fall need not be for ever, the Church's depressing dogma could be refuted in life.

Rousseau was not entirely original. In the English Peasants' Revolt, John Ball attempted a revolutionary appeal to Eden: 'When Adam delved and Eve span, who was then a gentleman?' But he lacked Rousseau's sophistication, and so did his audience.

The 'state of nature' far back in prehistory had also been canvassed in England, by Hobbes and Locke. Rousseau, however, idealized it. Supporting his views with ill-digested data on the unspoilt natives of the West Indies and other places, he proclaimed Natural Man, who was free, equal, and virtuous by instinct. So what had gone wrong? Inequality, said Rousseau, arose first from the differences that emerged in tribal activities such as singing and dancing. Some of the noble savages sang and danced better than others. Fan clubs gathered round them. Once privilege had crept in, it found further points of access. The division of labour tended to promote key workers, overseers, an accumulation of wealth by entrepreneurs. Humanity does progress, but the movement is really a non-progress into misery.

'Everything is good when it leaves the Creator's hands; everything degenerates in the hands of Man.' Arts and sciences are rooted in the worse side of human nature. Astronomy, for instance, is a product of astrology and therefore of superstition. Geometry would never have been invented if rich men had not needed land-surveying and kindred techniques. Civilization cannot wipe away the stains on its origins. It breeds disease and vice, it enslaves, it entangles even the higher impulses in religious and ethical systems that pervert them. Education and printing disseminate lies.

All this evil has been, so to speak, institutionalized by governments. Civil society began to take shape at an early stage, when private property gave a solid form to inequality, and made self-seeking advantageous. Human beings had to enter into a 'social contract' for mutual protection, and so the State was born. But some sections grew richer and more powerful than others. Dynasties, aristocracies, priestly castes, groups of plutocrats, built up civilization and their own privileges. The rulers of mankind now impose laws which are coercive in essence, and violate the natural law which is the only true principle of order. Hence, by a paradox, government is anarchy.

Ideally, the kings and priests and their institutions should all be sent packing. A new model State should be set up restoring the reign of natural law, and the spirit of the lost innocence. If the revolutionaries get this right, a just society can result, with a kind of culture which need not corrupt. Then, aided by reformed education, the natural goodness of men will reassert itself. In *The Social Contract* Rousseau is more cautious than the historical sequel might suggest. His new order is democracy, but he does not think democracy is feasible everywhere. Indeed he does not think that a complete democracy, with every citizen playing his full part, is feasible anywhere. In practice, the best that we can hope for is an elective republic in a small territory. The bigger the country, the worse the prospects.

When we ask what the voice of Nature actually says, the mythic compulsion shows more starkly. Rousseau strives for a direct and simple vision, but in the upshot he sees what he wants to see. He is none too clear as to whether even his Eden was literally real. It is a psychological axiom, a vital part of the mythical pattern. In his *Discourse on Inequality* he speaks of the state of nature as one which 'exists no longer, perhaps never existed, probably never will exist, and of which none the less it is necessary to have just ideas, in order to judge well of our present state'. He relies heavily on intuition and the dictates of the heart. According to Bertrand Russell, this was the crucial thing about him. He invented the appeal to feelings instead of arguments. After him we get romanticism, and a retreat from reason on several fronts, with a traceable line of descent to such spellbinders as Hitler.

That verdict is sadly reinforced by Rousseau's account of the State and what it should be. He believes that in any community, Nature speaks (or would if she could) through a sort of collective feeling called the general will. The general will is always right. Existing regimes and sectional interests thwart it. After the revolution, the new State will embody the general will. Thus Nature will resume her beneficent sway. But Rousseau never explains how we are to know what the general will is, in a given situation. He puts forward some suggestions, but betrays his real drift in passages praising Sparta and extolling the military virtues. What his advice comes to in practice is that the leaders, professing to be men of the people, will interpret the general will themselves, and suppress every association that may challenge them. And that is what the Jacobins tried to do. Robespierre was Rousseau's most eminent disciple.

Religion comes into all this, but heaven is annexed to earth, not the other way round. Rousseau changed his church affiliation twice to suit his convenience. The religion which he infused into his political system was chiefly an official cult, concocted to prop the earthly Utopia. Robespierre tried to plant it in France with a 'Festival of the Supreme Being', held in June 1794 as a ritual adjunct to the Terror.

3

In a piecemeal way, the French Revolution did realize some of Rousseau's desires. It did not, however, permanently restore natural virtue. Part of the trouble (if he had lived, he might have said the whole trouble) was that France was too big. *The Social Contract* itself would imply that the Jacobins were mistaken to try building an equal republic when they ought to have settled for a properly run monarchy. The first Rousseauan revolution, like the first Communist revolution, happened in the wrong country. Rousseau's own forecast had been that unspoilt Corsica would amaze the world; events fulfilled that prophecy after a fashion, but the fashion was not his.

Carlyle's insight in speaking of the *Saturnia regna* is exact. The

French Revolution, which destroyed or perverted most of Rousseau's reasoning, preserved his mystique; and the mystique was a variant on the theme epitomized in the British myth. France's size rapidly enlarged a split which was inherent anyhow. Because the Revolution occurred in the greatest and most brilliant kingdom of Europe, it was doomed from the outset as an essay in small-scale, simple-life republicanism. For exactly the same reason, it blazed with a splendour of inspiration which no mini-commonwealth could have produced. Wordsworth, looking back through a decade of disillusionment, could still remember that lifting of the heart:

> France standing at the top of golden hours,
> And human nature seeming born again . . .
> Bliss was it in that dawn to be alive,
> But to be young was very Heaven! O times,
> In which the meagre, stale, forbidding ways
> Of custom, law, and statute, took at once
> The attraction of a country in romance!
>
> (*The Prelude*, VI. 340-1,
> XI.108-112)

This is, precisely, the mystique of renewal, reinstatement, transfiguration: a fresh start.

Nor did the thrill die out everywhere as utterly as it did for Wordsworth. France's size conferred a second advantage. It enabled the Revolution to hold out, gloriously and for many years, against a threat which Rousseau foresaw but never faced – foreign intervention. No mini-commonwealth could have produced the national uprising of 1793, the Marseillaise, the rout of the invading kings, the victories of Napoleon. When Waterloo had been fought and the Holy Alliance was supreme at last, an heroic legend remained which seemed to vindicate Rousseau more than it did. For a generation the chains had actually fallen, men had actually been different. Through such retrospective apostles as Victor Hugo the legend survived. Even Waterloo, in Hugo's poetry, became *la fuite des géants* – a phrase recalling the Titans and the world's youth.

Alongside this legend, indeed, the modern idea of genuine if gradual progress was taking hold. It had descended from Locke to Condorcet, and to Jefferson and kindred Americans (who were by no means Rousseauans, despite notions to the contrary), and to

William Godwin and Jeremy Bentham and an assortment of Liberals and Socialists. There was no lost golden age, it declared; no past *Saturnia regna* or Arthurian Britain. Civilization was not degeneracy. Mankind moved forward. In Germany attempts were made to philosophize progress too, and combine it with revolution: whence the theories of Karl Marx and Friedrich Engels. But – and here we may end this aspect of the case, on a strange variant of the same mystique – the creators of Marxism, having rejected Rousseau's Paradise-lost-and-found-again, finally surrendered and smuggled it back in. The archetype was too strong for them, too pressing a need of human nature.

Their minds had been vaguely prepared for it – Marx's by Hegel, who adapted some of Rousseau's ideas, and Engels's by his friend and mentor Moses Hess, the philosopher of Zionism and the restoration of Israel. Still, when they wrote the *Communist Manifesto* in 1848, their picture of history had no room for any past 'rightness'. They portrayed 'all hitherto existing society' as lurching forward through a series of stages, each characterized by a different kind of economy and class structure, each dissolving and changing because of class conflict.

Their ancient world was a world of patricians and slave-owners oppressing plebeians and slaves. Then came feudalism, with its lords and guild-masters on top, its serfs and journeymen below. Economic expansion, a series of bourgeois revolutions, and the rise of mechanical industry, led to the modern Europe of capitalists and wage-slaves or proletarians. Its achievements were colossal, its evils also colossal. The next step would be for the proletariat to throw off its bosses and take over the means of production itself. The workers' triumph, placing a majority of the people in the saddle at last, would lead to a classless society.

Such was Marxism in its first phase: an ideology of progress, however jerky and painful. To each stage of society a different State and government corresponded. All of them so far had been repressive, because all upheld the authority of a dominant few. So far, however, government had always existed. Its evolution was part of society's. It would some day cease to be needed, but its end lay in a hypothetical future, after the workers' revolution, and (Marx appears to have decided) not even very soon after.

Marx in *Das Kapital*, he and Engels in a medley of other writings, enlarged the scheme with various proofs . . . or rationalizations.

The workers failed to respond. Even the Paris Commune of 1871, which Marx hailed, was doubtfully Marxist and confined to Paris. Then came a fresh development. In 1877 the American anthropologist Lewis H. Morgan published a book called *Ancient Society*. Basing his findings chiefly on the supposed customs of the seventeenth-century Iroquois, Morgan resurrected Rousseau's noble savages. The Iroquois, and most peoples at the same level, were alleged to have had a wise, free, equal society based on communal property, without any government. Primitive Man had been organized in 'gentes'; the national State came later.

Marx seized on this account eagerly. After his death in 1883, Engels used his notes on Morgan to compose a book of his own, *The Origin of the Family, Private Property and the State*. He announced that the State 'has not existed from all eternity'. It arose when economic growth, the division of labour, and kindred factors, split society into classes, and a sovereign authority was required, to keep the rulers safely on top of the ruled. This is Rousseau over again, and so is Engels's remarkable further point: that before government, before class conflict, before the history set forth in the *Communist Manifesto*, mankind lived in a semi-idyll of 'primitive communism'. Engels argued that the 'simple moral grandeur' of the old 'gens' society had been ruined by 'theft, violence, cunning, treason'. Economic progress had been started and kept in motion by 'the meanest impulses – vulgar covetousness, brutal lust, sordid avarice, selfish robbery of the common wealth'. To an English edition of the *Communist Manifesto*, published in 1888, he added a note explaining that the history which the *Manifesto* surveyed must now be construed as meaning written history only. Prehistory was otherwise.

So the future workers' revolution, leading toward a classless society, would not after all be a leap forward into the unknown. It would be a reinstatement. On a far superior level, of course, but a reinstatement still. The Saturnian golden age was back in the system; so was the Fall; so was the Return. Engels approvingly quoted Morgan himself on the trend of progress:

> Democracy in government, brotherhood in society, equality in rights and privileges, and universal education, foreshadow the next higher plane of society to which experience, intelligence and knowledge are steadily tending. It will be a revival, in a higher form, of the liberty, equality and fraternity of the ancient gentes.

Morgan's picture of ancient society was not in fact right. But it was too precious to drop. Marxists clung to it for many years in defiance of evidence against it, because it supplied something they could not do without.

The first Marxist who made a revolution was Lenin, and he paid special attention to *The Origin of the Family, Private Property and the State*, which he described as 'the most popular of Engels's works'. His own book *The State and Revolution*, written to rally Russian extremists in 1917, contains the ideas which he was then preaching on the subject. Here the revolutionary vision has become more vivid and dramatic. Given the Rousseauesque belief that mankind was once pure and classless, the subsequent rulers with their engines of power have become more sinister, more like usurpers. The State is a monster, an intrusion, an embodied corruption. In the morning of the world, this thing that upholds class tyranny with the knout and the chain did not exist. The workers are called to thrust it back into its proper oblivion. Through the famous 'withering away of the State', which Lenin prophesies in much more detail than Marx, our wronged species will recover its stolen inheritance.

Lenin's revolution was, so to speak, Prometheus Unbound; and it was Lenin's revolution that won.

7

The Anatomy of Compulsion

1

In one form or another, then, the mystique of reinstatement is obviously powerful. It is a recurring psychological fact, which the Arthur story happens to have expressed in mythical form. To say so is not to label it 'good' or 'bad', or commit oneself as to whether it is a true reflection of the human condition, or a dangerous fancy. Nor do the dicta of Confucius, Rousseau or Lenin show where the inner compulsion comes from.

If it gives power to movements of social change, does it ever do the same for movements of other kinds – nationalistic, for instance, or religious? And if so, do they shed any further light?

The mystique means the rebirth, in this world, of a former visionary 'rightness' that is dead-yet-not-dead, and the defeat of the evil that has seemed to destroy it. To find such a rebirth built into a nationalist programme and affecting millions of lives, we do not have to search far. The programme, indeed, is nationalistic and religious at once, at least in its origins. Arguably it has been the most successful programme in modern politics; successful, moreover, in such defiance of probability as to hint, even more strongly than Communism, at the working of what Jung might have called an archetype. I refer to Zionism, and the creation of the Republic of Israel.

For some time now, the Judaism of Reformed and Liberal synagogues has done its best to soft-pedal the Promised Land, to maintain that it is not an essential factor in the religion of Moses, and, latterly, to treat Zionism itself as a mere quest for a haven from persecution – a haven which might as well have been in

Africa or America. The prestige of Theodor Herzl, who organized Zionism in its narrowly political sense, helped to foster this view. Herzl tried to impose it on the movement. But (if a Gentile may be permitted to speak) it is wishful thinking. An assimilated western Jew may well feel happier to believe it, may excusably argue that matters ought to be so . . . but they are not.

The would-be de-mystifying of Zionism is quite at odds with the actual evolution of ancient Israel, with the growth of the Bible, and with the way in which Zionism did in fact produce its new state.[1] Jewish religion began with a conviction about the divinely bestowed Land. It developed round a series of efforts to reach that land, to hold it, and to grasp the implications of holding it.

A constant Old Testament theme is that Israel, God's chosen community, is 'right' when in possession of Palestine, 'wrong' and uprooted and alienated at other times. 'Israel in its divinely appointed home' is a psychological counterpart of the kingdom of Arthur, though, of course, the conception is more realistic. The great Rashi, medieval master of Jewish biblical scholars, states the primacy of the Land most frankly and astonishingly. Why, he asks, does the Bible start with the Creation? A reader might expect the answer that this is part of its teaching about God and the universe. But no. Rashi explains that the purpose of the opening section of *Genesis* is to prove an incontrovertible right to Palestine! The Israelites conquered the Promised Land by slaughtering the Canaanites who were already there. Only a divine command could justify this action, and only a divine command from which no appeal was possible: a command from the summit, from the Creator of the World. Therefore it had to be made clear that the God of Israel was the Creator, and that his will was law, for the unlucky Canaanites as for everyone else.

In the Bible's account of Abraham, and the patriarchal beginnings of the Israelite people, the same priority appears. God speaks to Abraham (or Abram, as he is called first) with a cryptic promise about the mighty nation which is to spring from him, and tells him to settle in a land that is to be shown him. He goes into Palestine, and at Shechem the Lord says: 'To your descendants I will give this land' (*Genesis* xii:7). Later the promise is repeated at more length (xiii: 14–17). Later again, the childless patriarch accepts the Lord's assurance that he will indeed have descendants;

[1] I have discussed these topics at more length in *The Land and the Book*.

and his faith is 'reckoned to him as righteousness' (xv:6). This is the first phrase in his story with any moral reference. The basic image of Abraham's family in Palestine, finding fulfilment living there with God's blessing, is prior to everything which modern religion regards as central.

In due course Abraham's descendants, the Israelites, sink into Egyptian bondage. God summons Moses to rescue them. Again the Land comes before ethics. God speaks of their restoration to it, and contrives their escape from Egypt, before he dictates the Ten Commandments. Israel occupies the Land under its divine covenant, and, for a while, prospers. David unites the tribes, Solomon builds the Lord a temple. Then, however, things go wrong. The kingdom falls apart. Both parts are harassed by stronger neighbours, and become semi-paganized and a prey to corruption and privilege.

Next comes the unique succession of prophets. Their vision, moral fervour, and transcendence of tribalism lay the foundation of a higher religion. Yet the occasion of their prophesying is still the crisis of Israel, and the break-up of the Palestinian commonwealth (a counterpart, if we care to press parallels, to the decline of the Round Table through sin). Their remedy is a spiritual revival, with an appeal to idealized traditions of the virtue and justice of the pioneer settlers.

Essentially the prophets are raising a question: 'If God planted us Israelites in the Land on the understanding that we should live and act in a certain way, doesn't this imply that our tenure is conditional on living and acting as required?' To which the prophets give their answer: 'Yes, it does. We must keep our side of the bargain. God still rules over events. The Covenant would be pointless if he relinquished control. And the way the Israelite monarchies have gone, with their wealth in a few hands, their paganized ritual, their foreign cults, is a standing menace. God in his righteous anger may allow other nations to conquer or even dispossess us.'

The dispossession occurred, as a matter of history. The northern Israelite kingdom was destroyed by the Assyrians. The southerners were deported to Babylon by Nebuchadnezzar, in such numbers as to leave only an impoverished peasantry. Their commonwealth appeared to be dead. But in 539 B.C. Babylon fell to the Persians and the exiles were allowed to go home. In the soaring rhetoric of that unknown prophet who wrote *Isaiah* xl–lv, the faith of Israel

promptly exploded into a fresh and imperishable splendour. Yet
his message remained centred on the Return, the Reinstatement,
the renewal of the blessing.

> The ransomed of the Lord shall return,
>   and come to Zion with singing,
>   everlasting joy shall be upon their heads . . .
> Awake, awake,
>   put on your strength, O Zion;
> put on your beautiful garments,
>   O Jerusalem, the holy city . . .
> Hark, your watchmen lift up their voice,
>   together they sing for joy;
> for eye to eye they see
>   the return of the Lord to Zion.
> Break forth together into singing,
>   you waste places of Jerusalem;
> for the Lord has comforted his people,
>   he has redeemed Jerusalem.

This most universal of Hebrew prophets is also the most passionately committed to the mystique of Zion, and Israel's vocation to
live there by God's law, enlightening the nations.

The exiles' actual return was less exalted. *Ezra* and *Nehemiah*
tell the tale. Still, a remnant did get back to Jerusalem and rebuild
the Temple, while many who did not go in person continued in
communion with them, and looked to Zion as their spiritual home.
It is from the faithful remnant and its scattered associate-members,
in Babylonia and elsewhere, that the Jewish people are descended.
Jewish identity itself was defined by this earlier 'Zionism'.

After their fatal rising against Rome, the Jews went into a longer
and sadder exile among the nations. But the Land was never forgotten. Prayers and ceremonies kept the yearning alive. In the
scattered Jewish communities of medieval Europe, little groups
would spend hours studying the topography of the lost Land,
listening to travellers who had seen it, gazing awe-stricken at the
trifling souvenirs which the travellers brought back. Poets composed homesick songs called 'Zionides'. Scholars and mystics
wandered eastward; thanks to Spanish persecution, the town of
Safed in Galilee harboured a distinguished rabbinic school.
Its leaders were refugees, yet they saw themselves as forerunners.
The in-gathering of the exiles to Palestine, and the restoration of

Israel's earthly splendour, would be the Messiah's task when he came.

The French Revolution and its sequels gave Jews in western Europe the new goal of assimilation. But this ideal had almost no impact on the larger, endlessly suffering Jewry farther east, and it was there that Zionism became a force. As a nineteenth-century nationalist movement it had its political intellectuals and sympathizers. But it effectively started about 1840 as a practical, do-it-yourself Back to Palestine campaign, and its promoters were two East European rabbis, Judah ben Alkalai and Zvi Hirsch Kalischer, who related it not to the nationalism of Germany or Italy but to the Messianic hope. The movement took its name from the societies of Lovers of Zion, Hovevei Zion, launched by Kalischer. These societies founded agricultural colonies in the Promised Land. They formed a federation, and its chairman Leo Pinsker supplied Zionism with a manifesto – a pamphlet entitled *Auto-Emancipation* – in 1882. Russian pogroms had grown so savage that Pinsker himself hesitated about Palestine, and allowed that a Jewish home might be sought in some other locale as a second-best. But such hesitations were short-lived. Zionist ideology after Pinsker was not a pragmatic refuge-seeking but a positive, spiritually charged vision of the Promised Land and Israel's calling.

When the celebrated Herzl arrived on the scene, his gifts as a publicist and political wire-puller put him in command of the movement. Like other assimilated Jews of the West, Herzl saw the need as simply to provide a haven. Scornful of the practical Zionists who were already quietly settling in Palestine, he aimed at a solution through some high-level political deal, and was prepared to consider other places. In 1903, however, the Sixth Zionist Congress compelled him to face the facts; and the Sixth Congress is the justification for this preamble.

Herzl had persuaded Joseph Chamberlain to sponsor a Zionist settlement under the British Crown, probably in Uganda. To his bewildered fury the scheme was rejected, even as an interim measure, and rejected by the votes of the Russian Jews who were to do the actual settling. These were the Jews who formed the backbone of Zionism, the downtrodden victims whom Herzl proposed to rescue . . . and they refused to be rescued. They preferred to go on being downtrodden, rather than contemplate any other sanctuary than the place of Israel's glory and predestined fulfilment. Herzl's dreams of liberated Jews advancing into a new land-scape did not touch them at all. The reinstatement of the lost glory was everything.

Herzl had done all he could, and his achievement was memorable. But he could go no farther along his chosen line. He died soon afterwards. Zionism's final triumph was largely the work of Chaim Weizmann, who united the political and practical factions, and secured the Balfour Declaration.

There is no point here in pursuing the tortuous sequels. Two things, however, are worth noting. A major part of the Zionist colonization of Palestine took the form of the famous *kibbutzim* – land settlements which functioned, at first, on a basis of voluntary communism. Mini-Utopias of this kind have been tried repeatedly elsewhere (nineteenth-century America had fully two hundred) and nearly all have failed. The *kibbutzim* succeeded. While they have somewhat changed their character, they have not dissolved even yet.

To account for the glaring contrast, many factors have been cited: good leadership, a sense of urgency, subsidies from overseas. None is adequate. The main explanation lies in a difference of attitude. The pioneers of the new Israel were not doing the same thing as the Utopia-builders of other countries. Few of the *kibbutzim* were ever religious in spirit, as Jews understand the term; but the strength of Jewish conditioning, the power of the mystique of restoration to Zion, supplied a sense of vocation and a resilience under pressure which no Utopian theorist has ever inspired. The word '*kibbutz*' itself means in-gathering, and is the word used down the centuries, in the Synagogue, for that in-gathering of the exiles which Jews stubbornly prayed for. All this was said many years ago by Aaron David Gordon, the founder of the prototype *kibbutz* at Deganya near the Lake of Tiberias. The *kibbutzim* confirmed his judgment; and Deganya flourishes to this day.

One thing more. Israel is a fiercely archaeological country. Digging for the national roots, at Masada and other sites, has been a democratic and patriotic pursuit to a greater degree than anywhere else on earth. One recognizes the Cadbury phenomenon on a vaster scale. The rising generation of born Israelis, the Sabra, are fast losing Jewishness and drifting away from Judaism. Yet the Bible lives on as the bond of unity through all countries and times. The historical mystique, the sense of collective character and vocation, the recovered Land at the heart of it all ... these can persist.

2

I think it important to dwell on the nature of Zionism at some length, because of the proof it gives of the potency of a revival-mystique once established, and the weakness of liberal and progressive ideas when in competition with it. An arresting sidelight is the frenzied anti-Zionism of many assimilated and would-be rational Jews. They attacked both Herzl and Weizmann as lunatic trouble-makers, and intrigued viciously against the latter. Not only did they fail, they betrayed the inferiority, in practice, of their own 'rational' judgment. The end of their policy in Europe was the colossal and awful disillusionment of the gas-chambers. In this case at least, the power of the mystique would seem to have come partly from a genuinely deeper insight that went with it.

But was Zionism special? It was a rare, perhaps unique blend of religion and nationalism. Do we find our pattern recurring in religion apart from nationalism, or in nationalism apart from religion? Or rather (since the two are seldom quite separate) in cases where one clearly predominates over the other?

Let us turn to Christianity, and the one revolutionary earthquake which the Church has gone through: the Reformation.

Christianity started as a Jewish Messianic movement that broke away. The Church soon became largely Gentile and anathema to the rabbis. Its converts had no national bond among them, and no ancestral link with the Holy Land. Hence the Church lost the territorial aspiration of Jews. The hope of Christ's Second Coming was not an equivalent. No earthly kingdom or golden age was associated with Jesus. Nevertheless, the Church did in time evolve its own golden age – its counterpart of the nostalgic vision of ancient Israel. This was the Apostolic Era, down to about the end of the first century A.D. In it, the New Testament had been written; in it, the Creed had been composed; in it, the lives of the faithful had been pure; and in it, most of the major legends were rooted.

The age of the Reformation was far from golden. It was hideous with Christian strife. Yet the common ground among the militants of change was considerable. All agreed as to the Catholic Church's corruption. There were those like Erasmus and Thomas More, who stayed in the Roman Communion (some, like More, heroically) and laboured to alter it. There were those like Luther and Calvin, who gave it up as an organized apostasy, and worked to reconstitute the true Church outside. There was also Henry VIII, who wanted only a limited reform to meet his own needs, though in practice he opened the door to Protestantism. There was, however, no notable reformer at all whose hope for the Church was 'progressive' or evolutionary.

All who agreed on Roman corruption also agreed on two remedial policies. One, of course, was to undo the evil. The other was to restore the apostolic purity which had existed once, and then faded under the shadow of papal abuses. Their appeal was to the dawn of the Christian era, when the Church was still close to its Founder and, as it were, 'right'. The proper object of reform was to bring this holy condition back, not, of course, as a carbon copy, but as the same thing reincarnate in the altered world.

Despite their bitter feuds over the implications of such a programme, the chief reformers showed their agreement on its nature by the activity they had in common: the revival of the New Testament, the handbook of Christians in the first century, as a handbook for Christians in the sixteenth. The Vulgate Latin of the Church was suspect as a tool of priestcraft. Erasmus edited and published the original Greek. Luther translated the entire Bible into German. Tyndale, using both Erasmus and Luther, produced a New Testament in English. Calvin poured out commentaries. Always the aim was to reunite Christendom to the Zion of its pristine beauty.

The Jewish parallel is not hindsight. Luther, for instance, was well aware of it, and his awareness was an outgrowth from hallowed precedents. Christians had long been disposed to treat Israel's relationship with the Promised Land as a symbolic foreshadowing of spiritual matters. In 1520 Luther entitled his main anti-papal manifesto *The Babylonish Captivity of the Church.* As the Chosen People were torn from Zion and condemned to exile in Babylonia, so the flock of Christ, once firmly established in the presence of God, had been dragged out of it by pontiffs who were no better than Nebuchadnezzar. It would follow (though the embattled Luther, at this stage, was too blind to the brighter side to say so) that the Reformation corresponded to Babylon's downfall and the repatriation of the captives, so radiantly proclaimed in *Isaiah*.

Among Protestants a subtler mental process also occurred, answering to the one that created the sleeping Arthur. Catholics challenged them with the question: 'If the Roman Church is false, where was the true Church during those centuries of darkness? Apparently it vanished. No true Church existed at all. Yet Christ promised that the gates of Hell should never prevail. How was his promise kept?' Reformers like More, who remained within the Catholic fold, maintained that Rome had never gone completely wrong. The divine sparks could be disinterred from under the rubbish and fanned into fire again. Luther's position precluded this. Where indeed had the Church of Christ been hiding, if the enforced alienation from holiness had been total?

The Protestant rejoinder was a little time coming. What is striking about it is the extent of its admission of the Catholic case. It would have been possible to say (as some later Protestants wisely did) that even while all Christians were in error, the Bible preserved the truth. Instead, many Protestants seem to have felt an inner compulsion to assert a far more dubious case. They claimed that the Apostolic Church had never died out. A faithful remnant – small, despised, oppressed, often silent – had always handed on the torch. The Reformation was not a novelty but a new blossoming of the secret and holy reality which had been there all the time.

Foxe's *Book of Martyrs*, that former mainstay of English popular piety, contains one of the attempts to give substance to this opinion. In effect, all the heretics persecuted by Rome – Albigenses, Waldenses, Lollards, Hussites, and so forth – came to be counted as proto-Protestants, transmitting an unbroken tradition. They *were* the primitive Church, powerless and unacknowledged and lied about, but living on in near-suspended animation and able to reassert its majesty . . . Arthur, as it were, waiting in his cave.

Protestants made skilful use of the Apocalypse. Their hope was an apocalyptic hope. Spenser, in *The Faerie Queene*, suggests that Elizabeth's championship of the Protestant cause is overthrowing Antichrist; and he connects it with her Arthurian claim, occasionally making Arthur himself symbolic of the true Christ restored to men by the Reformation.

3

Now for the other side of the coin. Do we find versions of the same mystique in nationalism, when religion is subordinate?

I think we must distinguish two kinds of nationalism, even

though they overlap. The chauvinistic or imperial kind starts with a nation already powerful and tries to increase its power. The more praiseworthy patriotic kind, such as Zionism itself at its best, starts with a downtrodden people and seeks their liberty and fulfilment. The baser kind has often exploited the finer kind. It reached an apex in Nazism.

In view of his presumed freedom from Semitic pollutions, and therefore from the influence of the biblical motifs we have been looking at, Hitler's style of propaganda is worth a glance. He called his Germany the Third Reich, or Empire. The Second Reich was the Kaiser's which fell in 1918. But what was the First, the proto-type?

Hitler meant the empire founded by Charlemagne, which briefly united most of western Christendom in the ninth century, and preserved a phantasm of unity for much longer. At first it included both Germany and France. It assumed the authority of the Caesars; hence its designation, throughout much of its career, as the Holy Roman Empire. Even after France was gone, the Empire embodied a claim by its German sovereigns to a secular suzerainty over all Christendom. Frederick Barbarossa, who reigned from 1152 to 1190, was the most successful. It was he who added the adjective 'Holy', and asserted a divine mandate linked with the Pope's. In the fifteenth century the declining Empire consoled itself with its famous if unsubtle imitation of the Arthur story. Barbarossa was not dead – he was asleep in a cavern in a mountain, the Kyffhäuser, and would wake up to restore his Germans to their rightful supremacy. At this time the imperial title was further enlarged. The Holy Roman Emperor became the Holy Roman Emperor 'of the German Nation'. Decline, however, continued.

Napoleon dissolved the last remnant of the moribund Reich. His own domain covered much the same ground as Charlemagne's, and he tried to play the role of a new Charlemagne himself. Inevitably, however, the Germans and not the French fell heir to the imperial dream in this form. When the Second Reich was proclaimed in 1871, its expansionists began recalling the First, remarking how much bigger and more majestic it had been in its heyday.

Their chauvinism did not conceive itself as a political novelty, but as a restoration after decay and eclipse. Thus Germany too followed the Arthurian pattern – even to invoking Germany's counterpart of Arthur. The Crown Prince Frederick, father of the future Kaiser Wilhelm II, was a liberal and peace-loving man. Yet he showed his son pictures of the medieval imperial insignia, saying: 'We have got to bring this back. The power of the Empire must be restored and the Imperial Crown regain its glamour. Barbarossa must be brought down again out of his mountain cave.'[1] The words show a sound grasp of Barbarossa's symbolic meaning, however unfortunate their likely effect, when addressed to that hearer.

As for Hitler, his talk of a Third Reich lasting a thousand years (the duration of the First), and his rhetorical glances at Charlemagne, were simply a repetition and refinement – if that is the word – of the same notion. The aristocrats of that First Reich were now supposed to have been 'pure', superior Aryans. Hitler's Russian campaign, which was intended to put Germany in a position of impregnable strength, was called Operation Barbarossa.

From the nightmare nationalism of a great nation perverted to conquer others, we may turn with relief to a great nation itself under foreign rule, and the nationalism that gave the first impulse to the Afro-Asian avalanche. India's attainment of independence will doubtless go on being debated among historians. But whatever the truth about the political twists and turns, the reawakening of India's masses from their long apathy was the achievement of one leader, Gandhi. It may be argued that after rousing them, he misled them. It may be argued that self-rule would have come in some other way, possibly sooner, without him. It is the testimony of all, including his enemies, that the villagers composing the bulk of India's population responded to him as to no other politician; and it is a matter of history that after the collapse of the Mutiny of 1857, India produced nothing like a national rising till the movement of 1921 under Gandhi's leadership.

Broadly speaking, the Indian patriotic renaissance passed through three phases before it reached maturity. The National Congress was founded in 1885, with British approval. An assemblage of professional men of liberal outlook, it edged slowly toward a radical stance. But the Indian lawyers, journalists and professors who belonged to it could see the future only in terms of India becoming westernized, with a parliamentary constitution. They and their opinions left the masses unstirred.

[1] Michael Balfour, *The Kaiser and his Times*, pp. 7, 69.

After 1900 a second school of thought encroached on the first. Its leader was Tilak, an apostle of militant Hinduism and anti-British national pride. Tilak split Congress with his condonation of terrorism. However, his appeal to religion, which the uneducated could understand, brought the first ripple of peasant conversion to nationalism. India's first major political strike was on Tilak's behalf, when his arrest provoked a mass walkout of Bombay mill-workers.

Gandhi, who had been living in South Africa for twenty years, returned finally to India in 1915. His successful and original battle for the civil rights of Indians in South Africa had predisposed many nationalists to welcome him. Rabindranath Tagore saluted him as a Mahatma or Great Soul. The spiritual implications of that Hindu title, plus Gandhi's own character and outlook, enabled him to repeat Tilak's religious appeal more effectively.

However, he repeated it in his own manner. The manifesto of his unique brand of nationalism was a pamphlet, *Hind Swaraj*, or in its English version, *Indian Home Rule*. In it he rejected both westernizing liberalism and Tilakite violence. The civilization which Britain had brought to India was, he declared, a corruption and a curse. India should refuse it and rediscover her true genius.

This, as portrayed by Gandhi, was an idealized form of the sub-continent's ancient village culture. It was quite true that Muslim and British rule had destroyed a flourishing system of village democracy; it was also true that factory-made British goods had ruined the village crafts, and created the worst seasonal unemployment on earth. In that context Gandhi was able to present his own programme as rekindling the spirit of a lost, glorious India of scholars and sages and wisely ordered village republics.

His political techniques, such as unarmed civil disobedience, gave substance (he claimed) to the ancient Hindu ideal of *Ahimsa* or non-violence. His do-it-yourself approach to social problems, his enlistment of the poorest people, brought back the murdered village self-rule in a new guise. His projects for reviving hand-spinning and other cottage industries were steps toward the restoration of the old village self-sufficiency, and freedom from bondage to the economy of the British overlords.

With this message Gandhi reached the peasants as no reforming liberal could. To quote Amaury de Riencourt, 'the secret of Gandhi's power was precisely the fact that he expressed the unconscious desire of India's mute masses', not to 'jump into an unknown future' but to 'dig deeper into India's cultural soil in order to retrieve all that had been presumably lost under British rule'.[1]

Gandhi's case against civilization as corruption bore some resemblance to Luther's attack on the falsified papal Christianity. But he was too honest to be dogmatic about an Indian golden age. He appealed to it as a fact in history, without giving it the exact date and locale which Protestants gave to the Apostolic Church. On the other hand he showed a far superior practical clarity about the steps to a renewal in the present. His constructive social programme in thousands of villages was the foundation and training ground for the national movement as long as he led it. The point, however, is that although the balance was different, Gandhi and the Protestant Reformers (to a large extent the Catholic ones also) thought in the same pattern; and it was by doing so, not by being progressive or gradualist, that they transformed millions of humble folk into revolutionaries.

Gandhi's religious language, his preaching of a clean break and a fresh start and a sort of conversion, gave the Indian form of the recurring mystique a special amplitude. But other nations in revolt against foreign rule have produced their own forms of it. Thus the prophets of the Risorgimento combined revolutionary fervour with a more specific image of the lost true Italy – Italy of the city-republics, Dante, the Renaissance; Italy which had civilized Europe – struggling to shine again through the murk of Hapsburg oppression. In Ireland, the constitutional Home Rule leaders lost control of their own movement to Sinn Fein, whose visionary Erin of saints and heroes was rooted fully a thousand years ago. Sinn Fein, not the Home Rule party, carried the Irish to independence.

With Italy and Ireland the concept of a lost glory, and a national vocation to bring it back, was easy to buttress historically. When Africa followed India's lead during the 1950s, a similar mystique was much harder to evolve; not because Africans had never produced anything, as whites maintained, but because the genuine achievements of some of them had left fewer known traces.

What is significant is that despite the difficulty of defining an African golden age, African nationalists felt impelled to try. They ransacked archaeology for early exhibits such as Benin bronzes.

[1] *The Soul of India*, p. 317.

They cited the large graduating class at the ancient University of Timbuktu. When the Gold Coast became independent, it was christened 'Ghana' after an early Empire of Ghana which may never have existed, and was somewhere else if it did. And so on to such malignant (if non-African) fictions as the Black Muslim myth – that the world was once black and happy; that the white man is an aberration produced by an evil-minded selective breeder; and that the overthrow of Whitey is the only revolution worth having.

The saner of these propaganda exercises were rebuttals of the charge that Africans were inferior and unable to rule themselves. Seen thus, they were often entirely proper, and more forceful than opponents cared to admit. (I have been told that after 1965 the white regime in Rhodesia discouraged study of the ruins of Zimbabwe.) But as critics pointed out, the ethical basis of such arguments is dubious. They seem to imply that human beings derive human rights from a cultural pedigree and not from simple humanity. In view of this objection, and in view of the parallels with the Italians and others who were under no obligation to prove anything, it is hard to resist the inference that African minds felt the same inner pressure, and invented the same type of restoration-mystique to fuel their activities.

8

The Undercurrent

1

All great mobilizers of mass discontent have tried to explain the evils they attack, and to hold up alternatives. In that spirit they have taught their followers new ways of looking at things; or revived old ways. They have traced what purport to be historical patterns, and projected them forward on to the future. By doing so, they have stirred up action on a vast scale and in a variety of fields – nationalism, religion, social or political revolution.

Yet through all the variety, one theme is repeated many times. Again and again the effective force is a mystique. Again and again it is the same mystique, variously articulated. Leaders seem to keep looking for the same pattern, and if it is not there, they put it there. This is the pattern to which the tale of King Arthur, with his Passing and his Return, gives a mythical form. We might speak of a Mystique of Transfiguration: *the reinstatement of a long-lost glory or promise, as the point of departure for a fresh start, with intervening corruption swept away.*

On the classical level, it is Virgil's return of the Saturnian age, and the gods before the gods. On the Arthurian level, it is the renewal of the Britons' kingdom, whether as imagined by Spenser or otherwise. But as a vision in action, it is Israel's re-possession of Zion; Luther's deliverance of the pure Faith from papal captivity; Hitler's revival of Charlemagne and Barbarossa; Gandhi's resurrection of buried India. It is Renaissance Italy, reborn; the Erin of saints and heroes, reborn; Ghana or Zimbabwe, reborn. It is the early Chou dynasty reincarnate in Confucius. It is Natural Humanity rising like an earthquake under the crust of pseudo-civilization. It is the ghost of the Iroquois confederacy striding into the Winter Palace.

Why does this mystique show such immense and self-generative power? It forces its way in where there are no good grounds for it. Even where the grounds are good, it seems so roundabout, and against common sense. The obvious goal for Man's collective endeavours, which most westerners would probably profess to approve, is far more down-to-earth. Surely what we should aim at is a steady utilitarian progress, based on the elementary things of life? The visible human fundamentals are birth, food, shelter, sex, death. Phrases like 'cradle to grave security' recognize that cycle. We can extend the meaning of the five headings to cover material conditions in general. Why not simply work to improve the management of these basic matters; plod on towards a world order that will preserve peace, with essential welfare for all; and harness science to an ever-widening mastery of the environment? What is wrong with rational humanism?

Most people might pay lip service to such a programme. Yet far fewer have ever responded to it in action than have responded to versions of the mystique. Even those who appear to do so, such as Oxfam workers, are usually moved by the moral demands of some particular elementary lack, rather than by any broad notions of general improvement.

Straightforward progress, on the face of it, is so palpably the right cause to work for that it should inspire everybody; and it inspires nobody. H. G. Wells was its arch-prophet. He made it sound more exciting than anyone else has done. Yet during the Second World War, George Orwell wrote a perceptive essay entitled 'Wells, Hitler, and the World State'. Orwell remarked that Wells had been talking about his sane world order for many years, and accomplished nothing. Here was a ghastly paradox. In support of the 'common-sense, essentially hedonistic view' which Wells urged (and which, according to Orwell, most thinking people accepted) nobody was willing to lift a finger or shed a pint of blood. Whereas Hitler, who was the utter negation of most of it, had millions of fanatical followers, and huge forces at his disposal.

There is something wrong, and at heart we know it. Aldous Huxley, in *Brave New World*, showed that a society might fulfil every Wellsian hope and still be horrifying. But if so, what else do

human beings want? Why should swarms of highly civilized speci-
mens forsake rational progress to embrace a crazy nightmare of
Teutonic resurgence, and the phantom of Barbarossa?

2

Part of the answer may come from anthropology. To judge from
the researches of Mircea Eliade, the mystique plunges us into
archetypal depths. It shades off into a region of ritual. Primitive
cults are full of notions about a return to a point of origin, a pristine good state. Cosmically, this is the freshness of Creation when
the world was born. For the individual, it is the unmarred integrity
of his own birth, before any decay or loss. Savages' initiation rituals
at such seasons as puberty are often dramas of symbolic death
and rebirth. Sometimes birth is actually simulated. The initiate
enters a hollow image and comes out. He has reverted to the dark
womb, which is equivalent to the chaos before the world, and he
emerges renewed for a fresh beginning. The wear and tear of time
is cancelled, the machine is wound up again.

In the more advanced of the ancient religions, the whole world
might be wound up again, physically or spiritually. This is said to
have been the purpose of the Babylonian New Year Festival, when
priests recited the Epic of Creation. The Aztec human sacrifices
which shocked the conquistadors were supposed to feed the gods,
and periodically revive their waning energies. A similar if brighter
thought underlies the Hindu myth of the avatars of the god Vishnu,
who goes through a series of widely spaced lives on earth. Manifest-
ing himself as Krishna in the *Bhagavad Gita* (Gandhi's favourite
book) he says: 'Whenever and wherever duty decays and unright-
eousness prospers, I shall be born in successive ages to destroy evil-
doers and re-establish the reign of the moral law.'

If we turn back and ask why common-sense progress is so much
less inspiring than the mystique, perhaps we have the beginning of
an answer. That sort of progress runs counter to what human
beings have always felt about their condition, and with reason. It
grounds itself on the elementary life which it proposes to improve,
the life of the visible fundamentals: birth, food, shelter, sex, death.
But this cradle-to-grave sequence, which is the only life we
are all sure of, does not itself go onward and upward. The
individual passes from youth to age, from innocence to corruption,

from freedom and hope to resignation and disillusion, from strength to decrepitude and finally death. There are temporary escapes but, on the face of it, no complete one.

Man is far more interested in fighting this trend than he is in progress. It is much to be doubted whether he ever really believes in progress. He has always seen the trend, and projected it outward on to the world and history. The Edens of his poetic imagination are at the dawn of time. Greek mythology, with its descent from the golden age into the silver into the bronze into the iron, is matched by the Hindu series of *Yugas* or cosmic epochs relentlessly contracting and darkening. Progress is a very recent invention. Certainly no ordinary person believes in it as he believes in earthly mortality, or sees what good it will do him when he is dead himself. People may believe in specific cases of it, may work devotedly and altruistically for them, and applaud them when they happen. But as an ideal it will never stir the depths till it has acquired new dimensions.

The rituals disclose what Man really wants. They are not rituals of linear progress, but of rebirth. They are attempts to undo the effects of time as Man knows them in practice, and make a fresh start. The perennial process of closing-in, cutting-down, withering-away – this is what he needs to confront and master, whether individually or cosmically. This is the trap he needs to escape from, into some undefined fulfilment. He gropes for weapons of defiance, for a tangible victory over the destroyer, a killing of the White Whale. Huxley's Brave New World offered every material good at the price of a faster, surer cutting-down, a stultifying death before birth, taking away not only the hope of regeneration but the power to hope at all. The price is too high.

At the ritual level there is an outright attempt to grapple with death itself, the final closing-in. Primitive initiates who leave their homes for a while, wandering off to the woods or a lonely hut, symbolically 'die'. Sometimes they enact their own destruction. Sometimes they submit to a token burial, and then behave as ghosts are supposed to behave, until the tribe receives them back. The object is to convert death from 'extinction' into 'death-to-something-that-must-be-transcended'. A girl who goes through initiation into womanhood is 'dying' to an outworn childhood and being reborn into fruitfulness. Death becomes functional instead of final, the rite of passage to a new life. Actual physical death is then merely a repetition of what has already happened in ritual, with, presumably, another rebirth beyond.

This mode of thinking rises into civilized myth, and farther. In Hinduism the last agony of the sinking universe is to usher in the last avatar of Vishnu, Kalki, who will reshape it into a new order. Chaos is the prerequisite of cosmos. Medieval rabbis consoled their oppressed flocks with the doctrine of the 'birth-pangs of the Messiah', saying that God's Chosen must endure the extreme of torment and apparent annihilation before their saviour could come; so that even pogroms made sense. The same idea appears, rationalized, in Marxism. The growing wretchedness of the masses is part of the theory. It is the necessary horror from which the revolution must spring . . . with the corollary, at times, that the Party should oppose reform, so as to ensure that the masses are as wretched as possible.

Primitive Man often seems to be successful in this ritual transformation of his own fate. Often he does see life and death as two states of being, rather than as existence and non-existence. He believes in the re-winding as he believes in the running down. On the other hand, in the earliest articulate cultures of Europe and the Middle East, the awareness of death has become manifest and poignant. In Homer, the earthly life which we know is the only life. The heroes look beyond it into nothing but a realm of shadows, an endless, joyless not-quite-extinction. With rare exceptions due to divine favour, the utmost they can hope for is to master death by heroically embracing it, as Achilles does, and surviving in fame. A similar outlook shows itself in the Babylonian epic of Gilgamesh, with similar yearnings.

When the epics were composed, the gods of the present dispensation were firmly enthroned. But now, in the light of the anthropological data, a new interest surely attaches to the evidence for a phase between – the actual Titan period. In Hesiod's eyes it was a feature of this golden age that men did not fear death in it, and passed to a real immortality in another state. The megalithic worship and the cult of the Great Goddess (a Titaness under some of her aspects) did promote such a faith. They carried on the primitive exorcism of death in a more sophisticated form. The Goddess was mistress of death as well as life, and all things were renewed in her. The temples were immense wombs. The dead who were laid to sleep in the passage-graves would wake up. When men under a sadder heaven reflected on the lost *Saturnia regna* which might return, were they dimly recalling a world that had possessed the secret of triumph over mortality? Gilgamesh, in the Babylonian epic, obtains this in the form of a magical plant from a kind of Titan named Utnapishtim, and loses it on the way home. A world that possessed the secret might regenerate itself out of slumber, and regenerate mankind with it.

Cronus himself, the British Cronus, lies asleep in a cavern which could originally have been a passage-grave or womb-temple. The Druids preserved something of the old outlook.[1] Arthur acquires the cave, and his alternative destiny is to pass to an island of immortality ruled by supernatural women: ultimately, perhaps, aspects of the Goddess?

At any rate, the transfer of the rebirth pattern from ritual and myth to politics, church affairs and social philosophy is easy to understand. Our mystique with all its variants is the same thing over again. It reflects the same world-picture inferred from mortal experience, and draws its strength from the same source. Man has a sense of 'things closing in', of doom and death. The rituals seek to defy this through a rebirth. The mystique, in one way and another, revives the ritual approach. It portrays our present discontents as due to the loss of a real good, and then says that the good is not finally lost, and can be reinstated.

More than once in history, the mystique can be seen taking shape as a belief in immortality wanes. Before Confucius, the Chinese assumed that their ancestors were alive and conscious. By Confucius's time an anxious debate was going on as to whether they were. Again, in the Old Testament nothing is said about immortality except in a few very late passages. Yet archaeology suggests that the early Hebrews did believe in it. Israel's religion, with its constant appeal to the restoration of the Lord's reign among his people, seems to be replacing a lost faith in individual survival with a doctrine of collective renewal.

So it has been in more recent times. The mystique has grown and proliferated as faith in Christian immortality has declined. Most of Rousseau's disciples still held to some sort of immortality, but not with the force of Christian dogma. Several writers have remarked on the return of total death as a factor in subsequent politics. Albert Camus in *The Rebel* presents modern insurrection

[1] Cf. S. von Cles-Reden. *The Realm of the Great Goddess,* pp. 122, 123, 259.

as a protest against it – sharpened, over the past century or so, by one very distinguished death, that of God. Orwell's tyrants speak as if they were the voice of the cosmos that crushes us: 'Man is infinitely malleable . . . *You* do not exist.' To which Camus's rebels retort that they are proving their own inviolable being: 'We rebel, therefore we are.'

Orwell himself stressed the waning of faith in immortality, and Koestler has assigned much of the blame to it for the failure of progress after 1918, and the appeal of ideologies such as Communism and Nazism. Human beings deprived of an eternal future lost patience and balance, wanted an instant earthly fruition, and were more willing to follow dangerous leads. The charge here is not against the poor and oppressed, whose outbreaks are always (at the very least) excusable, but against the millions above desperation level, who might have been expected to know better.

There is no doubt that the First World War did drive home the sense of corruptibility and mortality, and shake the foundations of whatever afterlife people still believed in. As Koestler points out, it was in the sequel to that war that the totalitarianisms, with their promises of life here and now, began to take hold. Meanwhile Fabian intellectuals such as Shaw and the Webbs, hitherto the arch-apostles of rational progress, swung toward a blind and mischievous adulation of Soviet Communism: they needed to see Socialist theory vindicated before they died.

But we can now see that the movements which Koestler speaks of were powerful through defiance of death, not simply (as he says) by promising an earthly fruition, but also by offering that fruition in a form which was itself a defiance, able to stir the unconscious depths. It was to take the shape of a resurrection, a grandiose proof that the destroyer Time could be defeated and an eclipsed rightness regained. The pure Aryan aristocracy, or classless unexploiting Man, as the case might be, would return from history's Avalon and recapture the earth.

All the variants of the mystique are challenges to the same gloomy inevitability. They excite human beings because they affirm that what seems to be lost is not lost; that a golden age not only existed, but can be disinterred from corruption with heightened glory; that the effects of time can be blotted out by some radical act; that the encroaching evil can be thrown off, and even made functional in the rebirth of what it crushed . . . as with Marx's crisis of capitalism which leads to the revolution. Further, some movements have had to twist themselves into this shape before they could acquire their full impact. If asked the meaning of life, a thoughtful revolutionary might well answer: 'The meaning of life is the overcoming of death.' Fully expounded, that statement can give him all he needs. By a remarkable flash of intuition Carlyle bracketed this very notion with his *Redeunt Saturnia regna*, in the paragraph on the French revolutionary mood which I quoted at the beginning of Chapter Six.

At its best, the appeal to a remote past is by no means reactionary or nostalgic. There need not be any idea of putting the clock back like Metternich. If the clock image is to be used at all, the process is as already described, a winding up after a running down. But it is described better in the words of the French Socialist Jean Jaurès: 'Take from the altars of the past the fire, not the ashes.' The long-lost glory is not a safe haven to withdraw into and dream about. It is a dynamism to carry forward into the present. To a Marxist, the primitive communist society of the past is not a static lotus-land, but the womb where the forces that propel history were generated; and the communist society of the future will have the same energies, and more. Or if we prefer a documented case, however far short of the ideal, then revolutionary France supplies it. When the corruption was swept away, and human nature, for a while, did seem born again, the result was not a lazy attempt to imitate noble savages, but the mass eruption of 1793 and the kings of Europe scattering in all directions.

3

To go back at last to the Arthurian Legend, with its absorption and development of the Titan theme – have we found the main reason for its potency? Does it convey a feeling that victory over loss, dissolution and death is what it is all about? People do not hope that King Arthur will be literally restored, or the Grail literally found. But the Legend is an image of life, partly as they know it to be, partly as they wish it to be. In haunting style, and with such powerful aids as the interwoven love-stories, the Legend portrays the sometime reality of a great good, its passing, and the possibility of getting it back.

Long ago, in the historical matrix where the British nation was formed, an actual and present splendour supposedly flourished. It vanished, yet survived. It is symbolized by the sleeping King in one phase of the cycle, by the hidden Grail in another. There is a realm of mystery and magic where a high quest was pursued and can perhaps be pursued still. The martyred hero who incarnates his people is preserved in a secret age-long immortality, and is destined to return and reign, with his wounds healed. Surely it is the halo of these associations, answering to a deep need of human nature, that confers a glamour even on the pottery scraps and post-holes of Cadbury? They have an imaginative charge which no science can neutralize; they are the buried splendour actually coming to light again.

As a check on this reading of the matter, can we detect any such inclination of mind in writers who have dealt with Arthur? Is the pattern of tragedy-yet-hope, mortality-yet-survival, visibly present in their thoughts?

Vast as the literature is, only two English authors have tried to organize it as a whole. They are Malory and Tennyson. To study the way Malory handled the stories is to see how far he redisposed them; and nearly always so as to heighten the effect of a golden age succumbing to forces of darkness. He not only unified the Legend, he gave it a new solidity and a new shape. Malory wrote during the Wars of the Roses, when a fairly successful feudal order was crumbling into ruin. Our Arthurian ideas are so much a result of his work in this context that it is not instantly obvious how much pointing-up he did, and in what spirit.

Among the older romances which he adapted, no single one gives anything approaching his entire story from start to finish. Furthermore, the source-material has a different moral atmosphere. Its world is one of 'open manslaughter and bold bawdry', in the words of the disapproving Roger Ascham. Generally the knights are violent, sensual men. The Round Table seldom embodies any distinct ethical ideal. Virtue is represented chiefly by hermits and kindred figures outside the court altogether. Malory's first great contribution is to insert another level of values. He still has the manslaughter and bawdry, he still has the bad laymen and good hermits, but he also shows how a layman can be good according to his own station in life. Thus Malory's Arthurian realm stands for a complete, valid earthly ethic, an ethic that can be realized in practice.

Also, as we noted before, he changes the order of events, giving time for the ideal to be shown in action. Geoffrey of Monmouth's Arthur seems to be constantly at war. Periods of peace are mentioned, but with only a meagre sketch of what happened in them. Arthur reaches his peak campaigning against Rome, and declines swiftly without even having got there. In Malory the Roman war is moved back. Arthur wins it, and then most of the adventures take place in a long peace that follows.

As a result, Malory evokes what is never delineated before – a British golden age that is not only romantic and chivalrous but, in a more serious way, good. Under Arthur a noble mode of life does to some extent flourish. Arthur's Britain therefore has relevance. Malory holds it up as a contrast and lesson to the distracted England he knows. His appeal is from knighthood and kingship as they are in the fifteenth century to knighthood and kingship as they should be, and, in King Arthur's reign, sometimes were.

Having established his golden age – his lost glory – Malory traces a well-defined process of corruption. The Round Table fails because of human vices and shortcomings. Even those separate attractions, the love-stories, are pressed into service for the overall theme. Guinevere's adultery with Lancelot is one of the main causes of trouble. Tristram throws the unknightliness of Mark into baleful relief. At last all is destroyed by civil war. When Caxton edited and printed Malory's writings, he called the book *Le Morte d'Arthur*. That title is not the author's but Caxton's. It is a vivid testimony to the effect Malory creates. In a sense, death is what the whole cycle is about. Malory makes it a tragedy taking its meaning from the fatal (or apparently fatal) end.

On the future rebirth, Malory is vaguer. He rejects Arthur's return, and prefers to 'leave him buried peacefully in his tomb at Glastonbury'. Yet his last allusion to the subject is the line said to have been inscribed on the tomb: 'Hic jacet Arthurus, rex quondam, rexque futurus' – Here lies Arthur, king that was, king that shall be. To Malory, perhaps, Arthur is symbolic. The earthly ideal is possible, because Arthur realized it enough to prove that it is. Hence there is no reason why his glory should not be revived in a regenerate England, given the will to do so: York and Lancaster, please note. This is the idea taken up by the Tudor propagandists and carried to its culmination in Spenser. *The Faerie Queene* spells out – or, at least, begins to spell out – what Malory's structuring of the Legend foreshadows.

Last, Tennyson. With him the case is clear, and all the more so because the clarity is unintended, a self-revelation. His Arthur is inseparable from another Arthur, the adored Hallam, whose sudden death and longed-for survival supplied Tennyson with the theme of his chief work. The *Idylls of the King* are linked with *In Memoriam*. Tennyson's first major treatment of the Legend was in the fragment *Morte d'Arthur*, describing the King's passing, with a curious epilogue about his return, as one who 'cannot die'. In the larger scheme of the *Idylls*, Malory's sequence of glory and decay is preserved, with new meanings added. The Legend is now a picture of 'ideal manhood closed in real man', its gradual eclipse through the encroachment of Sense on Soul, and a mysterious immortality for Arthur none the less, with a new sunrise at the close. Both Arthurs, the King and Hallam, are taken away yet really deathless, and destined to rejoin those who now mourn their going. In the late poem 'Merlin and the Gleam', they blend finally into one. We can no longer be sure, at every point, which of them the poet is talking about; presumably both.

For Tennyson, there can be no doubt where the initial attraction lay. Once attracted, he used the Legend as a vehicle for several ideas, religious, political and moral. But the name of Arthur kept his mind fixed on the imagery of loss that is not loss, death that is not death; of glory once experienced, and the dream of its triumphant renewal.

PART THREE

The Succession

9

Albion in Transition

1

Arthur, then, stands at the centre of what may fairly be called the British myth. For the reasons we now know, this fascinates and always will, so long as humanity thinks of itself as mortal and of its world as perishable. People may still believe in a Christian heaven, and personal salvation outside time and space – or they may not. Either way, their experience of earthly life is the same: and the resultant sorrows and longings may be different in urgency, but not in kind. Hence, in part at least, the more than archaeological spell of the hill where Arthur sleeps.

Yet one of Cadbury's lessons has been that there is far more to this than Arthur. The older and richer archaeological levels guide us toward the shadowy country of the gods before the gods, and (in Blake's language) the Giant Albion, whom Arthur brings to a human focus. Far back in that Titanic prehistory the British myth is rooted.

It stands alone among myths in its relationship to historical change, and collective human action. It vaguely resembles other myths of a god's departure and return; but in the Old World at any rate, these myths are cyclic – endlessly repetitive – and cannot be related to history with the same cogency. In the various revolutionary and national movements, human beings have acted uniquely, at real places and times: to reassemble dispersed Israel, to restore the Apostolic Church, or whatever the aim was. The British myth of a blessedness that flowers, withers, yet may flower again after a long lapse, once for all, is strangely intriguing because it has the same shape. It is a poetic statement of something which human beings constantly strive for – a triumph over mortality – and try to realize through their collective mythologies of action.

The British myth can of course be given a non-mythical

147

expression, as a special way of looking at things. It implies a belief that even in a situation seen to be badly wrong and tending down-hill, an original rightness is still, in some sense, 'there'. The rightness may be no more than a latent promise or possibility, but it endures, perhaps in the custody of a faithful few who have kept it alive. Corruption conceals it but can never destroy it. The solution to our present problems is to find a key which is lost, but exists.

Partly because of the observed movement of life from the safe and innocent womb through decay toward death, we find it easiest to think of the 'rightness' as having once blossomed openly: hence the past Edens and golden ages. However, the way-of-looking-at-things need not absolutely dictate such beliefs. Rousseau admitted that his past natural society might be chiefly a useful fiction for criticizing present society. The criticism remained sound. The natural state, in his view, was a potentiality, a kind of social vocation which so-called civilization thwarted. Man should be regarded as carrying it within him, whether literally Eden-derived or not. (Such an idea is frequent in religion applied to the indi-vidual. Hindus seek a true Self hidden behind the deceiving veil of appearances. Zen Buddhists desire an awakening which is the raising of a lost innocence back to the surface.)

For anybody who thinks in this way, whatever the extent of his faith in a past golden age, there can be no faith at all in automatic progress toward a future one. The buried rightness, the thing that ought to be, is probably quite at odds with the prevailing state of affairs after untold years of alienation from it. Existing trends do not lead towards it, except negatively by self-defeat. Very likely they cannot even be steered towards it. Whatever else is right as a remedy for evil, *laissez-faire* and trend-following are wrong. The aspiring world-betterer may accept portions of the present system, tinker with other portions, and try to make use of other portions. But his main business is to hunt out the buried rightness and reinstate it in action. True progress, if we are to employ that word, must be thought of in terms of defiance and a clean break and a fresh start.

It sounds impractical. Yet Zionism is a daunting object-lesson. The Zionist pioneers not only called for a transplanting of Jews and a revival of the ancestral vocation, they also denied that the Jewish problem could be solved through assimilation and liberal reform. In the eyes of their rational contemporaries they were mad.

Certainly they were the least 'trendy' of politicians. Yet, after their fashion, they were the most successful.

Obviously this way-of-looking-at-things can engender monsters of propagandist falsehood, like the noble and ancient Aryan strain which the Nazis proposed to rescue from mongrelism by selective breeding. On the other hand it can genuinely show what is the way of life rather than death. Whichever party we prefer in the Reformation, Luther's or Erasmus's, the recovery of the Church undoubtedly had to come as they said, through a quest for the Apostolic Faith, pursued in the conviction that it was still there under the millennial rubbish.

Is this attitude right or wrong in any absolute sense? If it appraises the human condition accurately, what about the lies and delusions it has led to? Could we explain, say, the Nazi mythology as an outcome of using the right approach for the wrong ends? Conversely, is the approach itself merely wishful thinking – a subtle expression of the craving to refute death, productive of zeal but not, reliably, of wisdom? At the heart of all this, is there a fundamental truth, or even a statement of fundamental issues?

I can conceive no short answer. But there is one thing we can do. We can look to Britain, the country that created the myth, and see whether any British minds have developed this way-of-looking-at-things any further, to a point of deeper elucidation. When studying the growth of the myth itself, we tested the insight of William Blake, and confirmed it. But his quoted remark on Albion and Arthur is only one small item in the copious mythology he invented. Blake, then, may surely help. And so may others, who have explored the same mythological paths, or looked at things in the same way. We have seen Arthur supplying a clue to historical events. Perhaps, though, Arthur is not the end of the story that seems to end in him. More clues may be waiting farther on.

2

In the light of all that has emerged, I make no apology for rejoining Blake and examining his ideas in more detail. Despite all the attention he has had (and deservedly), I do not know of anyone who has considered him in the way already suggested, as a myth-maker whose proved acumen justifies turning to him in all seriousness for a deeper comprehension of myth. What we have seen so far is that human beings persistently behave in a certain manner, which the British myth reflects, just as the Oedipus myth reflects another kind of behaviour. What we have to decide is whether we are confronting a truth or a delusion; whether human beings are right to detect something like their own mortality in the whole condition of the species, with the inference that a pattern of closing-in and defiance, rather than direct progress, must always be the real shape of history. Clearly this is a question about human nature itself. The closing-in, if it happens, is self-inflicted, whatever the compulsions that may seem to make it inevitable.

Now Blake, who grasped the point about Arthur and Albion, did in fact explore human nature under that very aspect. His imagination does take the British myth further, with implications, moreover, about modern Britain and society generally. He may still look eccentric, but less so than in the latter half of the nineteenth century, or even the first half of the twentieth. He is the only major English poet who has claimed to be a prophet in the Israelite style (not, of course, in the incidental sense of pretending to foretell future events). The course of time is bearing him out.

I think we may quite properly turn to Blake as a guide – a guide as well qualified for the present purpose as Virgil was to conduct Dante; though, like Virgil, he cannot go all the way.

Blake's work lies in the context of the Industrial Revolution and Napoleon. It was a scene of expanding capitalism, and distress that is familiar enough, accompanied by warfare and savage repression. As Edmund Burke observed, the sophists and calculators (Malthus, for instance) were coming into their own. Britain stood between empires. The American colonies had gone, the Victorian Empire was not yet fairly begun. But the foundations of 'greatness' and Kiplingite patriotism were being laid.

Blake's life extends from 1757 to 1827. Thus he was born before Wordsworth, Coleridge, Byron, Shelley and Keats, and survived three out of five of them – all five, perhaps, as poets. Yet he remained on the fringes of literature. His life, seen from outside, was uneventful. All we need glance at here is the little that is vital to understanding his poetry. Most of it was spent in London, except for three years at Felpham near Bognor, under the aegis of a patron. So far as contemporaries knew him at all, they knew him more as an artist than as a poet, and more as a commercial artist than as a creative one. His small income was earned chiefly by engraving and book illustration. His sole public exhibition of paintings was a failure, important mainly for the *Descriptive Catalogue*. It is in this catalogue that his dicta on Arthur and Albion appear, with much else.

Radical by temperament, he was friendly with Tom Paine. However, his political interests faded out. His marriage was tranquil. His biggest practical problem was how to reconcile his vocation with the need to make a living by accepting commissions. Lacking formal schooling, he studied French, Italian, Greek, Latin and Hebrew with immense gusto, as well as religious authors of a mystical kind – St Teresa of Avila, Jacob Boehme, William Law – and much history and antiquarianism. But he carried all his self-assumed burdens lightly. He is said to have died singing.

His anthology pieces, such as 'The Tyger', have of course always been read, and the hymn 'And did those feet in ancient time,' miscalled 'Jerusalem', has been widely if uncomprehendingly sung. The hazards start with his larger works. Partly because of them, he was long regarded as mad. Understanding and admiration have slowly dawned since his death. For many readers today, Blake is enthroned as a supreme poet and master-prophet. But even with the aid of his commentators he is hard to discuss as one might discuss, say, Wordsworth. It is doubtful whether anybody understands him all the way through (I do not). Also, while his ideas can be summed up in their main outlines, any such summing-up must lose the flavour. He will be made to appear more lucid, tidier, and smaller. The summing-up will be Blake minus Blake, and defensible only as an aid to reading him, not as a substitute for doing so.

He foreshadows Marshall McLuhan's distinction between 'hot' and 'cool' communication. The former is the clear-cut, spelt-out, sequential communication still normal for the printed word, as in a textbook. The latter is the kind alleged to characterize the TV era. Pioneered by James Joyce, it is an interplay between less-explicit language or imagery and a recipient who must do more himself if he is to grasp the message. Blake was a cool communicator, and knew it. In 1799 there was a project for him to illustrate the Rev. John Trusler, author of *The Way to be Rich and Respectable* and kindred works. This fell through. Mr Trusler wanted Blake's pictures to have a moral, and complained that he could make no sense of them. In reply, Blake wrote: 'The wisest of the Ancients consider'd what is not too Explicit as the fittest for Instruction, because it rouzes the faculties to act.' When we turn to his own prophetic books, this is putting it mildly. Their message is not so much 'what they say' as 'what you arrive at for yourself by a sustained effort to master them' – helped, naturally, by others who have made the same effort and arrived at a degree of consensus.

These prophetic, or symbolic, books are products of Blake's mature years. Before them comes the mainly lyrical verse in the *Songs of Innocence* and the *Songs of Experience*. Most of the published poetry was etched by the poet himself on whole-page plates, with text and pictures interwoven. Critics differ as to how far the pictures are necessary to the text. The prevailing view is that the text can be read alone without fatal loss.

The lyrical poems rhyme and scan. The symbolic ones never rhyme. At first they scan in a loose way, with three-beat or seven-beat lines recalling Hebrew verse and the bogus 'Ossian' epics of the eighteenth-century Celtic revival. Then the scansion dissolves in an endlessly variable rhythm. Besides poems, Blake's written work includes notebooks, commentaries on books he read, essays to go with his more ambitious paintings, and prose satires and fragments. The total bulk is not huge. Even with his letters, it all goes into one volume of manageable size.

From this body of material it is easy to extract what we need to start with: a few compact proofs that Blake did – or could – think in the pattern, practise the way-of-looking-at-things, which the British myth indicates. We may begin by noticing what he says of Arthur besides the Albion remark. Though not copious, it includes the theme of Arthur's magnificent reign, and the belief that he 'shall awake from sleep, and resume his dominion over earth and ocean'. That comes in the same section of the *Descriptive Catalogue* as the Albion passage itself. To show how Blake's mind could generalize the motif, there is an early poem, 'Gwin, King of Norway', in which a rising against a tyrant is led by a giant named Gordred, who wakes up from a long sleep in a cave. Again, Blake's serious thinking on revolutions – American, French, and otherwise – steadily approximates to the mystique as defined. In his earlier work, revolution is not a direct forward movement, but a break with the existing cycle leading to a fresh start. Later, he adds the statement that his own hope would be 'to Restore what the Ancients call'd the Golden Age', though, like Rousseau, he never commits himself too firmly to a literal belief in it.

More subtly indicative is the idea behind the titles of his two linked lyrical books. Man passes from the childlike 'innocence' of naïve ignorance to the sad 'experience' of reality, with the vision of the world darkening around him. But in Blake's mature thought there is a state beyond, 'organiz'd innocence'. We can come to terms with our disillusioning knowledge, and recapture the pristine joy on a new level, without self-deceit. This is a doctrine too weighty to dispose of in a sentence. The immediate point is simply that it fits the same basic scheme of loss that is not loss, and rebirth.

Blake shifted from belief in a violent revolution to hopes which were less naïve but no less revolutionary. His greatest works are about human nature, which he thinks of socially and historically as well as individually; and that is why they concern us here. He has been called an apocalyptic humanist. Very well: what is his own version of the recurrent mystique?

His grand theme is Man's 'fall into Division & his Resurrection to Unity'. To expound this, Blake deploys an array of invented characters who stand for human nature in various aspects. Sometimes they are like the gods of religion, but only because, for Blake, 'All deities reside in the human breast.' A 'Great Eternity', above space and time, is the true home of every being. 'God', however, means ideal humanity. In strict terms the only person we can rightly call God is Jesus, who embodies this. All specific gods, including Jehovah, are projections of human nature.

Attempts have been made to place Blake in a mystical tradition coming down from the Neo-Platonists through Paracelsus and Swedenborg. Source-hunting, however, can be overdone. Though he owes a debt to the esoteric Christian schools, he is not Christian in any approved sense. He is intensely religious, steeped in the Bible; but he supplies meanings of his own, which sometimes invert the orthodox meanings. In *The Everlasting Gospel* he says:

> Thou art a Man, God is no more,
> Thine own Humanity learn to Adore.

He connects his integrated, unfallen Man with Eden. But this is not the Eden of Scripture, and unfallen Man is not Adam, who is quite a late arrival in the Blakean cosmos, as is the Jehovah who pronounces doom on him. Blake goes back to the gods before the gods. In the world of Titans and giants he locates the primal forces of humanity, before they were disorganized and fettered. Even in his juvenile 'Gwin' poem, as we just saw, the liberating power is a giant from an Arthurian cave. In *The Marriage of Heaven and Hell* Blake speaks of the Giants now in chains who are the sources of all life and activity, and 'the Antediluvians who are our Energies'. In an epic fragment *The French Revolution* he suggests that the revolutionary forces are a stirring of the exiled Titans; and in the poem *America*, where his invented symbols begin to appear, he draws imagery from the fire-stealing Titan Prometheus.

We have traced the process which made Albion himself a Titan, combining Atlas and Cronus. In the *Descriptive Catalogue* passage, Arthur's empire is made out to be a legendary reflection of Albion's primeval realm. But also – and here the Blakean scheme is more palpably taking hold – the few traditional survivors of Camlann, Arthur's last battle, are made out to symbolize aspects of Primal Man. Clearly the question that arises is how Blake regards Albion, the prototype, and with what implications.

This Titan is in fact the chief of the symbolic figures in Blake's mythology, and the only one he explicitly takes from older mythology. In his earlier writings, 'Albion' is simply a name for Britain or England. But his delvings into antiquarian lore, Welsh triads, and similar matter, brought him face to face not only with Albion as a person but with the recent crop of Druid enthusiasts.

These were pushing the Druids farther and farther back in time, not merely to Stonehenge, but to a golden age remoter still. Theorists such as Edward Davies, author of *Celtic Researches*, ascribed all the wisdom of pagan antiquity to Druid masters. According to Davies, the Titan era was the period just after the Flood, when the families of the earth were undivided. The Druids were the sages of that era. They developed the pre-Deluge patriarchial wisdom, taught writing and other arts, and tried to establish a non-violent society. With the advent of violence, humanity declined. So, in their British headquarters, did the Druids themselves. But their teaching underlies the lore of the Celtic races, the philosophy of Greece, and also that of India (where, says Davies, the Brahmins have always known and revered the British Isles). Some of the bolder spirits of Davies's school included the Hebrews among the Druids' pupils and graduates, or, at any rate, argued that the revealed doctrine of Scripture and the Druid philosophy were all the same thing if you went back far enough.

The Greek part of this theory, at least, had a genuine pedigree. It appears in the writings of an eminent Father of the Church, Clement of Alexandria. Milton takes it up in *Areopagitica* and improves on it: 'Writers of good antiquity and ablest judgement have been perswaded that ev'n the school of Pythagoras, and the Persian wisdom took beginning from the old Philosophy of this Iland.' For Milton, Blake had a warm if critical admiration.

In his major works Blake adopts these notions and improves on them further yet. 'Adam', he declares, 'was a Druid, and Noah; also Abraham was called to succeed the Druidical age.' Again, 'All things Begin & End in Albion's Ancient Druid Rocky Shore.' During the Titan epoch, according to this remarkable expansion of the British myth, Britain humanized the whole earth, teaching eternal wisdom to a united mankind: united, partly because Atlantis was then above water, a Greater Britain joining America to Europe. This was not after the Flood as in Davies, but before, and indeed before the entire Scriptural history. All the world had one language and one religion, the Everlasting Gospel. The primordial culture created vast forgotten civilizations in Asia. All the surviving art works of antiquity, including the Greek, are simply copies and shadows of 'stupendous originals now lost or perhaps buried till some happier age.'

Albion's sages betrayed their trust. The Titans were scattered. Atlantis sank, its golden peaks vanished under the waves, the continents were split apart. Britain dwindled into an island. Nevertheless the drowned Atlantean ranges are still there below the surface, and still charged with Titanic energies, which surged up in the American and French Revolutions.

Hence, Blake's Albion is multiple. To begin with he is the Patriarch of Britain. The Arthurian Legend is a faint echo of what he once was and did. Several of his children, who stand (more or less) for the British people, are given names derived from Geoffrey of Monmouth. Blake is lovingly geographical; he has a mystique of places which would be hard to match outside the Old Testament.

But because of the theories which he exploits, Albion is more than a personified nation. He is lord of the Atlantic, with Atlas as one of his aspects. He is the culture-hero of all humanity; formerly all the nations of the earth were seen in his cities; his 'spiritual London' covered the world. Ultimately he *is* all humanity, the symbol of Man. Like Spenser's allegories, he has several levels of meaning.

As Man, Albion is a microcosm of Creation. In his first state, endowed with divine knowledge and life, he 'contain'd in his mighty limbs all things in Heaven & Earth'. Now that he has fallen, 'the Starry Heavens are fled from the mighty limbs of Albion'. Man has shrunk to the familiar naked ape. The biblical Adam was not the first human being but the limit of contraction. Blake describes his Titan in the notes to a picture ('A Vision of the Last Judgment') as 'Albion, our Ancestor, patriarch of the Atlantic Continent, whose History Preceded that of the Hebrews'.

Nobody knows how far Blake believed literally in the Celto-maniacs' Ancient Britain, or his own extension of it. The point which does need stressing is that the imaginative basis must not be pulled out from under the superstructure. While his Albion myth grows into a grandiose and enduring statement about the human condition, such a growth would have been impossible without the prior notion of Britain as the world's fountain-head. Furthermore Blake remains a patriot. Special meanings for Britain persist throughout. A firm continuity, however weird, links him with Arthur and all the rest.

3

Blake's account of Man, his fall, and his potential rebirth, is worked out through the series of symbolic books. Between 1789 and 1820 he composed ten short ones, a longer one called *Milton*, and two on a grand scale, *Vala or the Four Zoas* and *Jerusalem*. Albion himself is not placed squarely at the centre until *Jerusalem*, the last. He is present before, but Blake closed in on him gradually by way of the other characters. (This would appear to refute the view of some commentators, that Blake's real theme is the individual soul rather than mankind, and that his mythology is a mystical *Pilgrim's Progress*. If it were, surely Albion would be at the centre throughout.)

As the Eternal Man prior to all history and Creation itself as we know it, Albion is both human and divine, both male and female, enjoying complete balance and harmony. He is perfectly wise and perfectly innocent. Blake's reverent use of the figure of Jesus as symbol and representative of this perfection underlies his best-known lines, in the preface to *Milton*:

> And did those feet in ancient time
> Walk upon England's mountains green?
> And was the holy Lamb of God
> On England's pleasant pastures seen?

As usual, there are at least two layers of meaning. Blake may be referring to one of the odder offshoots of the Arthur-Grail imbroglio, the belief that Jesus visited Britain as a boy, lived at Priddy in the Mendips, and built the first wattle cabin at Glastonbury. This tale seems to have arisen quite recently – perhaps, indeed, too recently for Blake to have heard it – from a misunderstanding of one of the legends about the Old Church. Blake did show his interest in Glastonbury's more favoured legend by drawing a picture of 'Joseph of Arimathea among the Rocks of Albion'. But in any case the literal sense matters less than the symbolic. Christ walked in England because, in ancient time, the land of Albion contained the divine perfection of human nature.

Human nature has emphatically ceased to be perfect. Here we approach the heart of the present matter: Blake's belief that humanity has gone downhill; that this is a real trend, not merely a projection of individual mortality; and that the way to reverse it is through a restoration. His version of the recurrent mystique differs from most by piercing through all political and racial rationalizations, to the central issue of human nature itself. In spite of all quirks, perversities and obscurities, his poetic account of this deserves to be seriously and carefully studied. It does not depend on literal acceptance of the more bizarre portions of the history.

Man, for Blake, is fourfold. He is Intellect and Imagination and Emotion and Instinct. This Jungian scheme is related to the parts of the body and the points of the compass. Four characters called Zoas stand for the four aspects of Albion. 'Zoa' recalls the Greek word for 'life', and the four 'living creatures' in Ezekiel's vision of the Chariot (*Ezekiel* i:4–28), to which Jewish mysticism attaches great esoteric importance.

Man has fallen, in Blake's myth, through selfhood. Losing faith in the cosmic vision, he withdrew from Eternity into his own ego – the false, craving ego. Outgoing creativity gave way to possessiveness and subtler passions. The same act which divided Man from other beings also divided him from, and within, himself. The four Zoas sank into error and discord.

This inner disorganization of Man has dragged him down through four tiers of existence. Blake calls them Eden, Beulah, Generation, and Ulro. All four have been known to human beings at any given time in world history, but the tendency has been for more and more people to sink into the lower states for longer and longer. 'Eden' is the unfallen state of union with Eternity; we can still enjoy it in moments of vision. 'Beulah' is the best of ordinary life, the realm of peace, poetry, love. Bunyan made Beulah one of his allegorical countries in *The Pilgrim's Progress*. For Blake it is a region of moonlight by contrast with the sunlight of Eden, which would be unendurable going on without pause; a happy haven, but dangerous, because we can become relaxed and complacent in it (as some of the ancient aristocracies may have done, in Minoan Crete for instance). 'Generation' is, roughly, elementary life as most people undergo it most of the time – birth, food, shelter, sex, death – neither base nor exalted, but without final hope. 'Ulro' is the lowest state. Its inhabitants concern themselves with the material and measurable, with 'cash value', and are blind to anything else. This is the level of the wrong sort of practical common sense, and, in Blake's opinion, the wrong sort of science.[1]

The name 'Ulro' may be intended to suggest 'unruly.' Ulro is a state of delusion, with an air of disorder and bad dreaming. In modern language 'the materialistic rat-race' conveys a little of the notion. The image of Ulro's encroachment on mankind is a death-like sleep into which Albion falls – the Titanic slumber of Cronus and Arthur, invested with a Blakean meaning. Blake's story is more than an abstract picture of psychology. He portrays Man's gradual entrapment in the quicksand of Ulro, and the changes of his constituent Zoas, as actually happening through the centuries. They do not happen in a smooth sequence, any more than history does. In fact the story begins in an overlap between Eternity and Time, before the world existed; something like the Dream Time of Australian

[1] Jung broke with Freud in the same spirit. He did not quarrel with Freud's assertion that a religious doctrine (for example) was a sublimated genital image, but with his claim that it was *nothing but* that. The Ulro-dweller may be right in his facts. Where he goes wrong is in his *nothing but* attitude to them.

myth. But after a while, Albion's alienation starts revealing itself in earthly events, as the primal golden age breaks up. The decline goes on from there.

This plan might be expected to destroy itself, because Blake's prehistory is so unlike what we are accustomed to believe. However, he manages to close the door against that sort of criticism. He implies that we cannot think our way back to the Titan age, or grasp what was happening then, because we are involved in the fall ourselves. Our perceptions and mental habits have drifted too far from their original moorings. Lacking the spiritual key, we cannot reconstruct the prehistory from archaeological data; only, at best, by poetic insight. Which he supplies. (Nor is he quite so deeply at odds with science as might appear. 'The archaeologist', Sir Mortimer Wheeler has conceded, 'may find the tub, but altogether miss Diogenes.')

Blake's long-drawn fall of Man is not primarily a process of getting worse, but of getting smaller. Man, shut in and divided and subdivided, has found himself in a meaner and meaner universe, limited at last to the little he can glean from his myopic senses. As Blake once said in a letter, 'The tree which moves some to tears of joy is in the Eyes of others only a Green thing that stands in the way'. The 'Green thing' is the tree seen at the Ulro level, where, in a commercial civilization, more and more people spend their time.

4

But why and how is human nature supposed to have cut itself down like this? And, in fact, has it?

The four Zoas whose lack of harmony has caused all the trouble appear in Blake's poetry as complex, changeful figures with personalities of their own, not as mere allegories. They are Urizen (Intellect), Urthona or Los (Imagination), Luvah (Emotion), Tharmas (Instinct, and, in a sense, Man's physical being). The last two are less sharply focused. Tharmas, though important, fades out. Luvah is the source of the Dionysiac in life. When projected as a god, he is the ubiquitous nature-god worshipped with song and frenzy, known better to ourselves than to Blake through *The Golden Bough*.

Los takes shape as creative artist and seer, the father of inspiration. Los is the vital essence of Man; even when fallen he is the

Zoa who saves whatever can be saved, and prepares the way back. In that role he is also the spirit of Time, because, says Blake, 'Time is the mercy of Eternity.' Albion lost his vision in one terrible instant; history is the bitter working-out of that instant; but it also gives time for the forces of regeneration to rally, under Los's aegis.

Urizen – Intellect – is the chief agent of the fall. In his unfallen state he is the Prince of Light, but we do not hear very much about him as such. He is introduced already brooding in a realm of his own, the arch-villain of the story. Blake formed his name from a Greek verb meaning 'to limit', the same word from which 'horizon' is derived. Urizen stands for the abstract reasoning power when selfhood has torn it from the human harmony, and made it domineering. He is the source of law, uniformity, closed systems of every kind. This is his flaw. Cut off from his three colleagues, he is a frozen perfectionist. Blake draws him as an old man, and surrounds him with images of coldness, hardness and separation.

Urizen comes into view already obsessed with his delusion.

> 'From the depths of dark solitude, From
> The eternal abode in my holiness,
> Hidden, set apart, in my stern counsels,
> Reserv'd for the days of futurity,
> I have sought for a joy without pain,
> For a solid without fluctuation . . .
> Lo! I unfold my darkness, and on
> This rock place with strong hand the Book
> Of eternal brass, written in my solitude:
> Laws of peace, of love, of unity . . .
> One command, one joy, one desire,
> One curse, one weight, one measure,
> One King, one God, one Law.'

What the mind always hungers to do is to fit all experience into a single plan, with fixed principles – something it can computerize, so to speak. This is a false unity, not a true one. Haunted by fears of the irrational, Urizen constitutes himself 'God from Eternity to Eternity' and creates the 'Mundane Shell'. This, it appears, is the world of the ancient cosmology, when the vision of Eternity was not yet manifestly dimmed and the great sages were still at their height: a splendid starry dwelling-place for the human spirit, dimly recalled in the first chapter of *Genesis* and Plato's *Timaeus*, yet a descent, a contrived harmony only.

In due course it cracks. At some period still remote from ourselves, the sages degenerate into the Druids of history. The abuse of reason begins to poison their wisdom with the inhuman logic of rewards and punishments, and the insistence on rigid structure. They build monstrous temples such as Stonehenge, and invent the archetypal violence of human sacrifice; they break up the brotherhood of men, and dissect the human body itself on their altars. Whereupon the Flood sweeps over the earth, Atlantis is lost, and so forth.

As humanity declines, its noble cosmos losing cohesion, Urizen explores the abyss of irrationality that has yawned again. He has been devising a new system, the Net, or Web, of Religion. Disguised as Jehovah he has planted a beguiling garden, and now a tree springs up, the Tree of Mystery, on which Christ is afterwards crucified. Blake lays heavy stress on the evil effects of mystery, at least in the deliberate sense. Intellect, he suggests, has constantly been misapplied in harness with secrecy or pretence, to achieve an ascendancy over others, make them more docile, and conceal what is being done to them. Urizen as mystifier is the spirit of priesthood, trying to form a closed system by active falsification. Hence he is worse than in his previous phase. Concurrently, Los appears as Elijah and the succession of Hebrew poet-prophets, the last in Blake's eyes being not John the Baptist, but most interestingly, Joseph of Arimathea. Urizen seizes the truths uttered by Los, and codifies them in scriptures, so that the people whom the prophets enlightened shall transmit dogma instead.

Urizen's aim is always to control and consolidate. He is the 'restrainer', the 'great opposer of change', the net result of whose efforts is invariably a change for the worse. Besides his ingenuities as Jehovah, we gather that he has constructed other religions out of the dying embers of vision. One is that of the sky-gods led by Zeus, banisher and supplanter of the Titans.

Urizen roams about with his tablets inscribed 'Thou shalt not', preaching moral virtue instead of vision, and guilt instead of forgiveness. But he only repeats a discovery long since made – that none of his systems will really work.

> His soul sicken'd! he curs'd
> Both sons & daughters; for he saw
> That no flesh nor spirit could keep
> His iron laws one moment.

Every closed system refutes itself. Urizen is always having to re-write his books. He sinks into ever deeper frustration and gloom, as human turbulence cuts the ground from under his feet. Also the Hebrew prophetic genius is too strong for him. He becomes Satanic. Indeed Satan sometimes appears to *be* Urizen so far as he is anybody. Like the Satan of Milton, Urizen finally sinks to deceit and cunning. But he can also be violent, a persecutor. Afraid of the future, endlessly struggling to conserve, he sets up endless 'establishments'. Each embodies some principle or other: a religion (church Christianity, for instance), or in later times an ideology, or an enthroned fetish such as national greatness. Each establishment is coercive, and can only impose its kind of order by stamping its subjects down into Generation and Ulro. If they rise much above those states, their imagination will make them subversive. (A good example in a limited sphere is the original mass-production technique of Henry Ford. As a stable, functioning apparatus the factory depended – and Ford knew it depended – on having non-union robotized workers, pushed to the limit of endurance, with no breathing-space to think in.)

Blake's essential point here is that humanity should come first and all systems should yield to it. Urizen, the self-willed despotic mind, keeps inverting that priority and cutting human beings down to fit systems. Documented history shows Urizen at his best in Plato; at his worst, perhaps, in Stalin. The Russian dictator's alleged sneer 'How many divisions has the Pope?' is a choice bit of Ulronese in politics. But even Plato would have banned poets from his republic, conditioned its citizens by teaching them lies, and kept most of them at Blake's Generation level. The portrayal of Urizen is very acute.

And it becomes more acute as it enters its last phase. For a man of Blake's time, to look back on Plato was not an extraordinary feat. To foreshadow Stalin was. The most striking chapter in Urizen's career is the Age of Reason following the decline of the churches. The breakdown of his ecclesiastical phase is sketched in *The Four Zoas*. Trapped and warped by his own mysteries, Urizen turns into the Dragon of the Apocalypse, the mount of the harlot Babylon, palpably hateful (*Revelation* xvii). From the viewpoint of eighteenth-century enlightenment, this would have been the end of him. Christian priestcraft was his last guise, and Christian priestcraft was now exposed and doomed. In the era launched by Bacon, who taught experimental method; by Newton, who made sense of the universe; by Locke, who systematized the mind, and prompted the first ideas of progress . . . in that era, dogma had given way to rational 'Deism' and Natural Religion. Surely, then, full mental liberty had at last dawned? Surely the Urizenic perversion of intellect was at an end?

But Blake saw the case differently. In *The Four Zoas*, after Urizen's monstrous change –

> The Synagogue of Satan therefore, uniting against Mystery,/Satan dividing against Satan, resolv'd in open Sanhedrim/To burn Mystery with fire & form another from her ashes . . ./The ashes of Mystery began to animate; they call'd it Deism/And Natural Religion; as of old, so anew began/Babylon again.

Blake is looking ahead to the coming generations' disenchantment with science. Unless practised in the right spirit, science is not a release but another Urizenic trap. Again and again he names Bacon, Newton and Locke as the falsest of the false prophets, sometimes adding Voltaire as an auxiliary. They have brought back Urizen, the demon of closed systems, in another guise. Theirs is a science of uniformity, abstract law, calculation. It 'explains' Man with all his world by thrusting him down as near as possible to Ulro and keeping him there.

Locke's psychology, for instance, does work in a way, but only if you assume in advance that there is nothing for the mind to feed on but sense-impressions derived from material objects. Likewise, Newton's cosmic laws presuppose that nothing exists but the measurable. Their kind of science is a dissection in which everything that matters escapes, leaving Man dwarfed and helpless. And, of course, utterly and finally mortal. The 'allegoric heaven' which the churches still console him with is a barren fancy.

Eighteenth-century intellectuals, in Blake's eyes, betrayed their kinship to the priests by a shared contempt for inspiration. They dismissed even Methodists as 'enthusiasts.' Blake hints that the scientific thinkers are well on the way to becoming a priesthood themselves. Their science is divorced from the fullness of life and its needs. It fits in cosily with every real evil, just as the churches do. Both wither up humanity. Orthodox religion in the past bound men down,

Closing and restraining,
Till a Philosophy of Five Senses was complete.
Urizen wept & gave it into the hands of Newton & Locke.

Urizen weeps, because he can no longer enjoy anything. He is too busy hatching his nightmare inventions. As, in the past, he produced the tyranny of creeds and the wars of religion, so in Blake's world he is producing the doctrine of Adam Smith based on that abstract pygmy the Economic Man; he is producing Malthus; he is producing commercialism, warfare for profit, science misapplied by technical expertise in a hellish factory system. Blake's grim England is hallowed by the God of respectable Christians, who get on happily with the industrialists and political economists.

The famous 'Satanic mills' have the duality of many Blakean images. They are the mills of unholy logic, grinding down Reality into something infinitely less than it is. But the reader who thinks of the mills of Lancashire, child labour, and all the rest, is thinking of things that are contained in the larger idea: technology, the profit-and-loss account, the reduction of people to atomic units that can be dragooned into service.

The coming pseudo-scientific bureaucracies are in sight. So, indeed, are *Brave New World* and *Nineteen Eighty-Four*. Such Anti-Utopias belong to the realm of Urizen. He has been degrading human beings into sacrificial victims at one stage of history, slaves at another, factory-hands and cannon-fodder at another. Under his control they become functions. And always he has a ruling class keeping them in line, keeping the system closed as long as possible. He is glib (and anticipatory of Dickens) with his maxims for the bourgeoisie:

Urizen Read in his book of brass in sounding tones: . . .
"Listen to the Words of Wisdom,
So shall you govern over all; let Moral Duty tune your tongue.
But be your hearts harder than the nether millstone . . .
Compell the poor to live upon a Crust of bread, by soft mild arts.
Smile when they frown, frown when they smile; & when a man looks pale
With labour & abstinence, say he looks healthy & happy;
And when his children sicken, let them die; there are enough
Born, even too many, & our Earth will be overrun
Without these arts. If you would make the poor live with temper,
With pomp give every crust of bread you give; with gracious cunning

Magnify small gifts; reduce the man to want a gift, & then give with
  pomp.
Say he smiles if you hear him sigh. If pale, say he is ruddy.
Preach temperance: say he is overgorg'd & drowns his wit
In strong drink, tho' you know that bread & water are all
He can afford. Flatter his wife, pity his children, till we can
Reduce all to our will, as spaniels are taught with art."

As for the rational religion of the intellectuals, to Blake this is a
further lie. If we reason purely from what 'Science' accepts as
Nature, we shall never rise above that. In effect, the scientific
thinker defines the rules of proof in advance so as to exclude whatever he wants to exclude. Bacon, Newton and Locke may turn out
to be harbingers of revolution, but only because they have swept
aside the religious veil, and revealed what Man is cut down to,
when the imaginative and prophetic powers are denied scope. This
spectacle is so depressing that a change of heart may well ensue,
bringing the downfall of error, the renewal of imagination, a true
science instead of a false one.

There is in fact a limit to the distance that Man can fall. The
dormant potentiality of re-ascent has never been lost. Urizen himself can be saved, if he will only shed his mania for calculation and
continuity and intelligibility. The other three Zoas can rejoin him
in the harmony of a restored human nature. Man's rebirth out of the
depths of his own being – the awakening of Albion – is the climax
of Blake's visions.

5

The Blakean scheme of upward and downward pressures is complex. It ranges far outside the Urizen saga. Aware of the danger of
becoming Urizenic himself, the poet describes his purpose as
being to create a system to end systems. Part of the justification for
this claim is that his own system includes a being named Orc, a
sort of junior Prometheus who is a built-in revolt. Orc is
pictured at first as a deliverer, but later as only an initiator of cycles
which end by putting Urizen back – the French Revolution leading
via Napoleon to the Holy Alliance. Meanwhile Blake develops a
more profound concept of 'Spectres', the powers that drag down,
and 'Emanations', the powers that raise up. All his symbolic
personages have one of each, and so, we gather, does everybody.

The notion of the Spectre is close to Blake's personal problems as an artist and husband. The Spectre is the side of us that holds us in bondage to whatever Establishment we live under, and therefore unfulfilled, far below what we are meant to be. For those not absolutely shackled by need, and capable of doing better, this is chiefly practicality of the wrong kind: 'Looking after Number One', selfhood instead of humanity. The Spectre (in its calmer moods) is sensible, conformist, respectable. It involves us with property and prudence, drawing us down into the Ulro realm of cash value. It impels the artist to prostitute his gifts to money-making and the quest for fame and public esteem. Blake himself had to spend many hours on hack work for patrons, whose 'corporeal friend-ship' he saw as 'spiritual enmity'. He did not deny genuine responsibilities. One must pay the bills and not let dependants down. But no true progress can happen till one finds a method of integrating even this part of life with one's vocation, thereby getting rid of the spectral bondage.

> Each man is in his Spectre's power
> Until the arrival of that hour
> When his Humanity awake
> And cast his Spectre into the lake.

The Emanation is the opposing figure, and stands, in some degree, for the vocation which the Spectre thwarts. It holds the key to what one is meant to be and do, 'what I am for', in the words of Whitman. United with his Emanation, Man is fulfilled, and turned toward Eden. Blake introduces the Emanations of the four Zoas as characters in their own right. Urizen's is Ahania, a sub-goddess with antecedents in Jewish thought. She embodies the state of joyful wisdom in which the mind is active but not obsess-ively manipulative. Urizen casts her out, and this is the beginning of his major disasters.

The Emanations are female. Blake had strong views on sex, and could write boldly for his time. On the one hand, he regards the sexual relationship as a result of the fall. On the other, he believes in its saving power if it can be got right. It seldom is. He reverts often to the fallen 'female will' whose demands entangle Man with his Spectre. As Samuel Butler put it, too late for Blake, 'Brigands demand your money or your life; women require both.' From the female will comes a flood of woes – jealousy, acquisitiveness, inhibition, the bourgeois family. Lady Macbeth drives her husband to crime. Guinevere pushes hers too far into a spurious greatness. Merlin, the seer, is seduced and destroyed. The priests' Urizenic God, with his mysteries and confessionals, finds faithful allies in women, because 'Secresy gains females' loud applause.' Blake has a Nature-goddess called Vala, who is a deceiver.

All this is rather hard on women. Blake's sexual ideal is an outgoing, non-exclusive love free from the debased female will and its male correlative. Yet in *Visions of the Daughters of Albion* he voices this ideal through a female character. She proclaims liberty without jealousy or prudery: 'Arise, and drink your bliss, for every thing that lives is holy.' It must be added that except for a single ill-attested experiment, Blake remained affectionately content with one woman himself, and was careful to avoid hurting her. His views are not rationalizations. The femaleness of his Emanations is a genuinely radical motif, and cannot be undermined by raising personal queries. If the female will as we know it is damning, and yet the agents of salvation are female, then salvation must imply a change in the whole quality of life.

10

The Immortal City

1

Blake's finished version of the mystique relates humanity to the rightness which it has lost, and must hope to regain. It is the story of the fall and salvation of Albion, primarily as Man, but also (and not negligibly) as Britain. It is the extremest development of the British myth.

The fall of mankind is the working out of the consequences of Albion's. Urizen himself is only an aspect of Albion, as are the other actors. The Titan has been parted from his own Emanation, and his recovery must mean his reunion with her. Blake calls her Jerusalem. Hence the all-too-familiar lines about building Jerusalem in England's green and pleasant land. That is the revolutionary task which will bring England to fulfilment. Jerusalem is the buried rightness, lost yet not lost, which we have seen in so many other settings. The question is whether Blake's conception is a better-imagined one, that helps in evaluating the rest.

He does not portray Jerusalem as wholly distinct from Albion, a spouse or guardian angel. In one place he speaks of her as Albion's daughter. She is the glory which ancient Britain radiated to all mankind. When Jesus dwelt in England (figuratively, not literally) Jerusalem was first 'builded here'. Blake calls her by the name of the biblical Holy City because, in spirit, they are the same. Israel's faith came from Albion. In an address 'To the Jews' which he prefixes to Chapter Two of his symbolic book *Jerusalem*, he says:

Jerusalem the Emanation of the Giant Albion! Can it be? Is it a Truth that the Learned have explored? Was Britain the Primitive Seat of the

Patriarchal Religion? If it is true, my title-page is also True, that Jerusalem was & is the Emanation of the Giant Albion . . .

Your Ancestors derived their origin from Abraham, Heber, Shem and Noah, who were Druids, as the Druid Temples (which are the Patriarchal Pillars & Oak Groves) over the whole Earth witness to this day.

You have a tradition, that Man anciently contain'd in his mighty limbs all things in Heaven & Earth: this you recieved [sic] from the Druids.

'But now the Starry Heavens are fled from the mighty limbs of Albion.'

Albion was the Parent of the Druids.

The 'tradition' mentioned here is the Kabbalistic doctrine of Adam Kadmon, the mystical Primal Man, who was human nature and the embryonic universe at the same time. Scholars maintain that Albion is derived from Adam Kadmon; Blake, that Albion is the original and Adam Kadmon the copy.

Albion plus Jerusalem equals the golden age, dimly reflected in the legendary kingdom of Arthur. (Camelot would be Jerusalem's Arthurian counterpart, but I do not think Blake ever says so.) On the symbolic level, Jerusalem is an Emanation comprising all Emanations, an ideal comprising all ideals – the Celestial City of infinitely creative brotherhood. When the second building takes place, Britain will enlighten the earth again, and guide all humanity to fulfilment.

Jerusalem, Blake declares, 'is named Liberty among the sons of Albion'. Through the rebuilding, Britain will supply what the American and French liberty-lovers were groping for. In several prose passages Blake indicates that he does intend a real radical programme. The *Descriptive Catalogue* note to his picture 'The Ancient Britons' – the same that contains the Albion-Arthur text – offers some prefatory remarks.

The Britons (say historians) were naked civilized men, learned, studious, abstruse in thought and contemplation; naked, simple, plain in their acts and manners; wiser than after-ages. They were overwhelmed by brutal arms, all but a small remnant . . .

The British Antiquities are now in the Artist's hands; all his visionary contemplations, relating to his own country and its ancient glory, when it was, as it again shall be, the source of learning and inspiration. Arthur was a name for the constellation Arcturus, or Boötes, the keeper of the North Pole. And all the fables of Arthur and his round table; of the warlike naked Britons; of Merlin; of Arthur's conquest of the whole world; of his death, or sleep, and promise to return again; of the Druid monuments or temples; of the pavement of Watling-street; of London stone; of the caverns in Cornwall, Wales, Derbyshire, and Scotland; of the Giants of Ireland and Britain; of the elemental beings called by us by the general name of fairies . . . Mr. B. has in his hands poems of the highest antiquity. Adam was a Druid, and Noah; also Abraham was called to succeed the Druidical age, which began to turn allegoric and mental signification into corporeal command, whereby human sacrifice would have depopulated the earth. All these things are written in Eden. The artist is an inhabitant of that happy country; and if every thing goes on as it has begun, the world of vegetation and generation may expect to be opened again to Heaven, through Eden, as it was in the beginning . . .

How he [original Man] became divided is a subject of great sublimity and pathos. The Artist has written it under inspiration, and will, if God please, publish it; it is voluminous, and contains the ancient history of Britain, and the world of Satan and Adam.

In the mean time he has painted this Picture, which supposes that in the reign of that British Prince, who lived in the fifth century, there were remains of those naked Heroes in the Welch Mountains; they are there now, Gray saw them in the person of his bard on Snowdon; there they dwell in naked simplicity; happy is he who can see and converse with them above the shadows of generation and death. The giant Albion, was Patriarch of the Atlantic; he is the Atlas of the Greeks, one of those the Greeks called Titans. The stories of Arthur are the acts of Albion, applied to a Prince of the fifth century, who conquered Europe, and held the Empire of the world in the dark age, which the Romans never again recovered.

From this surprising manifesto, several leading ideas emerge. First, that the pre-Adamite Britain of Albion was 'the source of learning and inspiration', and Blake's programme includes restoring Britain to her old status. Second, that Celtic tradition preserves some of the ancient lore, and has expressed this through the 'fables' of Arthur and other media. (Blake improves them a little to suit himself. No actual legend makes Arthur become a universal ruler, but he is more like Albion if he does.) Third, the rebirth is to come through poetic imagination, in contact with the Blakean Eden. Lastly, there were actual Britons, even as late as Arthur's time, not utterly divorced from their golden antiquity, and therefore available as models. A faithful remnant in fact like

Plato's remnant of ancient Athenians; like the loyal Israelites; like the true Christians who supposedly kept the Gospel alive through the reign of the Romish Babylon. According to Blake their spirits linger among the Welsh mountains even yet. So, in Hesiod's Greece, did the spirits of the men of the Cronian golden age.

In spite of all the cloudy mythology, some sober thinking about the human condition shines through. What, for instance, does Blake mean by 'naked civilized men'? It is clear that his model Britons are figuratively naked in more senses than one. They lived simply, openly, uninhibitedly – and differently. That difference is the point of the phrase, which is a paradox; all known civilized men are clothed. But I am not sure that the literal meaning should be ruled out, either for the Britons, or for ourselves as their prospective imitators.

Nudism (or in the current parlance, Naturism) was not unknown in Blake's London. Thomas Jefferson Hogg, author of a memoir of Shelley, mentions it as a cult among the intelligentsia. A friend who visited Blake himself alleged afterwards that he had found the poet and his wife reading in their summer-house with no clothes on. Blake handled the situation with aplomb. As an artist he is at his strongest when most anatomical. The picture 'The Ancient Britons' is lost, but some of the central figures were undoubtedly nude. At least there is a hint in all this at the need for a fresh attitude to human nature, bodily as well as mental.

The 'voluminous' work mentioned in the note is *Jerusalem*, Blake's last and greatest symbolic book, elaborating his version of the British myth. He conceived it as a prophecy in the Hebrew manner. In fact it is not only prophetic but apocalyptic, going beyond the prophetic style of the Old Testament. Blake sees this corrupt world coming to an end in a total transfiguration. By the time he wrote *Jerusalem* he had veered so far from politics as to think even Christ unduly political. He expressed his revolutionary hopes through the apocalyptic genre instead, combining it with the Celtic theme of the sleeping and awakening Titan.

The result is a work of towering extraordinariness. *Jerusalem* does not yield fully to a single reading, or to half a dozen, or to any assignable number. It is best approached with that foreknowledge. The reader can then skim through it and catch its main drift, without getting held up by hopeless attempts to fathom the details.

A second reading will bring out more, a third will bring out more again, and so on without limit according to taste.

Jerusalem is oriented toward the final redemption. Hence, Urizen recedes except as an influence, and instead there is a great deal about Los, the Zoa of imagination who preserves hope; also about Jesus. The story of the fall is repeated, however, with a more human and more British bias than hitherto, and with prose prefaces to each chapter.

Blake begins by stating his theme:

> Of the Sleep of Ulro! and of the passage through
> Eternal Death! and of the awaking to Eternal Life.

Albion's fall is a shutting-in and sealing-off of himself, followed by disintegration. The poem does not follow a chronological order. Often it counterpoints one period against another, or combines several in a montage. But it does start with the effects of Albion's loss of faith in the divine vision, far back before Adam; and it does end with the eighteenth century, and the transformation which Blake hopes for in the nineteenth.

At the outset Albion says:

> 'Jerusalem is not: her daughters are indefinite:
> By demonstration man alone can live, and not by faith.
> My mountains are my own, and I will keep them to myself:
> The Malvern and the Cheviot, the Wolds, Plinlimmon & Snowdon
> Are mine: here will I build my Laws of Moral Virtue.
> Humanity shall be no more, but war & princedom & victory!'

As a general human symbol, Albion has withdrawn into selfhood. He is neglecting creation, thirsting for power. But Albion is also the Titan, Patriarch of Britain, whose error brought the decline of mankind. 'My mountains are my own', he says, naming them; he has abandoned his mission for narrow, pugnacious nationalism. Most of *Jerusalem* is ardently British. Arthur appears in it, as archetypal monarch – that is, in a phase of his legend which reflects Albion's error, rather than his glory. Personified British towns, personified rivers, slightly altered names from Geoffrey of Monmouth, slightly altered names of obscure contemporaries of Blake himself, mingle in strange profusion on page after page.

Albion sinks into self-inflicted despair and a deathlike trance – the Titanic sleep. He is taken up by the merciful hands of Jesus and laid on a rock in the sea, 'closed apart from all Nations'. In historical terms, Britain is reduced to a mere island. Jerusalem, Albion's estranged Emanation, takes refuge in the 'Spaces of Erin': Erin, perhaps, as being the abode – in Blake's time – of a Celtic remnant holding out against the tyranny of a darkened England.

Meanwhile Albion's sons and daughters run riot. They succumb to the cruel and orgiastic Nature-worship of fallen Druidism. They set up Stonehenge. Arthur institutes kingship. Britain passes through the phases traced in the story of Urizen, ending with a calculating ethic, a prohibitive Christianity, and the rise of Bacon, Newton and Locke, that trio of Englishmen who embody Albion's 'spectral' side, and prove the saying that the corruption of the best is the worst.

Blake produces startling effects by telescoping his images. In a single passage he draws together the collapse of craftsmanship under the impact of machines, the growth of dehumanized factories (with a preview of mass-production), the Napoleonic Wars which British industry kept going, and the brutalities of the press-gang.

> Then left the Sons of Urizen the plow & harrow, the loom,
> The hammer & the chisel & the rule & compasses; from London fleeing,
> They forg'd the sword on Cheviot, the chariot of war & the battle-ax,
> The trumpet fitted to mortal battle, & the Flute of summer in Annandale;
> And all the Arts of Life they chang'd into the Arts of Death in Albion.
> The hour-glass contemn'd because its simple workmanship
> Was like the workmanship of the plowman, & the water wheel
> That raises water into cisterns, broken & burn'd with fire
> Because its workmanship was like the workmanship of the shepherd;
> And in their stead, intricate wheels invented, wheel without wheel,
> To perplex youth in their outgoings & to bind to labours in Albion
> Of day & night the myriads of eternity: that they may grind
> And polish brass & iron hour after hour, laborious task,
> Kept ignorant of its use: that they may spend the days of wisdom
> In sorrowful drudgery to obtain a scanty pittance of bread,
> In ignorance to view a small portion & think that All,
> And call it Demonstration, blind to all the simple rules of life.
> 'Now, now the battle rages round thy tender limbs, O Vala!
> Now smile among thy bitter tears, now put on all thy beauty.
> Is not the wound of the sword sweet & the broken bone delightful?

Wilt thou now smile among the scythes when the wounded groan in
the field?
We were carried away in thousands from London & in tens
Of thousands from Westminster & Marybone, in ships clos'd up,
Chain'd hand & foot, compell'd to fight under the iron whips
Of our captains, fearing our officers more than the enemy . . .'

Throughout the horrors, hints at a faithful remnant persist.
Besides the Celts, there is an unexplained Someone hidden in
Albion's forests who will found a future religion. The topographical lore stresses England's cathedral cities as still possessing
spiritual power even in their debasement.

Allying himself to these obscure trends, the figure of Los
carries on cyclopean labours. To some extent he is a dramatization
of Blake himself, a creative artist toiling at a metaphorical smithy,
in a storm of fire and passion. Los is prophetic insight, art, culture,
and so forth, keeping the divine vision in time of trouble. He
sustains a view of the universe which is above the level of mere
Generation. As a Shelleyan 'unacknowledged legislator' he notes
such processes as

'The Briton, Saxon, Roman, Norman amalgamating
In my Furnaces into One Nation, the English . . .'

A nation formed by cultural fusion during the dark ages. At the
height of his powers Los can master the Spectre; he can turn even
the baser world to account. He builds a citadel which is a place of
precision in the 'land of death eternal', the desert of the abstract.
Los's function is not so much to destroy error as to clarify it by
word and image so that it will be seen for what it is. The age of
'Bacon, Newton, Locke' brings what Blake optimistically regards
as the final self-revelation and self-refutation, the darkest hour
before dawn. If their dismal philosophy is taking hold, says Los,

'Is it not that Signal of the Morning which was told us in the Beginning?'

So – in the poem – it proves to be. Personified England repents
her crimes and accuses herself as Albion's murderess. But he is not
gone for ever.

Her voice pierc'd Albion's clay cold ear; he moved upon the Rock.
The Breath Divine went forth upon the morning hills. Albion mov'd
Upon the Rock, he open'd his eyelids in pain, in pain he mov'd

His stony members, he saw England. Ah! shall the Dead live again?
The Breath Divine went forth over the morning hills. Albion rose
In anger, the wrath of God breaking, bright flaming on all sides
    around
His awful limbs; into the Heavens he walked . . .
Then Jesus appeared standing by Albion as the Good Shepherd
By the lost Sheep that he hath found, & Albion knew that it
Was the Lord, the Universal Humanity; & Albion saw his Form
A Man, & they conversed as Man with Man in Ages of Eternity.
And the Divine Appearance was the likeness & similitude of Los.

Of Los, because salvation must come through vision. The Christ of conventional religion has no power to save.

The four Zoas return to unity in Albion's bosom. Jerusalem rejoins him and 'overspreads all Nations as in Ancient Time'. The world is reborn in love and forgiveness, enlightened again by Albion. The golden age is rekindled. Every man 'stands Fourfold', a harmony of the Zoas. Perhaps the most characteristic feature of Blake's apocalypse is that it destroys nothing – except error. The whole achievement of the ages is saved. Jerusalem contains the Emanations of all beings. No person is condemned or excluded. Even Bacon, Newton and Locke appear beside Milton, Shakespeare and Chaucer, transmuted and immortal in the Titanic energies of the new dawn.

2

The question is still the same: whether Blake is merely giving one more version of a recurrent attitude to the world, or whether he is significantly and thoughtfully enlarging the myth so as to pierce deeper. One test is to look at the results. Does he offer anything more specific than gestures? Does his appraisal of the human condition actually produce anything like a programme?

If read with care, he does give an impression of bedrock under the exotic growths and puzzling topsoil. He has a quite definite style of radicalism. Furthermore, it is not a freak ideology of his own. It is later repeated with variations by other radicals, and is much less a museum piece today than the radicalism of Bentham, Gladstone, or the Webbs.

In sober terms, Blake is a patriot who rejects virtually all the paraphernalia of patriotism, at least as it was understood in the heyday of the British Empire. The corruption which Albion's arousal is to sweep away includes nationalistic pride and prowess in war (though Blake, like Gandhi, could respect such martial heroes as Nelson). It includes respectable family life, the Church of England, and, one suspects, the Monarchy. It also includes most of the Victorian idols which Blake did not live to see fully fashioned: the public-school virtues, and philanthropy, and classical education, and the White Man's Burden, and the capitalistic progress that inspired the Great Exhibition. These all belong to the state of error. As for science, Blake's objections to Bacon, Newton and Locke would extend to Darwin. Possibly with more justice. The Survival of the Fittest, when invoked to support such doctrines as racial superiority, did visibly degrade its exponents.

The British Establishment which Blake sees taking shape around him is of course not the only thing of its kind. It is simply the latest among the Urizenic structures of power, falsehood and debasement which the fall has produced. Possessiveness will always be wrong. The calculating spirit will always be wrong. The ethics of guilt and veto will always be wrong. The cutting-down of men to fit systems will always be wrong.

On the positive side, it would perhaps be unfair to expect a literal spelling-out of 'what will happen when Albion wakes up'. However, it is fair to ask what 'building Jerusalem' means, because Blake exhorts his readers to do it. 'To Labour in Knowledge is to Build up Jerusalem . . . Let every Christian, as much as in him lies, engage himself openly & publicly before all the World in some Mental pursuit for the Building up of Jerusalem.' We might say of Blake, as of some others who have united the religious and radical temper, that the key to his revolution is *living differently*: not only in the inward sense of personal conversion, but in the outward sense of active and constructive dissent from a sick society. If enough people undertake this, a new, alternative society will grow up within the old, and, in the fullness of time, transfigure it.

The new life-style must re-create the golden age, with hints from the traditions preserved among the Celtic remnant, and coming down from the 'naked civilized men' of early Britain. 'The Primeval State of Man was Wisdom, Art and Science' – that is, the right sort of science. Not that Blake declares for the Simple Life in a doctrinaire way. He seldom if ever denounces material goods as such. The point, rather, is to get our priorities right. A higher standard of living for the poor and hungry is a proper goal of human endeavour. So is a higher standard of living for artists, as Blake is honest enough to say outright. But a higher standard of living will not do as the object of life. In one place, Blake defines hell as being 'shut up in the possession of corporeal desires'. Certainly the modern consumer's corporeal desires tend to shut him up in the Urizenic prison of mass-production and mass-media.

Deliverance, on this showing, implies pursuing the right sort of aims – those that restore human nature to its presumed lost grandeur and integrity, not those that shrink it and split it up into functions. Jerusalem is Liberty, and the secret of liberty, as Albion's children once knew, is to aim upwards. Urizen cannot trap people who live for imagination, creation, adventure, the heightening of the spirit. He cannot trap them, because he cannot invent a system which even pretends to give what they want.

Jerusalem contains the query, 'Are not Religion and Politics the same thing?' At our normal level, they are two faces of the same tyranny. At the higher level the identity will persist, but altered. Jerusalem will be both religious and political, yet without sect or party. Its building might seem to necessitate new sects, new parties, and therefore new engines of coercion. Though not very explicit in facing this difficulty, Blake hints at what might today be called a philosophy of non-violence. However, it is anything but passive. Blake is all for conflict, and for any action whatever rather than quietism. Without contraries, he says, there is no progression. But in the new life-style, 'corporeal fight' will give way to 'mental fight', the flashing interplay of aroused minds.

Blake proposes to defeat Urizen, and restore him to his senses, by cultivating the things he hates. Thus, openness must replace mystery: there must be no secret doctrines and no conspiracies. Spontaneity and impulse must replace deliberation. When authority strikes back, courageous martyrdom will be better than counter-violence.

> For a Tear is an Intellectual Thing,
> And a Sigh is the Sword of an Angel King,
> And the bitter groan of the Martyr's woe
> Is an Arrow from the Almightie's Bow.

The new world, if it ever comes, will be a world of fulfilment;

of diversity; and of absolution. Blake's vision is positive and passionate. All life must flower to the full, ecstatically, without restraint. 'Energy is Eternal Delight.' The new society will practise a high degree of sexual freedom. Further, extremes must co-exist. Jerusalem is not a grey blur, it is the sum of all fulfilments. Uniformity is anathema; general rules are *ipso facto* wrong (the opposite of Kant); and likewise the States and Churches that try to enforce them. 'One Law for the Lion & Ox is Oppression.' Or, in *Jerusalem*: 'General Good is the plea of the scoundrel, hypocrite and flatterer.' Good can only be done in particular.

Every citizen of the new order, every grouping of citizens, will presumably be a special case. People will diverge far more sharply from each other than they do now, as they work out their assorted vocations. Yet all will be harmony. If we want a specific example, there is little doubt that a realized Jerusalem will comprise every race under the sun on equal terms, each with its own culture. It will not be (for instance) a white liberal republic that confers civil rights on Negroes and assimilates them to itself, however gently.

To speak of 'absolution' as a quality of Blake's new order is to use a Catholic word; but he praised the Catholic Church on this very point. When a priest absolves a penitent, it is as if the sin had never been. In Jerusalem absolution will be the norm. The moral chain will be broken. Injuries may still be committed, but they will come and go and be forgotten. Guilt will cease in mutual pardon.

> & Throughout all Eternity
> I forgive you, you forgive me.
> As our dear Redeemer said:
> 'This the Wine & this the Bread.'

For Blake, forgiveness is Christ's essential teaching. Through it the Jesus of history comes in as the master-spirit of the new world, and is one with the poetic Saviour. Blake's devotion to Jesus was deep and sincere, but idiosyncratic. In an unfinished poem, *The Everlasting Gospel*, he argues from Scripture that Jesus taught nothing new in the way of moral virtue and was not conventionally virtuous himself, but acted from inspired impulse. Forgiveness is not merely *in* the Gospel; it *is* the Gospel.

Blake's ethics would seem to excuse complete nihilism, opting-out from civilized life, amorality. But he had more than a touch of practical sanity. He knew that some of the emancipated souls of his time actually had thrown over morality in the name of nebulous higher things. In our present state, he said, no such leap can be approved.

> Many Persons, such as Paine & Voltaire, with some of the Ancient Greeks, say: 'we will not converse concerning Good & Evil; we will live in Paradise & Liberty.' You may do so in Spirit, but not in the Mortal Body as you pretend, till after the Last Judgment . . .

That is, after the spiritual revolution. It remains true that the tendency of Blake's Gospel is to disentangle humanity from the priestly 'Thou shalt not', and steer it along the path to freedom. As Jerusalem is built, so the bondage to rules and laws will relax. Some day Man will live by a single commandment for which Blake might have found the words ready-made in St Augustine: 'Love, and do what you will.'

3

Taken alongside other apostles of change, Blake might seem closest to Rousseau. Both evoke a golden age, corrupted largely by the spurious triumphs of the mind; both connect civilization as we know it with tyranny; and so on. It is thus a shade disconcerting to find Blake consigning Rousseau to the scrap-heap with his other villains. But the reason for the rejection brings us face to face, at last, with what is really his own crucial idea, and the thing he adds to our understanding of the mystique.

> Mock on, Mock on Voltaire, Rousseau:
> Mock on, Mock on: 'tis all in vain!
> You throw the sand against the wind,
> And the wind blows it back again.
>
> And every sand becomes a Gem
> Reflected in the beams divine;
> Blown back they blind the mocking Eye,
> But still in Israel's paths they shine.
>
> The Atoms of Democritus
> And Newton's Particles of light
> Are sands upon the Red sea shore,
> Where Israel's tents do shine so bright.

The 'facts' which the social critic scatters as ammunition, like the atoms of a false science, tell a different story when looked at together in the right way. Rousseau never does this. Having proved present society to be self-destructive, he discards what he dislikes, and tries to put together a 'natural state' or 'good life' out of what he keeps. To Blake it is all futile. The materials, and the means of reconstruction, are not there any more. If we confine ourselves to Man as he is – fallen, cut down, divided from Eternity and himself – Eden will elude us. Rousseau can pick up his grains of sand, but he will never see Israel's tents. He can pull society apart, but his would-be regeneration is, in effect, an attempt to restore Albion's reign without waking him up. What his Jacobin disciples wanted to do cannot be done without the prophetic vision which alone will reveal the nature of the lost glory, and the original human plenitude.

The same would apply to other revolutionaries; Lenin, for instance. A doctrine that starts from abstract proletarians and material motives, confessedly formed by bourgeois society, will not, unaided, produce anything better. Its adherents may talk of a classless communist world, but their view of their own world makes them unable to give it substance.

Blake's contribution to the British myth is to take the 'sleep' of the Titan and Arthur, and make it symbolize a fact about the human condition; the precise fact which Rousseau and the rest have been groping for but never quite catching. Albion is lord of the golden age, and with his fall and subsequent sleep, this is lost. Albion is also Man, and the process of decline, which people so stubbornly see in history, is really his own falling below the golden-age state which was the summit of his powers. To put things right demands, first of all, that Man shall grow above what he is now; shall grow up out of Ulro, and back toward his almost forgotten potentialities. Albion's waking cannot mean simply a social upheaval or national liberation, though such events might well follow. It implies the return of human beings to full human stature and integrity: their becoming what they were always meant to be. That is the first step towards any true revolution.

At least to some extent, Blake is right. A downward tendency, in his terms, certainly is more than a mere projection of individual life on to society. We need not believe in his Hesiodic picture of a vast slide from a mythical golden age. He has laid his finger on something that does happen, piecemeal, but with dismal monotony.

Man does most persistently prove his high capacities and then fall below them because of his cravings and limitations; after which the capacities themselves carry him farther down on a vicious spiral. The good does not last. This is what everybody feels about the Renaissance, the French Revolution, and many similar dawns. They are not false dawns. They give authentic and ever-renewed glimpses of what Man is capable of. But always the darkness closes in again. Which is exactly what Malory portrayed in his handling of the Arthurian Legend.

It may not be a law of nature, or a real norm of history. But it answers so poignantly to the individual's feeling about his own life that people are likely to go on treating it as a norm. All the variants of the mystique, at any rate, can be construed as relating this vaguely apprehended truth to a special problem. Israel, or India, or the Church, is *seen as* an entity in which a glorious human fulfilment once occurred and then succumbed. The effort to revive it has the galvanic quality of defiance and victory over death. But in all the cases we have looked at, the deeper point made by Blake is obscured. If the original human failure took place, there can be no simple recovery by reconstituting an Israel (or India, or whatever) out of the wreckage that remains from the first loss. There will be a partial achievement at best and another breakdown. Somehow, human beings must recapture the lost glory in themselves, must transcend their present state, if they are to change the world. The way up is through Eden . . . or Avalon.

In Blake's own scheme of things, we might well ask how. The Jacobins and the Communists at least tried out their ideas. They had an immense amount of evil to work on, and could stir the masses to act. But what will power Blake's revolution? Why should it ever start?

His answer, in a word, would be 'clarification'. On the negative side, Time will turn evil into good by defining and thus exposing it. Voltaire's Age of Reason dispelled the religious mystery that once obscured issues. Now, the world of pseudo-science is so plainly at fault that a reaction must set in. But the fact that it has not done so effectively after a century and a half prompts us to look for the positive side of Blake's answer. It is summed up in the appearance of the Saviour under the likeness of Los. The clarification that will induce change must come through imagination – not mere fancy, but the creative vision, as in the Hebrew prophets. To

Blake the artistic impulse, if genuine, is one with the prophetic. He urges poets, painters, sculptors and architects to lead the revolution.

Such a vanguard scarcely inspires confidence. Blake seems to think that if artists will surrender fully to the spiritual power, their soaring lucidity will not only whirl them up toward Eden but carry society with them. To find an artist believing such a thing himself excites a suspicion that his own artistic experiences were unusual. And Blake's were.

Hence, in part, the hard-dying notion of his insanity. As with the Hebrew prophets, his inspiration invaded him from sources that were not in his conscious self. He 'saw' scenes and 'heard' words. It is abundantly clear, from his manuscripts and other evidence, that he was no scribbling 'automatic writer'. But a vivid and complex image of some kind would flash on him spontaneously, charged with meaning. As a conscious artist he then visualized it or verbalized it or both. In due course he would receive another image, and another and another, till his current theme was exhausted. It has been suggested that some of these images were hypnagogic – that they came in the borderland between sleep and waking. (This was the case with the only Blakean vision I ever had myself.) Blake believed that he was being granted insights that overleaped space and time, pierced the veils of illusion, and brought him face to face with the lost golden world and the rich and fiery origins of all beings.

He may have been deluded, but he was not inventing. A recent case-history parallels not only his experience but the quality attaching to it. Minnie Evans[1] is an American Negro folk-artist in her seventies. She is without formal education and has never travelled. She began painting late in life, impelled by experiences that were unforeseen and unsought. In 1962 she told part of the story: 'In a dream it was shown to me what I have to do, of paintings. The whole entire horizon all the way across the whole earth was put together like this with pictures. All over my yard, all up the side of trees and everywhere were pictures.' Mrs Evans 'never plans a drawing', they 'just happen'. Some portray recognizable figures and objects, though often with a surrealist effect; some are symmetrical designs. One of the latter type resulted from

[1] See Nina Howell Starr, 'The Lost World of Minnie Evans,' *The Bennington Review*, Summer 1969, pp. 41–58.

a dream in which she was inside a log with ants bustling around her. But not all her experiences occur in sleep. A very Blakean picture, 'The Prophets in the Air', recalls a waking vision. Several human forms appeared to her, flying, and singing to her in words she could not understand.

She has offered a statement about the source of her inspiration. Under the circumstances it is startling. 'This art that I have put out has come from nations I suppose might have been destroyed before the Flood . . . No one knows anything about them, but God has given it to me to bring them back into the world.' Not even 'destroyed *in* the Flood', as a naïve Bible Christian might have been expected to say, but 'destroyed *before* the Flood'.

Whatever it is that has happened to Minnie Evans, it is surely the same thing that happened to Blake – only, in his case, the recipient was a person of rare natural gifts and wide reading, so that a system grew from it.

His experience was no shapeless emotional thrill. He defined it. Vision can be single, twofold, threefold or fourfold. Single vision corresponds to Ulro, the level of cash value, Newtonian physics, and Locke's psychology. At the other extreme, fourfold vision penetrates Eden, and the Eternal Now above time and space.

> Now I a fourfold vision see,
> And a fourfold vision is given to me;
> 'Tis fourfold in my supreme delight
> And threefold in soft Beulah's night
> And twofold Always. May God us keep
> From Single vision & Newton's sleep!

Or in a more famous passage:

'What,' it will be Question'd, 'When the Sun rises, do you not see a round disk of fire somewhat like a Guinea?' O no, no, I see an Innumerable company of the Heavenly host crying 'Holy, Holy, Holy is the Lord God Almighty.'

Blake (to use his own words again) actually did see a world in a grain of sand, a heaven in a wild flower. His favourite contemporary poet was Wordsworth, to whom the 'meanest flower' could give thoughts too deep for tears. But Blake went beyond Wordsworthian reflection. He considered that to perceive by the senses only, as we now have them, is to live in illusion.

183

How do you know but ev'ry Bird that cuts the airy way,
Is an immense world of delight, clos'd by your senses five?

The relevance of all this to Blake's idea of human regeneration is, first, that the heightened vision is needed; secondly, that it is not a superhuman gift somehow added to us, but the way human beings ought to perceive all the time, and, in the golden age, actually did.

If the doors of perception were cleansed every thing would appear to man as it is, infinite. For man has closed himself up, till he sees all things thro' narrow chinks of his cavern.

This is the belief explored by Aldous Huxley through mescalin, and in various ways by later drug-takers.

Our commonplace shut-in life is Paradise Lost. In the beginning, Blake says, Man's awareness was far greater in its scope. To recover the vanished vision, or a little of it, is the first step toward Albion's awakening. The full blaze of reconquered Eternity is too much to hope for yet. But the true artist is always moving that way. He is an agent of public redemption. He communicates his insights to some extent, and those who cannot see directly can approach wisdom by following up the clues he drops.

I give you the end of a golden string,
    Only wind it into a ball,
It will lead you in at Heaven's gate
    Built in Jerusalem's wall.

The direct vision of Truth is *ipso facto* radical. As with the Hebrew prophets, so with the poetic seer, his insight reveals so agonizing a contrast between what Is and what is Meant to Be – between the surface facts and the imprisoned splendour – that he is always a rebel. Therefore Milton wrote finely of Hell but constrainedly of Heaven because, being a true poet, he was 'of the Devil's party without knowing it.'

Blake did not use drugs. But he did believe in special aid of another kind. It is here that we reach the root of his spiritual patriotism and his role as a continuator of the British myth. He transferred the quality of Zion to Britain. For the Hebrew prophets, at least before Israel's exile, the sovereign holiness of the Holy Land consisted in its being the one place where valid inspiration could happen. There alone the Lord spoke to men.

The same belief appears in such Jewish books as *Ecclesiasticus*, where Wisdom makes her home in Jerusalem, and it reappears in the rabbinic mysticism of later times. Blake plants his own Jerusalem in Britain, with all the implications. (He is too fond of using 'England' as a synonym, but that fault is not confined to him.)

Albion's isle enlightened the world, and will again, because it is the place where the highest vision occurred, and still can; not the only place, but the pre-eminent place. Thanks partly to the Celts and their bardic tradition, to Joseph of Arimathea and Arthur, the ancient presences still hover around us. The ancient quests can still be renewed. Even with Urizen enthroned, the cathedral cities retain a trace of the Everlasting Gospel, and in wilder spots the 'elemental beings called by us by the general name of fairies' still invisibly befriend.

London is indeed the dark commercial metropolis of 'charter'd streets' and misery, depicted in a Song of Experience. But under the disguise it is also the spiritual capital that once civilized the world. The glory was here, the earthly fall happened here, the restoration can happen here. Those who inhabit Albion's land can see it all, if they will only look, and because they can see it they can labour in knowledge.

> The fields from Islington to Marybone,
> To Primrose Hill and Saint John's Wood,
>   Were builded over with pillars of gold,
>   And there Jerusalem's pillars stood.
>
> Her Little-ones ran on the fields,
> The Lamb of God among them seen,
>   And fair Jerusalem his Bride,
>   Among the little meadows green.
>
> Pancrass & Kentish-town repose
> Among her golden pillars high,
>   Among her golden arches which
>   Shine upon the starry sky.

11

The Dissentient Radicals

1

With Blake, then, the British myth is carried much farther; the way-of-looking-at-things is highly articulated. He puts forward a view of history and a sort of programme. It repeats much the same pattern as Rousseau, the Zionists, and the rest. But he builds it round his transforming conviction that the real problem lies in human nature. Man, as given, is less than he ought to be and has been. Not only is he (as Blake puts it) a 'mortal worm' oppressed by his own subjection to age and death; this state goes with a downward tendency in the whole species, a withering and shrinkage due to its own inner disarray. Blake summons Man to an act of spiritual defiance, a transfiguring insight, a rebirth above his present level. On this showing, the various revolutions have been half-blind attempts at such an act. But no revolution will succeed lastingly till human beings grow back to what they are meant to be. And this implies far more than platitudes about 'bringing morality into politics' or the like.

Whatever our verdict on Blake's mythology and his programme in detail, the downward tendency is a fact, if not a universal fact. The revolutions themselves have shown it in action, after their golden effervescence dies down. It follows that the asserted need for a kind of human transcendence is at least plausible. In Arthurian terms, Malory's tale of tragedy has given classic form to the fact, while Arthur's 'healing' and return symbolize the transcendence.

Here we might halt. But I remarked that Blake's programme does not stand alone. After him a series of English minds, and minds under English influence, can be seen evolving heterodox

186

programmes rather like his, and expressing the same way-of-looking-at-things in their own context. We might associate these thinkers with Blake himself as 'Dissentient Radicals'. I do not claim that there is any inevitable logic about their thinking, or that they amount to a rival school alongside the Utilitarians and Socialists whom they dissent from. The links between them are mostly frail, the disagreements are sweeping. But they are worth glancing at by way of postscript: not because they can be discussed and disposed of in a few pages apiece – each one has had books written about him, and very properly – but because of their convergence on the Blakean theme of a human shortcoming, and the need for a human reconstitution. They circle round this along orbits suggesting a centre of attraction, an impersonal constant. If our study of Arthur ends in a fresh approach to the mental processes of the sons of Albion, it will have had its value.

2

Several commentators on Blake have traced parallels with a second poet, and exclaimed at the absence of evidence that either of them read the other. The poet in question is that laureate of the Left, Percy Bysshe Shelley.

After an ardently subversive youth, Shelley died before he was thirty. Even by then his prose meditations on politics had become more cautious. In poetry, however, he did not recant. A mystique of revolution continued to bloom in it, with a more specific response than Blake's to the news of the day – more specific, and, among readers, more influential. Shelley has been claimed as a proto-Socialist, as a Neo-Platonist, and as an Anarchist moulded by William Godwin (who was his hero at one stage and his cadging father-in-law at another, but not simultaneously). Most certainly he was a Dissentient Radical. Blake, who did not influence him, sheds more light on his mental workings than almost any author who did.

Shelley's constant concern is Liberty, which he too personifies, though not in a complex creation like Blake's Jerusalem. Against Liberty he ranges the whole coercive Establishment, especially established religion. He was sent down from Oxford for his pamphlet *The Necessity of Atheism*, and proceeded to write the long blank-verse poem *Queen Mab*, with the banned pamphlet incorporated in the notes at the back. *Queen Mab* is a rehash of Godwin and Rousseau. Besides tirades against the 'kings, priests and statesmen' who 'blast the human flower', and against the 'Almighty Fiend' foisted on us by religion, the poem alleges a further cause of social corruption – meat-eating. With Shelley we get a hint, one of the first, that human nature has fallen because of a bodily degeneration due to wrong diet. But in *Queen Mab* he has not yet arrived at a radical doctrine of his own. He follows Godwin in predicting that the mere march of progress will somehow dissolve the assorted evils.

As he matured, Shelley moved toward a belief that the trend of society is not upward after all, and that liberation must come through action against it. There is a struggling spirit of good in the world, more or less equated with Liberty, which a superficially stronger spirit of evil is always crushing. Shelley's major myth of regeneration, his counterpart to *Jerusalem*, is the lyric drama *Prometheus Unbound*. This was composed in Italy during 1818–19. In the light of Blake, one of its most arresting features is that Shelley goes to the same realm for his central conception – to the realm of the Titans.

It is not as if the Titans were obvious revolutionary symbols. Cronus indeed was the deity of slaves, but this aspect of him is inconspicuous. If one looks at Greek myth alone, the Titans' chief attributes are obsolescence and failure, hardly encouraging qualifications. When Keats took them up in *Hyperion* he depicted them as a worn-out dynasty, in process of replacement by the more brilliant Olympians.

Shelley, however, sees the Titanic era in quite a Blakean way, not merely as the golden age, but as the source of energies now fettered which will break free and bring it back. The second idea, as we have seen, is foreign to Greece. Aeschylus wrote a trilogy on Prometheus, but portrayed the Titan making his peace with the new order. Shelley had no use for such a feeble end, and said so.

His own Prometheus is like Albion, the patriarch and culture-hero of the human race, standing for the highest of human nature in its remote origins. As Albion, in the beginning, was united to Jerusalem, so Prometheus was united to a consort named Asia, standing for the Platonic 'Intellectual Beauty' hailed by Shelley in a separate hymn. Prometheus's golden age – a development from Saturn's – had the same instability as in Blake and was more a potentiality than a fact. Prometheus, through some error within himself, had already enthroned the evil pseudo-God Jupiter, who is the embodiment of all oppression and the source of all misery: Shelley's Urizen, though he is worse than Blake's. Because Prometheus fought for humanity, Jupiter banished him to the distant mountain where he was chained to a rock and tortured. Humanity fell with him and came under Jupiter's obscurantist tyranny.

When the play begins, mankind, deprived of Prometheus, has been suffering and sinking for thousands of years. Attempts at recovery such as the French Revolution have been grisly fiascos. What the world's inhabitants think of as life is a false 'painted veil' masking reality: Shelley's equivalent of the Blakean withering-up of perception. Prometheus is still defiant. It transpires that during the early days of his punishment, he alarmed the earth by pronouncing a terrible curse on Jupiter. It also transpires, though not at once, that this curse was a factor in his own fall, because it was a surrender to passion and hatred. When it is repeated to him, the wisdom that has come with his long ordeal impels him to retract.

> It doth repent me; words are quick and vain;
> Grief for a while is blind, and so was mine.
> I wish no living thing to suffer pain.

He has not capitulated. His moral strength is now all the greater. For a moment, however, he seems to have capitulated. Jupiter tries to complete his own victory by a final assault on Man, but instead is overthrown. Prometheus's change of heart has brought a shift in the cosmic order. Love, named as one of the eldest of beings, is fully reborn in him. He is unbound and reunited to Asia, as Albion to Jerusalem. Meanwhile the divine absolutes are reasserting themselves. Mankind (and in fact the whole solar system) surges into an expansion of consciousness, an explosion of joy. The world of this apocalypse is no novelty, but the familiar world transfigured by Eternity bursting through it –

> The pine boughs are singing
> Old songs with new gladness.

Man flowers again into what he was always meant to be, and the evils of society disappear.

> The painted veil, by those who were, called life,
> Which mimicked, as with colours idly spread,
> All men believed or hoped, is torn aside;

The loathsome mask has fallen, the man remains
Sceptreless, free, uncircumscribed, but man
Equal, unclassed, tribeless, and nationless,
Exempt from awe, worship, degree, the king
Over himself; just, gentle, wise: but man
Passionless? – no, yet free from guilt or pain,
Which were, for his will made or suffered them.

In *Prometheus Unbound* Shelley dwells, like Blake, on martyr-dom as a moral force, and on forgiveness. Prometheus's forgive-ness of Jupiter – or at any rate, his abandonment of the wish to punish him – sets the process of liberation in motion. Shelley has decided that revolution must come through abjuring violence of mind as well as body. Jupiter's rise and fall imply that human beings create their own oppressors. When they cease to hate and fear, they will soon cease to be oppressed. The last lines of the drama are among the best known:

To suffer woes which Hope thinks infinite;
To forgive wrongs darker than death or night;
　　To defy Power, which seems omnipotent;
To love, and bear; to hope till Hope creates
From its own wreck the thing it contemplates;
　　Neither to change, nor falter, nor repent;
This, like thy glory, Titan, is to be
Good, great and joyous, beautiful and free;
This is alone Life, Joy, Empire, and Victory.

Prometheus's unbinding, like Albion's awakening, might be taken as no more than a metaphor for revolution; but as with Albion, it implies something happening to mankind. The Titan's reunion with Asia is the restoration of Man to the almost incon-ceivable fullness of his nature. In the *Hymn to Intellectual Beauty*, which Asia personifies, Shelley says:

Man were immortal, and omnipotent,
Didst thou, unknown and awful as thou art,
Keep with thy glorious train firm state within his heart.

Shelley enlarged on this view in his *Defence of Poetry*, an essay even more Blakean in spirit. Here he suggests that the motive power for regenerating society must come, not from its official legislators, but from its unacknowledged ones; and these are the poets. Shelley gives poetry a wide meaning. It covers the works of creative imagination in general, which he contrasts with the rather limited products of reason.

The exertions of Locke, Hume, Gibbon, Voltaire, Rousseau, and their disciples, in favour of oppressed and deluded humanity, are entitled to the gratitude of mankind. Yet it is easy to calculate the degree of moral and intellectual improvement which the world would have exhibited, had they never lived. A little more nonsense would have been talked for a century or two; and perhaps a few more men, women, and children burnt as heretics . . . But it exceeds all imagination to conceive what would have been the moral condition of the world if neither Dante, Petrarch, Boccaccio, Chaucer, Shakespeare, Calderon, Lord Bacon, nor Milton, had ever existed; if Raphael and Michael Angelo had never been born; if the Hebrew poetry had never been translated; if a revival of the study of Greek literature had never taken place; if no monuments of ancient sculpture had been handed down to us; and if the poetry of the religion of the ancient world had been extinguished together with its belief.

Shelley dissents from Blake about the classification of Bacon. But his ideal poet is, in Blakean terms, a son of Los, with much the same function. He is the seer who understands in depth. Transcending the common round, he attains insights which are more potent, more lasting, than the calculations and demonstrations of the Urizenic practical thinker. Whatever the inspiration may be that will change history's course, it will come resplendently through a poet, not analytically through an accountant.

In 1821 Shelley was stirred, as Byron was, by an actual political upheaval. After centuries of abject silence the Greeks rose against the Turks. No event could have been better fitted to excite the author of *Prometheus Unbound*. Devouring such reports as he could get from the papers, Shelley composed another drama, *Hellas*. Like *Prometheus* it is a reminiscence of Aeschylus, who saluted the Greek victory at Salamis in *The Persians*. As in Aeschylus, the action takes place at the tyrant's court and the Greek warriors are offstage. The battles have to be orthodox battles, with no hint of trusting to non-violence or moral power. But a mystic reveals to the Sultan that superhuman forces out of the past are at work, as Shelley meant to make clearer in a prologue, which he never finished.

The idealized Greek patriots are, in the world context, Shelley's 'faithful remnant'. Ancient Greece was the cradle of Liberty, and gave substance to the Prometheus myth by civilizing mankind. Christ himself, we are informed in the prologue, was a Platonist. The light was trampled out, yet the loss was not final. In 1821 the Greek rebels are renewing immortal Hellas after the long eclipse, and rekindling hope for every nation.

Aware, at the moment of writing, that the outcome remains doubtful, Shelley concludes his play by shifting on to another level. Even if the Greeks lose, their valour is a revelation of Hellas, henceforth built on a rock that 'frowns above the idle foam of Time'. In the last chorus, after the triumphant cry 'Greece, which was dead, is arisen', we have the famous verses that moved H. G. Wells and Bertrand Russell:

> The world's great age begins anew,
>   The golden years return,
> The earth doth like a snake renew
>   Her winter weeds outworn:
> Heaven smiles, and faiths and empires gleam,
> Like wrecks of a dissolving dream . . .
>
> Another Athens shall arise,
>   And to remoter time
> Bequeath, like sunset to the skies,
>   The splendour of its prime;
> And leave, if nought so bright may live,
> All earth can take or Heaven can give.

This rebirth has more than a parallelism of form with those we have already reviewed. A few lines later we are back among the Titans, and in the presence of the great slumberer himself, waking up (as he never does in classical myth) like Albion.

> Saturn and Love their long repose
>   Shall burst, more bright and good
> Than all who fell, than One who rose,
>   Than many unsubdued:
> Not gold, not blood, their altar dowers,
> But votive tears and symbol flowers.

'All who fell' are the pagan gods supplanted by Christ; 'One who rose' is Christ himself, whom Shelley places lower than Blake does; 'many unsubdued' are the gods outside the Hellenic sphere of influence, who will yield to the restored Titans. 'Love' was mentioned in *Prometheus* as prior to the Olympian gods; Shelley must mean Aphrodite, who, in the earliest myths, does antedate them. But he sees her as more than a patroness of sex. She stands for the single archetypal Love, of which the loves of fallen mankind, sacred and profane, are no more than shadows.

Shelley's England did not revolt, though he exhorted it to do so. He saw his own country much as Blake did, and denounced much the same things. War, capitalism, factories, the educational system, the approved sexual ethic, the Established Church – all are blights. Only once, but most memorably, Shelley was moved to translate his general outlook into a full-scale poetic appeal to Englishmen.

In 1819 a peaceful assembly of Manchester working people, protesting at hunger and unemployment, was attacked by mounted yeomanry. About a dozen were killed, and hundreds hurt, in what is known to history as the Peterloo Massacre. The Government went on to pass the repressive Six Acts as a check to further demonstrations. Shelley, in Italy, poured out a long, indignant and astonishing poem, *The Mask of Anarchy*. It calls for a revolution which has nothing to do with 'progress', but is to revive the spirit of an older and better England. The workers have been dispossessed of their birthright. They must regain it by moral heroism, raising them above the everyday level: heroism leading to non-violent direct action and martyrdom, till the evil has spent itself against them, and its agents surrender or are converted.

> Men of England, heirs of Glory,
> Heroes of unwritten story,
> Nurslings of one mighty Mother,
> Hopes of her, and one another;
>
> Rise like Lions after slumber
> In unvanquishable number,
> Shake your chains to earth like dew
> Which in sleep had fallen on you –
> Ye are many – they are few . . .
>
> Let a vast assembly be,
> And with great solemnity
> Declare with measured words that ye
> Are, as God has made ye, free . . .
>
> Let the tyrants pour around
> With a quick and startling sound,

Like the loosening of a sea,
Troops of armed emblazonry . . .

Stand ye calm and resolute,
Like a forest close and mute,
With folded arms and looks which are
Weapons of unvanquished war,

And let Panic, who outspeeds
The career of armèd steeds
Pass, a disregarded shade
Through your phalanx undismayed.

Let the laws of your own land,
Good or ill, between ye stand
Hand to hand, and foot to foot,
Arbiters of the dispute.

The old laws of England – they
Whose reverend heads with age are gray,
Children of a wiser day;
And whose solemn voice must be
Thine own echo – Liberty! . . .

And if then the tyrants dare
Let them ride among you there,
Slash, and stab, and maim, and hew, –
What they like, that let them do.

With folded arms and steady eyes,
And little fear, and less surprise,
Look upon them as they slay
Till their rage has died away.

Then they will return with shame
To the place from which they came,
And the blood thus shed will speak
In hot blushes on their cheek . . .

And that slaughter to the Nation
Shall steam up like inspiration,
Eloquent, oracular;
A volcano heard afar.

The Dissentient Radicals

It would be unwise to collect Shelley's revolutionary writings and squeeze a doctrine out of them. They are not systematic and they are not even quite consistent. Thus he has several golden ages, variously placed and dated according to subject-matter. If the good life was at least possible in Athens, or in the vague Merrie England of the 'old laws', then the catastrophe of losing Prometheus's golden age seems less decisive. One of the *Hellas* choruses traces the spirit of Liberty through the centuries, mounting a series of local counter-attacks against encroaching evil. Each creates an enclave of partial recovery, but never for long. This fits the Greek and kindred flowerings into the larger scheme, but also makes it more complicated.

There is no doubt, however, as to Shelley's attitude. The motif of a human fall, and a counter-attack via spiritual regeneration, is central. He has several of the Blakean corollaries – the stress on poetic imagination, for instance, and on martyrdom, and on shedding the mortal worm's fear of death. The thing that never takes shape in Shelley is the constructive work, the building of Jerusalem. His exalted English rebels are to take direct action by confronting authority. But, however exalted, they cannot be doing this all the time. Shelley's appeal leaves them almost in the dark as to how they can begin re-creating England themselves. His major step beyond Blake was to greet the new industrial masses as a source of hope; he did not live long enough to carry this idea further.

3

Shelley's own talent for 'unacknowledged legislation' is proved by the careers of a number of his readers. One of them was Robert Owen, sometimes regarded as the father of Socialism. Owen supplied what Shelley did not, a constructive programme for forming a new society within the old. But his peculiar interest extends much further than that. He was utterly unlike Shelley and Blake, a successful factory manager, a most un-visionary person. Yet the social theory which he invented – and spent his fortune testing – shows several of the main features of the poets' Dissentient Radicalism. It could be adapted and fitted into Blake's system more readily than into the political Socialism which has claimed to annex it. The word 'Socialism' was coined by followers of Owen; the shift in its meaning is seldom noticed.

Born in 1771, the son of a saddler, he was a self-made man – one of those who were quick to grasp the potentialities of the new machines, and rose to wealth and power amazingly young. If the poets give an impression that their ideas are the fancies of impractical dreamers, Owen should dispel it. As chief executive of the mill at New Lanark, he was an immensely efficient pioneer of enlightened self-interest.

His work force was recruited largely from deracinated crofters. In general they were resentful, dirty, drunken, thievish, and irresponsible. Most employers would have treated them as riff-raff. Owen did not. He provided decent living quarters, proper drainage, an honest company store, a school and a nursery. He improved standards of conduct on the job by a scheme of merit-rating. Paternal as his attitude was, it was far ahead of the brutal indifference of his competitors. It paid in human terms; it paid even in money terms. New Lanark acquired a stability that carried it through the savage ups and downs of early capitalism with unusual smoothness. The mill became a show place, admired, though seldom imitated, by visitors from all over Europe.

An employer like this was rare enough. One who reflected on the results was rarer still. Owen (unlike Blake) welcomed the advent of the machine age. But he knew that under the *laissez-faire* economics which the machine-owners favoured, it was serving the interests of a few only, and impoverishing and degrading a far greater number. The problem that engrossed him was how to harness technology for the common welfare.

His New Lanark experience led him to suggest 'co-operation', then an unfamiliar word, instead of individualism. At first he thought of this as arranged from above by a benevolent oligarchy. He proposed a national programme for checking the anarchic growth of industrial towns, and substituting planned 'villages of co-operation', with a healthy balance between industry and agriculture, and proper amenities.

He managed to enlist a fair-sized body of influential support, including a royal duke and several bishops. But he lost a great deal of it in 1817 by publicly blaming religion for society's failure to solve its problems. His speech was not a sudden outburst. For some years he had been working at a highly subversive theory based on his own success in improving human material. In a pamphlet entitled *A New View of Society* he had already propounded it.

Man, Owen announces, has the power to solve his problems . . . but not as he is now. He has been rendered incapable by the great lie of religion: that each person is responsible for what he is and does. On the contrary, character is made *for* people, not *by* them. They are formed by their circumstances. The result of the lie in Owen's England was, in his view, a vicious spiral. Employers forced people to work and live in conditions which made them poor, ignorant, dishonest, and so forth. While these conditions prevailed, the victims could never improve themselves or master their environment. The employer, for his part, was conditioned to be a heartless profiteer. Furthermore he could always refuse to do anything for the workers, and rationalize his refusal, because the Church assured him that their shortcomings and poverty were their own fault, and it would be futile trying to make them other than they were. As their proved superior he had every right to exploit them; if he was at the top, he deserved to be there. Many of the workers, as good Christians, acquiesced.

Owen had caught a glimpse of Urizen, with his 'laws of moral virtue' which, in practice, no one can keep. Owen's remedy was to alter the social structure. He believed in an original sanity of human nature, though he was too down-to-earth to speculate about golden ages. The first step was, as with Blake and Shelley, a kind of conversion. Human beings must break free from the conditioning of thousands of years of priestcraft, and turn their moral world upside down, or rather right side up. The next step, logically following from the first, was to make a fresh start. Those who had embraced the truth must set to work creating different communities, different factories, different schools, where they could perfect their own inner reconstruction and enable others to pursue theirs. In the new society people would recover full human stature, and learn to control their destiny.

After several disillusionments Owen gave up hope of remodelling society from above. Through friendly MP's he sponsored the first Factory Act in 1819, but it was a toothless measure with no value except as a precedent, and he showed little interest in the more effective Acts that came later. In 1825 he withdrew from New Lanark with £50,000 and launched a social experiment himself.

It took the form of a model community in America, a forerunner of the swarm of mini-Utopias that dotted the United States during the nineteenth century. New Harmony, Indiana, was to demonstrate mankind in the making. Owen bought 30,000 acres and assembled a party of colonists. His faith in his own theory, however, was excessive. Confident that a co-operatively run settlement would turn all the settlers into co-operators, he took every applicant who came. Within three years New Harmony was a discord. Something of the founder's spirit survived to create other communities elsewhere. Owen himself, however, returned to England, still well-off by the standards of the day, but much less so.

On reaching home he discovered a new field for experiment. The working class was learning to organize. Some of its more thoughtful members were taking up his ideas. Owen threw himself into the struggles of labour. From 1832 to '34 he was the workers' leader so far as anyone was. He advised them to by-pass the capitalists entirely and build their own economic system, based on association instead of individual ownership. They should start their own co-operative stores, self-governing workshops, and builders' guilds. A federation of trade unions would give the movement cohesion and strength. In due course the superior power of co-operation would squeeze the capitalists out.

The Owenites did get as far as launching a co-operative store in London, and a builders' guild, which managed a little actual building. But in 1834 the Government struck at unionism. After the Tolpuddle martyrdoms the back of the movement was broken and resolution crumbled. Working-class militants saw no hope until they could exert pressure on governments as their masters did. They swung over to Chartism and political action. Owenism petered out. The Rochdale pioneers of consumer co-operation were Owenites, but their programme was a poor ghost of Owen's. In Disraeli's novel *Sybil*, written in 1845, the Owenite diehard among the working-class characters is a lonely figure whom nobody listens to. The activists around him are political radicals who foreshadow the Liberal and Labour reformers of the next hundred years.

Owen drifted away into crankishness, and lived on till 1858, writing and talking to the last. His final phase is usually dismissed as a dotage. After the poets, however, it is interesting to see the form his crankishness took. It became apocalyptic. In the absence of constructive projects, he laid more stress on the basic conversion. He imagined that it could happen widely and suddenly, and for

Blake's reason: that the error was becoming so starkly plain as to make a reaction certain. Also he looked for aid from sources outside the blinded generation around him. Having been a pioneer of enlightened management, co-operation, educational reform, Secularism and Socialism, he ended as a pioneer of Spiritualism. Shelley, Thomas Jefferson and the Duke of Kent came to him at seances with comforting words. The living, still hamstrung by religion, had proved inadequate; so the dead, who knew better, were returning to supply the lack. It does not appear that he ever raised King Arthur.

4

It was the Chartist stream that swelled into the river of orthodox radical politics. In 1884 the Fabian Society was founded, to pursue what its members called Socialism by constitutional methods and Acts of Parliament. Out of this, after various contortions, the programme of the Labour Party emerged. But during the 1880s and '90s, while Fabianism was growing under the aegis of the Webbs and Shaw, there was a surge of intellectual unrest that took a different line. Some of its leaders were half in, half out of Fabianism, but they tended to be more and more out.

This almost forgotten ferment was hardly a movement. It splintered in all directions. Yet its effects were considerable. The common feature was a questioning of the whole way of life and conception of Man upheld by the Victorian Establishment. Most of the Fabians who persevered in their Fabianism were, by and large, respectable. The heretics were much less so. Instead of studying administrative reform, they insisted on querying more fundamental matters: religion, sex, food.

On the first of these issues, some were agnostics or freethinkers on the model of Charles Bradlaugh; others sought new religions, especially eastern ones – often under the influence of Edwin Arnold, author of *The Light of Asia*. The most famous, Annie Besant, not only moved away from early Fabianism but went through both the other phases, ending as high-priestess of Theosophy. On the second issue, sex, some favoured free love as Shelley had done, some a Tolstoyan neo-puritanism, some a more lenient view of deviation; their common enemy was Victorian marriage. Havelock Ellis had his beginnings here. On the third issue, food, this was the heyday of diet theories and, in particular, vegetarianism, which involved the Shelleyan claim that Man had degenerated because of bad eating habits. 'Nature Cure' systems, and a distrust of orthodox medicine, often went with it.

From a distance of eighty-odd years this flurry has a faddish look; its importance lies chiefly in the eminence of some of the people whom it set thinking. But in view of what several of them afterwards did, it is worth recalling the man who was the head of the school, so far as it had one: Edward Carpenter, the apostle of the Simple Life. In 1888 he read a controversial paper to the Fabians. The following year, under heavy fire, he published it with further material under the title *Civilization : its Cause and Cure*.

Carpenter, a mathematician and science teacher, had reacted against the physical sciences and turned to anthropology. It led him to literal belief in a past golden age – an age of healthy savagery, when Man was 'whole'. Civilization, he said, does bring progress, but at the price of inner disorganization. It is a phase to be outgrown. Man must not retreat from it, but he must push on past it. Human nature must recover its lost integrity. Simplicity must return on a higher plane.

The dream of a world 'reconverted into Paradise' was also affirmed by such diet-theorists as Anna Kingsford, a woman doctor whose career remains a classic case-history of the *mélange* of vegetarianism, Theosophy, and offbeat apocalypticism which swept over a section of the English intelligentsia. Some were less offbeat than others, and more disposed to discuss practical politics; though even these leaned toward voluntary communism and non-violence – it was the day of William Morris, whose *News from Nowhere* appeared in 1891. Often they were catalytic to a degree now seldom realized. Such was Henry Stephens Salt, founder of the Humanitarian League, who held regular open house at a vegetarian restaurant, and to whom Shaw and other notables always acknowledged a debt, even if they went the Fabian way.

Shelley was adoringly read in these circles, and Henry Salt was an authority on him, yet the trend was far more than a mere muddled discipleship of Shelley. Heterodox radicals thinking for themselves arrived, not at the same ideas, but at essentially the same pattern; and they moved on, not into a common philosophy, but into variations on the old theme. This Dissentient Radicalism of the Eighties and Nineties never cohered at all. Its leading figures drifted apart.

5

Among their audience were some who launched movements of their own. One who was largely formed in this milieu, who revolted against it into an amused love-hate, yet who re-created the pattern in still another guise, was Gilbert Keith Chesterton. Himself a poet and artist besides much else, he wrote a book on Blake, and admired Shelley. But the book was imperceptive and the admiration was tempered. 'G.K.C.' was more deeply influenced by another favourite author of the Carpenter school, Walt Whitman; mainly as the voice of a direct, buoyant vision of reality.

Chesterton was a revolutionary who decided that the Left was not going his way. Like Blake he disliked generalizations and abstractions. He was ardent for discrete things in themselves, 'minute particulars'. But progressive thinkers, such as the Fabians, seemed to him to fuse everything together into a shapeless grey mass that supposedly 'evolved'. Furthermore most of them had little real use for liberty, and cut away the ground for belief in it. Chesterton challenged the term 'freethought', current among the agnostics of the Left. Far from making the mind free, he argued, it shut it up in a prison cell of determinism, and forbade it to admit anything which science could not demonstrate. Chesterton did not use the Blakean word Ulro, but he defined that state for himself. As for the alleged forward evolution of society, he could not see that this was the tendency at all.

How then could a revolution come, how could Man be set free? In *Orthodoxy*, a defence of what he regarded as Christianity, Chesterton gave the first instalment of his answer. Society can only be changed by something distinct from it, a powerful agency which is above it and not 'evolving', at any rate in the same sense. That means a rebirth of the true Church.

More and more Chesterton came to believe in what Hindus call *maya*, the covering of illusion that hides reality, Shelley's 'painted veil'. Chesterton located it in the eye of the beholder. Man does not see, because, conditioned by the accumulation of habits, he is unable to see. The remedy lies in absolute freshness, a kind of innocence, that will open his eyes to his actual state. In a novel,

Manalive, Chesterton has a character whose life is changed by a journey round the world, because he comes back to his own country from the opposite side and sees it as he would a new one.

Much of Chesterton's early wildness of style, his fantastic humour and love of paradox, reflect his desire to startle the reader into seeing things without the myopia due to a conditioned response. The dull mental atmosphere of the time, the cruel and deadening civilization that went with it, blinded Man to the world. As Blake had said, vision must be restored. Again Chesterton turned toward Christianity. With examples such as St Francis in mind, he argued that the man who regards all things as made by God can see them more truly than the would-be objective scientist, and live with them more wisely and richly.

For some years Chesterton was active in Liberal politics and journalism. His mentors were his brother Cecil and Hilaire Belloc, who entered the Commons as a Liberal in 1906 and withdrew, embittered, in 1910. Belloc wrote *The Servile State*, an attack on parliamentary Leftism, and (with Cecil Chesterton) *The Party System*, an attack on Parliament itself. We might construe both as footnotes to the public career of Urizen. The Fabian approach, in Belloc's view, could lead only to a bureaucracy – whether called Socialist or not – with the same class on top. Everybody else would be planned and classified, cut down and coerced, in the name of welfare. Moreover, the whole scheme was bound up with large-scale capitalism, the British Empire, the fetish of bigger and bigger units. It would squeeze the individual into nonentity.

G.K.C. agreed. He dropped politics and began considering direct action as the correlative of direct vision. Instinctively he had always favoured direct action anyhow. Another of his novels, *The Napoleon of Notting Hill*, is a prophetic comedy championing the small unit against the big one, Notting Hill against London, and extolling the spiritual magic of engaging in a struggle yourself instead of merely campaigning and wire-pulling. Chesterton became convinced that the only retort to the advancing Servile State was private property – small property in many hands, with as many citizens as possible controlling their own fate – and that the only real revolution would be a devolution. As Socialists said, the giant capitalist and the slum landlord must go; but the State must not replace them. Liberty must mean small capitalists, householders owning their homes, little farms, a balanced economy. The worst of the evil was recent. It must not be encouraged to 'evolve', it must be done away with.

This colossal task presupposed human beings restored to vision and spiritual grandeur. Chesterton's version of the recurrent theme, converging with many other interests and thoughts, led him to a somewhat personal Catholicism. He was received into the Church in 1922 and loyally contended for Rome ever afterwards. He described his conversion in a sonnet as 'one moment when I bowed my head, And the whole world turned over and came upright': an echo of Robert Owen, ironically for both of them.

His mature radicalism was bound up with his religion. The Church was the one credible icebreaker, the one power that could lift Man out of delusion and deadlock, and form the apostles of a renovated social order. But it was also the key to an actual English golden age, and to the problem of getting England right again. Like Shelley, Chesterton admitted more golden ages than one, and as a Christian he saw their archetype in Eden; but in English history he looked to the thirteenth and fourteenth centuries.

Although he often wrote with wishful inaccuracy, Chesterton never deluded himself into fancying that medieval life was happy. He was less naïve on that score than the Socialist Morris, or William Cobbett. In *A Short History of England* he conjectured that medieval life could have become happy if the Peasants' Revolt had succeeded . . . but it didn't. However, medieval England did have the potentiality for going right; it had the Faith, and certain attitudes, and certain institutions (guilds, for instance) putting them into practice. Medieval England was wrecked by plutocracy in alliance with Protestantism. The enclosures of common land, and the confiscation of the monastic wealth, created huge private fortunes and an army of uprooted peasants as cheap labour. The Industrial Revolution was simply a second dose. It was time to reverse the process.

Faced with the fact that the Catholic Church did not look very radical, Chesterton singled out such special pronouncements as Leo XIII's encyclical *Rerum Novarum*, which does advocate small property in many hands. But although he never said so outright, his own brand of Catholicism depended on the fact that England was not Catholic, had persecuted the minority loyal to Rome, and still harboured prejudice against them. Hence he could feel his chosen religion to be adventurous and even seditious. The Catholics in England, who had kept the Faith quietly and staunchly, became the faithful remnant with whom he could work.

They viewed him with mixed feelings. However, he worked. In 1926 he launched his equivalent of Owen's constructive programme with some Catholic aid. He called it (rather reluctantly) Distributism. It was offered as a third way, by-passing Capitalism and Socialism, and corresponding to natural human desires and to what was best in the Middle Ages. Attempts were made to realize the Chestertonian society – small property, back-to-the-land, grass-roots co-operation – in settlements and communities. In England these attempts petered out, like Owen's. Distributism had more effect across the Atlantic, but chiefly as a philosophy of self-help during the depression of the 1930s, as in the Antigonish movement of Nova Scotia.

In view of Chesterton's abysses of difference from Blake, it is intriguing how alike they are in their unlikeness, how a whole cluster of archetypes seems to take control of both. Chesterton too is a patriot who rejects the Empire, commercial greatness, and all the rest, and opts for a Little England. He too detests the calculating spirit, and the debasement and enslavement of Man by pseudo-science. He shares Blake's dislike of mystery as a tool of domination.

He is mystically fascinated by places, above all by London places. He is also fascinated by British mythology, though Glastonbury interests him more than Arthur. We have noted what he says about Albion, and his stress on that neglected yet vital concept of 'gods before the gods'. Even as a Catholic he pictures a Christ unusually close to *The Everlasting Gospel* – a strange, disturbing, unpredictable Christ, whom no ordinary rules will define; and his book containing this portrait is called *The Everlasting Man*.

Chesterton diverged most sharply from Blake and Shelley in his approval of violence. He preferred soldiers to pacifists, and his best long poems are about war. Still, in his final judgment the greatest of Englishmen was not a warrior but the pacific Thomas More, that wise and brave prophet who saw the corruption when it was taking hold, denounced it, and died for resisting it. Also, G.K.C. had an unconscious share in starting the greatest non-violent movement of all. It is a further symptom of recurrent patterns of thinking that he, of all people, gave a crucial push to Gandhi.

6

On 18 September 1909 the *Illustrated London News* carried an article by Chesterton on the demand for self-rule which some Indians were already voicing. His theme was that he would respect them if they would consent to be genuinely Indian. Western civilization, imposed on their country by the English, might well be a blight. What troubled him was that the nationalists did not want to get rid of the blight and go their own way; they wanted to plunge further into civilization, to ape England and call it freedom.

> When young Indians talk of independence for India, I get a feeling that they do not understand what they are talking about. I admit that they who demand *swarajya* are fine fellows; most young idealists are fine fellows. I do not doubt that many of our officials are stupid and oppressive. Most of such officials are stupid and oppressive. But when I see the actual papers and know the views of Indian nationalists, I get bored and feel dubious about them. What they want is not very Indian and not very national. They talk about Herbert Spencer's philosophy and other similar matters. What is the good of the Indian national spirit if they cannot protect themselves from Herbert Spencer? . . . One of their papers is called *The Indian Sociologist*. Do the Indian youths want to pollute their ancient villages and poison their kindly homes by introducing Spencer's philosophy into them?

As it happened, Gandhi was in England, on a mission for his compatriots in South Africa. The article burst on him like a revelation. He made a Gujarati translation and sent it to the paper he was editing. On the voyage back to South Africa he poured out the pamphlet *Hind Swaraj* sketching the new kind of nationalism which he was to preach, with only slight modifications, to the end of his days.

It horrified Indian politicians, but gave him unequalled strength with the masses. As we saw, he found his Chestertonian 'true India' far back in a legendary epoch of heroes and sages, god-given Vedas and village-communes, before the various conquerors had trampled down Hindu society. There he discovered his own social ideals. The true India still struggled on feebly in the villages, under millennial corruption. Modern civilization as imposed by the English was the last and blackest curse of all. The business of nationalism was to throw it off and reunite India to her ancient vocation.

Actually, it was not so very strange that Chesterton should have had a message for Gandhi. G.K.C. had never wholly turned away from the milieu of Edward Carpenter, Annie Besant, Edwin Arnold and the others; and it was in the same milieu that Gandhi had moved (timidly but thoughtfully) during his time as a law student in London. He testifies in his autobiography to the way this English circle brought his ideas into focus as his own people could not. Thus he did not believe in the Hindu doctrine of vegetarianism till he read a pamphlet by Henry Salt. His convictions about self-help and simplicity can be traced largely to the Simple Life teachings of Carpenter. He discovered his own religion through Edwin Arnold's translation of the *Bhagavad Gita*. The western authors who influenced him most, Tolstoy and Ruskin, were both favourites in the same circle.

What Gandhi did, in effect, was to pick up bits and pieces of Dissentient Radicalism in England, and transplant them to a soil where they could take root as expressions of a living culture. He applied the notions of a clique in one country to mobilize millions in another. The handicrafts, the non-violence, the critique of civilization, the anti-imperialism, the near-anarchist social ideal, the dietary theories, the distrust of medical science, the Gandhian version of Hinduism – all were being expounded in London during the 1890s. But whereas in London they became less and less effectual, more and more crankish, in India they could waken responsive chords and appear to reflect the suppressed national genius.

Gandhi considered that he had plunged back into formative depths, so to speak, and risen to the surface with the key in his hand. He declined the role of Mahatma and Messiah which the masses thrust upon him. Yet as a living legend, he came as near to being an equivalent of Arthur returned as any leader has ever been: the incarnation of the lost glory of a conquered people, come back to deliver them, haloed with epic imagery.

But he did not blame everything on foreigners. As the years passed, he campaigned more and more passionately against the corruptions of Hinduism itself, above all against Untouchability, which condemned fifty million Hindus to a sub-human status and taught the others that it was virtuous to keep them there. Indians themselves had fallen, and their regeneration must come partly by recapturing the purer religion of the past. Gandhi sought his 'faithful remnant' in the villages, where (as the orientalist Max Müller had assured him) the glowing embers of ancient India could still be found. Among the villagers he pursued his main apostolate.

It is against the background of Dissentient Radicalism that we can now, in conclusion, take stock of the most famous thing about him – his non-violent technique of *Satyagraha*, otherwise 'Truth-Force' or 'Soul-Force'. He insisted that this was India's proper weapon and grew out of her own best traditions. The claim was dubious. Hinduism had always preached *Ahimsa* or non-violence, but only in the negative sense of not inflicting injury. Gandhi developed *Satyagraha* in South Africa, not India, and it was more Shelleyan than Hindu.

To equate it with random civil disobedience or anarchic disruption is a mistake. Gandhi said that, in a situation seen to be wrong, the *Satyagrahi* must seek a precise insight into the nature of the wrong. He must pierce the veils of illusion and propaganda, and achieve a direct apprehension of the Truth, the heart of the situation. Having defined the Wrong, and the Right that should replace it, he must affirm his insight in action. Thus in 1930, as a protest against the British salt monopoly, Gandhi exhorted Indians to boycott Government salt and make illegal, duty-free salt for themselves. If enough people go on doing this sort of thing, without violence of body or mind, and if they endure all the consequences long enough, their opponents will be converted; the mind of society will change; the Wrong will end in adjustment and mutual pardon.

In Gandhi's eyes this was a religious process. Non-violence was not simply a tactic. Truth in this context means Truth with a capital T, and Truth is God. The *Satyagrahi's* strength comes from a touch of the Absolute, and his divine insight is a kind of conversion in itself. Gandhi and his disciples saw the parallels with Shelley. They quoted *Prometheus Unbound* and *The Mask of Anarchy*, and they translated *The Mask of Anarchy* into something very like fact, walking unarmed toward armed police, and falling in waves without striking a blow.

Truth-Force had its positive aspect in the 'constructive programme' which Gandhi declared to be the key to success. He seriously tried to build Jerusalem, or its Indian counterpart, from the ground up. His campaigns for hand-spinning, hand-weaving, cottage industry, basic education in villages, the emancipation of women and Untouchables – all were aimed at re-creating the harmonious society which would embody Truth and the vocation of India. A Counter-Establishment was to grow up within the Raj and slowly displace it: an equivalent of Owen's co-operatives and Chesterton's Distributist land schemes. The fact that the programme crumbled after his death, surviving only in patches and fragments, does not refute his genius as the one Indian leader with an idea which could get the masses on the move.

Until about 1935 *Satyagraha* was effective in mobilizing Indians and training them in courage and self-reliance. Gandhi can also be credited with achieving a very real shift in British attitudes, the precondition of independence, though not the substance of it. But the fratricidal horrors of the last year of the Raj drove him to admit what Blake and others imply: that Man has been cut down and conditioned to a point where no technique will be enough. A profound inner regeneration was needed, and *Satyagraha*, though on the right track, had not produced one.

For most of his public career Gandhi had a boundless faith in ordinary people, a boundless respect for them, and an amazing gift for turning them into heroes and martyrs. But the magic of his personality was not unlimited. He realized at last that he had expected too much. As imperial power withdrew, the Indians who began slaughtering each other proved that they could be as violent as anyone else. The number who had absorbed Gandhi's lesson turned out to be tragically small.

He was not the man to despair utterly. One of the last problems which engaged him was how human beings could be made equal to the stern imperatives of Truth and Non-Violence. Experimentation in his own life had suggested various ideas. He had taken a vow of *Brahmacharya* or self-control, including sexual continence. In his autobiography he speaks of everyday sensual life as 'animal-like' and below full humanity. The self-controlled man, then, is not so much adding to humanity as re-entering it; and if enough men took the vow . . . ?

At the age of seventy-seven, when Gandhi undertook his lonely missions of pacification in riot zones, *Brahmacharya* was at the centre of his thoughts. If he could reduce himself to zero, God would 'possess' him and he would at last become adequate to his undertakings. He succeeded, and faced the resulting martyrdom, at the hands of a resentful fanatic, with perfect calm. His communion with what the religions call God did raise him above normal humanity; in whatever way that fact should be interpreted.

But he could not do the same for others, and the kind of conduct which made him magnificent made many of his followers merely priggish. In his musings on human shortcomings, he grasped a point which we have seen hovering in the background of mass action generally, and the reinstatement mystique in particular. At the heart of the problem, Gandhi realized, was the human attitude to death. Often he told his followers to stop being afraid of it. If Indians could break out of the prison of that fear, the revolution would be theirs. 'Life', he remarked, 'is perpetual triumph over the grave.' In his last years he was moving toward a position like Bernard Shaw's: that Man could be changed by the assurance of a much longer and healthier life.

He did not agree with Shaw in hoping for an evolutionary leap forward to a race of Neo-Methuselahs. He preferred to think that in the golden Vedic era men had been closer to full humanity than they were now. Hindu sacred writings hint at a longer natural lifespan. Gandhi argued that we only fail to attain this because of our vices and unhealthy habits. Putting the full span at 125 years, he half-seriously proposed to aim at it himself, and resumed study of the nature-cure theories which he had heard as a student in England.

It was no more than the groping of a good and disillusioned man. But we can now see it in relation to similar gropings, and do the same with the whole Gandhian movement. Even the remotest linkages persist strangely. Thus the dramatist Laurence Housman, one of Gandhi's warmest admirers, was also an Arthurian revivalist, deeply involved with the Glastonbury Festival of the 1920s.

Epilogue

The Return of Arthur

1

To recapitulate. When Welsh and Breton bards concocted their legendary King Arthur, between the sixth century and the twelfth, they were expressing what Gandhi was to express long afterwards, however differently: the unsubdued spirit of a race conquered by the English. The conscious process was fairly straightforward. As plenty of early triads show, Arthur belonged among the bards' equivalents of the 'gods before the gods' – the noble Britons, their own ancestors, who held Britain before the accursed Saxon came. That ever-receding epoch was the golden age of the Island. Arthur was its chief historical figure, the chief chastiser of the Saxon, the victor of Badon. Around him, therefore, the consoling legends gathered. He grew into a mighty prince embodying the soul of his people, the hero of many exploits which were not originally his.

A query overhung his death and place of burial. It was possible, therefore, to imagine him as still alive, doubtless through enchantment. Some day he would surely come back to aid the struggling remnant in the hills of the west. He would crush the Saxon and restore all the Island to the Britons.

But once this naïve Celtic Messiah had been invented, once the golden age had become linked with him, vast traditional and subconscious depths began yawning. The Christian myth-making of the British Isles was unlike that of the Continent. Because the Church had not suffered as much or as long under a pagan priesthood, the pagan gods were not always suppressed or changed out of recognition. They survived in story as kings or heroes, and with them survived a mythology of Otherworlds and ambiguous powers, such as the rest of Christendom usually preferred not to admit.

More has come down from Ireland than from Britain, but enough has come from Britain to show what happened.

The complete legendary Arthur was formed out of materials prior to his actual lifetime and to Christianity – some of them, perhaps, prior to the Celts' advent in Britain. The original lords of the golden age were Cronus's Titans. Themes from their world, of which Britain was sketchily a part, descended on Arthur's shoulders through such intermediaries as the god Bran and the sea-spirit Barinthus. When Geoffrey of Monmouth passed him on to the romancers, he was a composite thousands of years deep. Stonehenge had got into his legend, and so, probably, had some of the smaller monuments and natural features which bear his name now. He was sovereign of an ocean realm, and went on Otherworld quests by water.

His kingdom was not only glorious but tragically so, doomed to dissolution in his own reign like Cronus's; and he too departed westward. In Lyonesse he had a vestigial Atlantis which sank after his time. Fallen, he passed undying to an Elysian Atlantic isle where he lived on, or else to a cave where he slept through the centuries, again reproducing the fate of Cronus – that is, the British Cronus, whoever he was – in either event. His Avalon was a place of supernatural women. Their ancestry runs back, through the secret sea-realms of the Irish, to the age of the Great Goddess who was Cronus's consort. A medieval Italian fancy which placed his cavern under the crater of Etna was curiously sound. Etna was the home of the Cyclopes, who belonged to the Titan world.

Some day Arthur will wake up, or return from Avalon, and restore Britain's golden age. In his waking he is like the Atlantic giant in Brendan's voyage. As restorer of the golden age he is like the renascent Saturn, that possibly Druidic Titan, in Virgil.

When this unique figure had been put together – as he could not have been outside the countries of the insular Celts – he symbolized deeper, more universal yearnings than the daydream of a *revanche* which had occasioned him. The Plantagenet kings of England annexed him and claimed the Arthurian succession. Romancers on both sides of the Channel transformed him into a medieval sovereign with an order of chivalry. Their stories drew in more of the Celtic mythology, including the cryptic motifs behind the Grail. They disguised it, but seldom effaced its birthmarks. The hovering Camelot of romance is not to be definitely pinned down at Cadbury or anywhere else. But it is still the focus of a doomed golden age. At many removes, yet recognizably, King Arthur and his Knights of the Round Table are the Titans over again; as Blake darkly perceived. It is an odd irony, if no more, that some of the romancers made Arthur beget his own over-thrower Modred, as Cronus begot Zeus.

The Return, which meant less to the confident rulers of medieval England, dropped into partial abeyance for a while. Officially the grave at Glastonbury disposed of it. However, it went on flourishing as a popular belief, not only in Wales and Cornwall but in parts of England, where, as in Somerset, the Celtic element was strong. In the fifteenth century the French disasters and the Wars of the Roses helped to prompt Malory's resurrection of the Arthurian kingdom, as the model for a degenerate England. The Tudors found vitality enough in the Return to exploit it as propaganda; and their greatest narrative poet, Spenser, took it seriously enough in its Tudor version to place it at the centre of his principal work.

As we have seen, to note this conscious use of the motif is to open the door on a long vista of unconscious parallels. The pattern of the completed Arthur story may be called 'the British myth'. It expresses a way of looking at things which has moulded human behaviour many times, and swayed many minds seemingly lucid and well-informed: a compulsion to see society's unhappiness in terms of past glories followed by loss and corruption, but also to see a reinstatement as possible, and as the true path forward. Anthropology confirms what common sense might suggest, that human beings project the closing-in and extinction of their own lives, and the longing for rebirth and renewal, on to history; though with solid support from the actual collapse of many hopes. The prophets and champions of Israel, the Christian Reformers, Confucius and Rousseau and the rest – each saw the evil around as the darkening of an earlier noon, each offered a revolution that was a counter-thrust, a restoration, a turning back of the night. The ideas of Blake and other English radicals suggest further that the myth is essentially 'about' human nature, and that the only true rebirth would be a profound overhaul of Man.

Perhaps Arthur, last of the Titans, was able to be immortal and an earnest of resurrection because his roots were in a culture that actually had no fear of death, no sense of extinction. So Hesiod says when he describes the Cronian golden age; so the archaeology of the Goddess's realm may imply; and hints at the same mystery, lingering among the Celts, appear in what little we know of the Druids' lore, in the wonderful islands of the Irish, and – possibly – in the pre-Christian aspects of the Grail.

However the legendary Arthur acquired his magic, he did acquire it. He has lodged himself in countless imaginations with the whisper that death is not always death, that defeat is not always defeat, that there are buried treasures of the past which can be brought back to sunlight. Whether he casts his spell over a Tennyson grieving for his lost friend, or over a visitor to Cadbury enraptured by 'Arthurian' objects which ought to disappoint but do not, he is answering to the same need, in a universe of change and decay.

2

So far as Arthur's Return can have a precise meaning, I would say it is happening now: not so much because of the general revival of interest, as because of the form this is taking – a convergence of different kinds of interest, making him single (if complex) instead of multiple. Until recently, Arthurian literature was a special study; Britain's post-Roman history was another; dark-age archaeology was another; and so forth. The assorted specialists hardly even met or conversed. But lately they have begun doing so. The Cadbury project has played its part in this new intercommunication, which remains valid, whatever conclusions may be drawn as to Arthur's presence there. In 1969 the triennial Congress of the International Arthurian Society was held in Cardiff, and the assembled scholars went to Glastonbury and Cadbury. The notable point was not that they went, but that they had never gone, as a body, before. From this convergence among the experts, and the new Arthurian fiction and drama, a fresh coherence is coming.

Today we can at least begin to see the theme as a whole. In the 1950s there was still an 'Arthur of romance' and an 'Arthur of Welsh legend' and an 'Arthur of poetry' and a cloudy 'historical Arthur' – several wildly diverse figures whom hardly anybody, apart from a few suspect amateurs, cared much about fitting together. The Arthur of the 1970s approaches his fifteenth centenary as one person, an actual man enlarged into a perennial symbol.

And he is more than an academic construct. If we pursue the

issue he raises when thus grasped, he actually has the power to affect our thoughts on society, and therefore, perhaps, society itself in time. He forces us to think of the role of the mass mystique, and especially a certain kind of mystique, in human affairs. Orwell's bitter question is still vital. When rational, temperate progress seems so manifestly good, why will hardly anyone live for it when millions will live – and die – for a Hitler? From Orwell himself, and Camus and Koestler, we may accept the idea that loss of belief in immortality has something to do with this. Modern Man sees himself, more than ever, as in a plight, heading for gradual or rapid annihilation, and he clutches at hopes of fulfilment here and now. From the British myth, equally, we may infer that this sense of doom is crucial. But the myth takes us further. It helps us to see how the ideologies themselves, again and again, have been more than promises of a good time. The good time itself has the nature of a victory over decay and loss and the powers of destruction. The recurrent mystique defies death as Arthur does, and as mortals want to do.

So the comparatively cool humanist, like Orwell, is apt to be battling against the current. He can show that progress is no mirage, that it has happened and does happen, sometimes gradually, sometimes through a sudden upheaval. Yet in their hearts, people seldom feel this. Reforms are fought for and won, yet they seldom taste as they ought to. The reformers, however public-spirited, do not light a lasting fire, because human beings do not see the world in that way. Their own life – the elementary life of birth, food, shelter, sex, death – does not advance, it perishes. For more and more of them this has become a stark fact without softening; and the shape of society gives their sense of defeat all the confirmation it needs.

To look for a literal answer in the myth would be ill-advised. To look for aids to reflection in, say, Blake's version of it, is perhaps less so. Thus we can read Blake as implying that humanists, in the modern agnostic sense, have no answer which is likely to work. And very probably they have not. They defeat themselves by their own exclusions. The 'science' which they appeal to is on the level of what Blake calls Generation, if not Ulro – 'single vision and Newton's sleep'. The 'humanity' which they believe in is the humanity of the Blakean mortal worm; and the worm's mind is unlikely to be changed, except through persuasion that he can be more than a worm. Humanists, and the scientists they invoke, have been fairly successful in persuading him of the opposite: that he is (to alter the image) a naked ape with no personal future or self-transcendence. But he seldom responds with a generous dedication to the progress of his species. He is more liable to react into an excusable apathy, looking after Number One, playing it safe and passing the buck; or else into conduct offering instant fulfilment, however dubious – revolution, drugs, violence, mysticism, or hypertrophic sex.

In fighting such perversities the humanist starts with one hand tied behind his back. (Sometimes, it must be added with regret, his own Urizenic leanings tie the other hand too.) Ever since Rousseau supplanted Voltaire, the various forms of the rebirth mystique have won more rounds than they have lost in the battle for minds. That does not mean that they are true, or beneficial – any of them. Even those which are not plainly noxious may well end up, as Communism has done, in a Urizenic trap. Further, they tend to fly to extremes. The revolutionary dramatizes his way of looking at things. He builds up inflated images of the hostile and corrupting Establishment. He resorts to endless rationalizations, Marxist or otherwise, to prove that anything short of total revolution is totally futile. He conjures up phantasms of unspoilt humanity and past golden ages which are at best selective, at worst absurd and hateful, as in the original Black Muslim myth. The humanist will dispute these golden ages; he will produce historical facts to explode them; but the result will always be deadlock.

The real age of the Titans and the Great Goddess at least went to the heart of the matter if it banished the fear of death. Arthur, its apparent heir, embodies the yearned-for victory which is at the root of so much. He triumphs over death in his own person. The golden age which he stands for departs and returns as an extension of his undying self. Hence he anchors our thoughts firmly on what the trouble is. As the emblem of a mortal need, he can be summed up very simply as the man who was dead but wouldn't lie down.

The farthest we can go toward de-mystifying the attitude which human nature seems to aspire to might be this: 'Yes, the world closes in on us, Man goes down to defeat, great and good things can be lost and have been lost. Still there is *something* we can turn to; something through which we can triumph over decay and death, recover what is lost, and push on. It may lie dormant but it is there, and we can act in that faith.' To put it another way: an attitude which acknowledges the tragedy of the human condition, yet maintains defiance with a firmer basis than mere bravado.

Historically this attitude has been clearest in the long endurance of the Jews, the 'something' here being the divine blessing inherited from Abraham. It was also habitual with Gandhi, who insisted (and proved more than once) that while *Satyagraha* might seem to fail, it was capable of sudden and confounding recoveries. He said it drew strength from God, who took command at critical moments. Apart from such public instances, it is an attitude which has often nerved individual courage and inspired many adventures and forlorn hopes. Have we travelled such a long distance to end up with an idealistic cliché? Not quite. We have learnt to unpack the cliché and realize the vastness of its contents.

3

The mystique which we have seen operative in so many forms has led to undoubted good as well as the horrors and delusions bewailed by Orwell. Which is the right course – to combat the tendency to think and act thus; or to accept it and see if it can be kept benign?

The dilemma is genuine. I can conceive no formula for combining this attitude with humanism of the liberal-progressive sort. In the first place, the humanist will hardly admit the closing-in as a norm of history. He is not disposed to believe in golden ages, or great and good things in the past, now vanished. Except as an incidental the tragedy of loss cannot be fitted into his scheme of things. Therefore the counter-thrust cannot, either.

And he need not always have reason on his side. It is quite possible to picture a Dissentient Radicalism like Blake's or Chesterton's with no far-fetched mythology to weaken it. A person taking such a stand would allow that great and good things (or potentialities) have indeed been, to all appearances, lost. He would not reject everything in the past as obsolete and contemptible. He would consider what the great and good things are, what the accumulated evils are that have fought against them, how the good can be reinstated as a new point of departure. The result might well turn out to be thoroughly subversive. This kind of thinking would diverge from the usual habits of humanism by mistrusting all trends and systems, and aiming to renew society from its roots, probably with a Blakean stress on Man himself. The advice of Jean Jaurès already quoted – 'Take from the altars of the past the fire, not the ashes' – would make more sense to a person of this outlook than it does to most latter-day Socialists.

If the foregoing sounds merely speculative, we have only to turn back to the actual Dissentient Radicals to see how detailed their inferences were as to what was good and bad for England, and how much of a consensus there was among them. It would be interesting to try charting a new national course today on the basis of their values.

Beyond all this, however, there is a deeper split between the humanist (always using that term in its current sense) and anybody who stands in the Blakean succession. The posture of creative defiance has to be grounded on that 'something' – the reality, outside everyday existence, which the undying Arthur presumably symbolizes. Can it be defined? Is it God, either in himself, or in some agency such as a church? Is it a saving power embedded in human nature? Are such notions as the unquenchable spirit of a nation or race ever more than romantic verbiage?

Humanists would contend that the 'something' is illusory and the attitude therefore baseless. All versions of the mystique, however potent in practice, are in that case merely incantations and exorcisms against mortality. Certainly there is no easy definition of what the ground of defiance is if it is anything. Individual, spiritual immortality of the Christian type has only a very doubtful bearing here. What Blake dismissed as the 'allegoric heaven' is no retort to the fact of earthly extinction. Pie-in-the-sky, when widely believed in, may have preserved Christians from seeking more dangerous consolations. But this is a negative quality; and the readiness of Communists, with no faith in immortality, to die for the Cause, proves that such supreme moral strength does not depend on an afterlife.

Psychologically the most impressive case of defiance, the case to which the whole problem keeps leading back, is the indestructible life of Israel from the Bible onward, often against all rational expectation. The Hebraic power of self-resurrection does not come from a faith in personal immortality (which the Hebrews of the prophetic age had no clear notions about), or even from religion (since many of the most fervent Zionists were not, in the Jewish sense, religious at all). Rather, the strength is the strength of the community, of Israel as an undying collective person, in whom each member transcends his own petty existence. As one of the great rabbinic teachers put it, 'All the generations of Israel were present at Sinai.' Or as another said, speaking of the Passover ritual, 'Every Jew should feel that *he himself* was delivered from Egypt.'

This sacred solidarity of the whole people is a commonplace of Jewish teaching, and the world has seen how the conditioning can persist after the religion fades. But the Jewish case can be generalized. The person who takes part in the death-conquering collective act – the revolution, or whatever it is – often does so as one of a group. The act is the act of a social class or a racial minority or a church or a party. Hence that recurring idea of a faithful remnant, those few in a fallen society who have not bowed the knee to Baal. There is an impulse to look for a defiant handful, a potential quasi-Israel already in being, to join up with. In the group, the individual finds a greater life than his own; and this, frequently, is the 'something' he has faith in.

Humanists of an earlier vintage showed some awareness of the need. Comte proposed what looks, for a moment, like a reconciliation of the humanist outlook with the propensities that upset it. He preached a cult of Humanity itself, the immortal 'Great Being' of which we are all members. One must sadly confess that this has not worked, and shows no sign of working. Humanity is too big and vague. But even if it were smaller, the distressing truth is that the mystique requires an enemy, a death-force. Jewish identity has endured through thousands of years, partly because Jews have been persecuted. To be a black militant entails being anti-white. There must always, it seems, as in the Dead Sea Scrolls, be Sons of Light and Sons of Darkness; or at any rate, recognized powers of darkness. Gandhi said the British must not be hated, but he described the British Raj as satanic. Prometheus implies Zeus. Arthur implies the Saxons and Modred. We cannot be partisans for Humanity, only for sections of it.

This was the main weakness of Robert Owen. His enemy was abstract error. The fact – the stubborn and rather terrible fact – is that the co-operative life which he kept trying to plant on earth has flourished only in one place and under one set of circumstances: in the Zionist settlements of Palestine, the *kibbutzim*, instruments of a national vocation with beleaguering enemies around. To move mankind you must have a tangible cause and a tangible opposition. The result may be good, or atrocious.

But we are at last in sight of the ultimate question. People who today label themselves as humanists maintain that ordinary life, as each individual knows it, is all there is, and death is the end. But there are many ways of being concerned with human problems without thinking this; and a pervasive common factor – underlying, especially, the mystique we have been exploring – is the belief in a greater life, a transcendent life, which the individual can (so to speak) grow into and relate to himself. It may be the life of God, or the gods. It may be a collective life which is more real than the individual's: the life of a church, or race, or nation, or institution. There may be a linkage of souls through reincarnation, as taught by Theosophists; or a presence of the dead alongside the living, as taught by Spiritualists (including Owen in his old age). There may be a Blakean Great Eternity of which we are all citizens. There may be personal immortality; there may not.

Through this greater life, however conceived, human beings can face the encroaching forces of darkness and defy them, with a triumphant defiance which individual life gives no warrant for. It may itself undergo eclipse and apparent death, yet it comes back again like Arthur. Chesterton, in *The Everlasting Man*, laid eloquent stress on this attribute of the Catholic Church. Others may think of the spirit of a nation surviving conquest, or a trampled race surviving enslavement. Whatever it is, it must surely be pictured as a source of that spiritual regeneration called for by Blake and the other Dissentient Radicals.

But *is* there a greater life, a 'something', or not? Orwell caught a glimpse of this ultimate issue. Near the end of *Nineteen Eighty-Four*, his hero Winston Smith tells a Party inquisitor that the regime cannot last for ever. Anything so frightful must fail. The inquisitor asks why it should, what reason for hope the rebel has. Belief in God might be a reason; Orwell has seen, however, that this is not the only possible reason. Winston tries such retorts as 'the spirit of Man will defeat you', even 'Life will defeat you'. But he realizes that they will not stand up. As a twentieth-century man and a Party member, he has been taught that the mortal life of individuals is the only life. If so, there is nothing to base defiance on. 'God' and 'Man' are only words. The tyranny of the Party which controls every individual may perfectly well last for ever. The only adequate retort would be to invoke a life greater than that of individuals. Winston might do it in several ways, religious or otherwise, but he is powerless to bring logic or conviction to any. The Party meanwhile has its own ghastly version of the greater life, confined to its own committed membership, and against that, he is nothing.

The debate continues, or should continue. It is not a debate between agnostics and religious believers, but between Enclosers and Enlargers. It is a debate which has meaning, as theological debates, for the present, have not. The reality or otherwise of a greater life can be seriously discussed. It can even be investigated. If we consider the saints and martyrs and patriots, the artists and mystics and revolutionaries, who have believed in it in one form or another; if we study the record of movements embodying that belief – do we find that the humanist science which denies it can explain all the facts, psychological, historical, and, in the Shelleyan sense, poetic? And should it fail to do so, what are the implications of the residual mysteries?

If science succeeds and there are no mysteries, then the sooner such illusions are shed, the better. But their dismissal will leave the victorious humanist facing his old problem: how the 'mortal worms' in their billions can be brought to accept mortality, and care about an infinite vista of progress when their own lives are finite and unprogressive. The only obvious solution would be the science-fiction one, so curiously foreshadowed by Carlyle in his sketch of the French revolutionary mood. Science may conquer death physically and visibly, and create new human beings who can live as long as they choose in perfect health. Then perhaps the mystique will die itself, and humanism will have its way. It will have got rid of Arthur by turning everybody into an Arthur.

That is one solution. Another would be to establish a real ground for the mystique, a real greater life through which lesser lives can fulfil themselves, acknowledging the tragedy of their state but defying it; and then, having found what the reality is, to keep its influence benign. Whether this would mean inventing a religion, or re-stating a religion already existing, or devising a new philosophy or psychology, I will not now discuss. In any case the overcoming of darkness and death is the grand theme. To this the sleeper of Camelot can direct our thoughts, and, I believe, fruitfully.

Bibliographical Note

It will be clear that *Camelot and the Vision of Albion* is in part a reprise of several topics which have interested me personally, and which have turned out, when studied together, to converge. My own earlier books contain fuller discussions, with bibliographies too long to reproduce here. *The Quest for Arthur's Britain* (1968) reviews various aspects of King Arthur. More of the Cadbury story may be found in Leslie Alcock's annual excavation reports, published by the Society of Antiquaries of London from 1967 onward. Of other books by myself, *Land to the West* (1962) explores the Atlantic mythos. *The Land and the Book* (1965) deals with the background of Zionism. *Gandhi* (1968) surveys the career of the Mahatma.

The following works may be added, either because they are not in the bibliographies of the foregoing, or because there is special reason to draw attention to them. The list is highly selective, *ad hoc* and personal. I make no apology for the glaring absences from it.

1. For the early mythology and religion:
CAMPBELL, Joseph (ed.). *Man and Transformation.* 1964. This symposium includes an important paper by Mircea Eliade, several of whose books help to elucidate the mystique of renewal.

CLES-REDEN, Sibylle von. *The Realm of the Great Goddess.* 1961.

GRAVES, Robert. *The Greek Myths.* 2 vols. 1960, 1962.

LUCE, J. V. *The End of Atlantis.* 1969.

WILLETTS, R. F. *Cretan Cults and Festivals.* 1962.

2. For Celtic and Roman Britain:
BROMWICH, Rachel. *Trioedd Ynys Prydein.* 1961. The Welsh triads, with translation and very full notes.

221

CHADWICK, Nora K. *The Druids.* 1966.
FRERE, Sheppard. *Britannia.* 1967.
NEWSTEAD, Helaine. *Bran the Blessed in Arthurian Romance.* 1939.
PIGGOTT, Stuart. *The Druids.* 1968.

3. For the ideologies and the ideological figures (besides their own works):
BALFOUR, Michael. *The Kaiser and his Times.* 1964.
CAMUS, Albert. *The Rebel.* 1953.
CATLIN, George. *A History of the Political Philosophers.* 1950.
COHN, Norman. *The Pursuit of the Millennium.* 1970.
COLE, G. D. H. *The Life of Robert Owen.* 1930.
CREEL, H. G. *Confucius: the Man and the Myth.* 1951.
MALCOLM X. *The Autobiography of Malcolm X.* 1966.
REISCHAUER, Edwin O., and FAIRBANK, John K. *East Asia: the Great Tradition.* 1960.
RUSSELL, Bertrand. *A History of Western Philosophy.* 1948.
WILSON, Edmund. *To the Finland Station.* 1941.

4. For Blake:
BLOOM, Harold. *Blake's Apocalypse.* 1963.
DAMON, S. Foster. *William Blake: his Philosophy and Symbols.* 1924.
ERDMAN, David. *Blake: Prophet against Empire.* 1954.
FISHER, Peter F. *The Valley of Vision.* 1961.
FRYE, Northrop. *Fearful Symmetry.* 1947.
HUGHES, William R. *Jerusalem by William Blake.* 1964.
PERCIVAL, Milton O. *William Blake's Circle of Destiny.* 1938.
STARR, Nina Howell. 'The Lost World of Minnie Evans.' In *The Bennington Review,* Summer 1969.
TODD, Ruthven. *Tracks in the Snow.* 1946.
WILSON, Mona. *The Life of William Blake.* 1948.

Finally I would mention C. G. Jung's *Memories, Dreams, Reflections* (1967); Marghanita Laski's *Ecstasy* (1961), which gives an account of a recurrent psychological state described as 'adamic', that seems to go with Utopian visions; and the encyclopaedia *Man, Myth and Magic* (1970), edited by Richard Cavendish, which contains several relevant articles.

Index

Abraham, 121, 216
Achilles, 138
Acts of Pilate, The, 95
Adam Kadmon, Kabbalistic doctrine of, 169
Aeschylus, 29, 35, 188
 The Persians, 191
 Prometheus Unbound, 36
Africa, seeking golden age in past of, 132–3
Aidan, St, 82
Albion, 26, 46, 87, 147, 188, 189, 190, 192
 as a Titan, 35
 Blake on, 14, 24, 25, 35, 36–7, 51–2, 154, 155–6, 160, 168–70, 172, 175, 180
 first mention of, 25, 36
 Holinshed on, 36
 Patriarch of the Atlantic, 46, 52, 156, 170
 Spenser on, 36
Alcock, Leslie, 7, 76
Alkalai, Judah bèn, 124
Amesbury monastery, 95
Ancient Society, Lewis H. Morgan's, 118, 119
Anglo-Saxon Chronicle, 79
Annales Cambriae, 73
Annwn, realm of, 63, 88
Aphrodite, 26, 37
 Shelley's, 193
Ari Frode, 47
Aristotle, 25

Arnold, Edwin, 199, 206
Arthur, King, 52, 62, 72, 185, 213, 220
 as a Titan, 212, 215
 as projection of Albion, 38, 86, 87, 147, 170
 Blake on, 14, 15, 25
 burial place of, 1
 cave of, 4–5, 64
 Cronus myth attached to, 90–3, 105
 dates of, 6, 82
 historical facts, 73–4, 77–8, 80–2
 immortality of, 84–8, 210, 212, 217
 in Blake's *Jerusalem,* 172
 legend of magic cauldron and, 97–8
 mystique of transfiguration and, 134
 'northern' Arthur, 79
 potency of his legend, 141–2
 reincarnated in Henry VII, 103
 return of, 212, 213
 tomb of, 84–5
Arthur (Tudor), Prince, 104
Arthurian Literature in the Middle Ages, R. S. Loomis', 75, 97
Ascham, Roger, 142
Asia, Prometheus' consort, 188, 189, 190
Athene, 26
Athens, 31, 34
Atkinson, Prof. R. J. C., 23

223

Atlantic, named after Atlas, 28
Atlantis, 29–34, 39, 68, 105, 106, 155
  Britain as, 32, 33
  Crete as, 31–2
  defeated by Athens, 31
  inundation of, 31
  rulers of, 30
Atlas, 24, 26, 28, 29, 30, 34, 90
  equated with Albion, 37, 51, 52, 170
Augustine of Canterbury, St, 82
Augustine of Hippo, St, 179
Aurelius Ambrosius, King, 22, 23, 72, 73, 78
Auto-Emancipation, 124
Avalon, 1, 8, 12, 19, 63, 88, 98, 100, 181, 211
  site of, 90

Bacon, Francis, 163, 165, 173, 174, 175, 176, 191
Badon, Mt, battle of, 73, 79
  possible site, 81
Ball, John, 113
Bard, The, Thomas Gray's, 105, 170
Barinthus, 90, 211
Bedevere, Sir, 80
Belenus, 61–2
Belgae, the, 41
Belloc, Hilaire, 202
  The Party System, 202
  The Servile State, 202
Benin bronzes, 132
Bennington Review, The, 182n
Bentham, Jeremy, 117, 175
Besant, Annie, 199, 206
Beulah, Blake's, 158
Bhagavad Gita, 136, 206
Black Book of Carmarthen, 85
Blake, William, 46, 51–2, 78, 212
  admires Milton, 155

America, 154
Descriptive Catalogue, 151, 152, 169
Emanations of, 166–7
The Everlasting Gospel, 153, 178, 204
The French Revolution, 154
his Albion, 14, 24, 25, 35, 36–7, 51–2, 154, 155–6, 160, 168–70, 172, 175, 180
his Orc, 165
Jerusalem, 52, 156, 168, 171–4 177, 178, 188
The Marriage of Heaven and Hell, 154
Milton, 157
on Arthur and Albion, 14, 15, 24, 25, 60, 86, 91, 149–50, 152, 170, 180
on Christ in England, 157
on Man, 156–9
patriotism of, 175–6, 184
philosophy of, 152–3, 153–85
poetry of, 151, 152
'Satanic mills' of, 164
Songs of Experience, 152
Songs of Innocence, 152
Spectres of, 165–6
Vala or the Four Zoas, 156, 162, 163
Visions of the Daughters of Albion, 167
zoas of, 157, 158, 159
Boccaccio, 191
Book of Martyrs, Foxe's, 128
Bradlaugh, Charles, 199
Bran, 51, 68, 90, 100, 101, 211
  identified with Cronus, 92
  legend of, 65–7, 87, 88
Brave New World, Aldous Huxley's, 135, 137, 164
Brendan, St, 90, 101
  his voyage, 67–8, 99
Brennus, 51

Index

Britain,
  Albion-figure as god of, 37
  and Atlantis, 29, 32, 33
  as Hyperborean land, 32–3, 61
  barbarian invasions of, 59–60,
    71, 72, 73
  Celtic invasion of, 39–40, 41
  decline of Roman Britain, 56–60
  early geography of, 19–20
  early links with Mediterranean,
    33–4
  early man in, 21
  enters Iron Age, 39
  first called Albion, 25
  Geoffrey of Monmouth on, 35
  Malory's golden age of, 143
  Procopius on, 63
  Roman invasions and conquest,
    41
Brutus, King, 35
Burke, Edmund, 150
Butler, Samuel, 166
Byron, Lord, 191

Cadbury Castle, 1, 2
  as Camelot, 6–7, 74
  as Iron Age citadel, 41–3
  aspect of landscape from, 19
  captured by Vespasian, 41
  described, 2–3
  findings at, 21–2
  first excavation of, 5, 6
  first inhabited, 21
  human sacrifice in, 43
  King Arthur's Palace at, 77
  latest excavations of, 8, 9, 13,
    75–7
  Leland and Stukeley on, 4
  mint at, 5–6
  Roman finds at, 56
  start of recent dig, 7
  temple at, 57, 58, 59
  visitors to, 8
  wells at, 5

Cadwallader, 4, 103, 104
Cadwy, 4, 80
Calderon, 191
Caesar, Julius, 53
  invades Britain, 41
  on Druids, 44
Calvin, Jean, 126, 127
Calypso, 26, 47
Cam, river, 4, 5
Camelot, 1, 12, 169, 211
  Cadbury Castle as, 6–7, 74, 211–
    12
  location of, 70–71
Camelot Research Committee, 7
Camlann, battle of, 5, 73, 85, 88,
    90
Camus, Albert, 139, 214
Cantref, Lost, 20
Canute, King, 6
Cape Breton Island, 50
Cape Farewell, 50
Cape Wrath, 50
Carausius, 57
Carlyle, Thomas, 109, 112, 115,
    141, 220
Carpenter, Edward, 200, 206
  Civilization : its Cause and Cure,
    200
Carthaginians, the, 39
Caxton, William, 102, 103, 143
Celtic Researches, Edward Davies',
    154
Celts, the,
  Christianity of, 64, 82, 94–6, 97,
    210
  forts of, 39–40
  gods of, 61–3
  invade Britain, 39
  La Tène culture of, 40
  monks of, 96
  sack Rome, 40
  spread of, 40
Ceridwen, 62, 64
Chamberlain, Joseph, 124

225

Charlemagne, 84, 93, 129
Chartism, 198, 199
Chaucer, Geoffrey, 175, 191
Chesterton, Cecil, 202
  The Party System, 202
Chesterton, G. K., 8, 11, 15, 28, 201–4
  becomes a Catholic, 203
  The Everlasting Man, 204, 219
  Manalive, 202
  The Napoleon of Notting Hill, 202
  on Indian home rule, 205
  Orthodoxy, 201
  philosophy of, 201–2, 203
  politics of, 202
  A Short History of England, 9, 203
China, 110
Chou dynasty, 110
Chrétien de Troyes, 6, 70
  Conte du Graal, 98
Christ,
  Blake on, 168, 178
  Chesterton on, 204
  Shelley on, 192
Claudius, Emperor, 41
Clement of Alexandria, 155
Cnossus, 31
Coligny Calendar, 44
Collen, St, 61
Communist Manifesto, 117, 118
Communists, the, 181
Comte, Auguste, 218
Condorcet, Marquis de, 116
Confucius, 110–12, 120, 139, 212
  programme of, 111
  Tao and, 110
Constantine the Great, Emperor, 57
Constantine, King, 23, 62, 71–2
Cordelia, 61
Cox, J. Stevens, 6
Cretan Cults and Festivals, R. F. Willetts's, 49n

Crete, as Atlantis, 31–2
Cronus, 26–7, 29, 35, 49, 90, 91, 139, 211
  Dionysius of Halicarnassus on, 54
  exile of, 28
  god of slaves, 27, 188
  golden age of, 29, 34
  myths of his island of exile, 48, 51, 68
  ousted by Zeus, 27
Culhwch and Olwen, 83, 87
Custennin Gorneu (Constantine III), 62, 72
Cybele, 57
Cyclopes, the, 27
  their home in Etna, 211
Cymbeline, 13, 52, 104

Dante, 191
  Divine Comedy, 99
Darwin, Charles, 176
David, King, 122
David, St, 64, 96
Davies, Edward, 154
Davis Strait, 50
Death, ritual and, 137–8
Deluge, legends of the, 20
Demetrius, 48, 51, 52
De Riencourt, Amaury, 131
  The Soul of India, 132n
Deucalion, 26
Dicuil, 47
Diet theories, 200
Dio Chrysostom, 45
Diogenes Laertius, 45
Distributism, Chesterton's, 204
Dogger Bank, 20, 32
Don Quixote, 88
Donnelly, Ignatius, 31, 34
Dream of Prince Macsen, The, 62
Druids, 44–6, 161, 170
  as sages, 154–5
  belief in immortality of, 44–5

Druids–*cont.*
  Blake's, 173
  traditions of, 20, 139
Druids, The, Nora K. Chadwick's,
  45n
Dunstan, St, 95
Dunwich, 20
Durotriges, the, 3, 41
Dyfed, kingdom of, 73

Ecclesiasticus, 185
Eden, Blake's, 153, 162, 170, 180,
  181, 182, 183
Edward I, King, 85
Elen, 62, 64
Eliade, Mircea, 136
Elizabeth I, Queen, 104
Ellis, Havelock, 199
Elysium, 28, 34
Elmet, kingdom of, 73
Engels, Friedrich, 117
  *Origin of the Family, Private
  Property and the State,* 118,
  119
Epimetheus, 26, 29
Erasmus, 126, 127, 149
Ethelred the Unready, King, 5–6
Evans, Minnie, 182, 183

Fabian Society, 199, 201
Fazio degli Uberti, 70
Fisher King, the, 99, 100
Ford, Henry, 162
Frederick Barbarossa, 93
  legend of his immortality, 129
Frederick, Crown Prince of Prussia,
  130
Frederick the Great, 112
French Revolution, 109–10, 115,
  116
  and the Jews, 124
Freud, Sigmund, 158n

Galahad, Sir, 99

Gandhi, 10, 12, 130, 176, 210, 216,
  218
  compared to Arthur, 206
  condemns untouchability, 206
  considers civilization corrupting,
  132
  doctrine of non-violence, 207
  fights for Indian independence,
  131–2, 206–9
  Indian Home Rule (Hind Swaraj)
  pamphlet, 131, 205
  influenced by Chesterton, 204,
  205–6
  vow of self-control, 208–9
Gaul, 40
Generation, Blake's, 158, 162, 214
Genesis, 160
Geoffrey of Monmouth, 13–14, 25,
  27, 62, 71, 72, 78, 83, 85, 103,
  104, 143, 155
  his Avalon, 90
  History of the Kings of Britain,
  13, 35, 85, 86
  The Life of Merlin, 90
  on Stonehenge, 22–3
George V, King, 10
George VI, King, 10
Germany, the three reichs of, 129
Ghana, 133
Gibbon, Edward, 191
Gildas, 78, 82
Gilgamesh, 138, 139
Gladstone, William Ewart, 175
Glastonbury, 2, 9, 20, 106, 212
  Abbey, 11, 94
  as Avalon, 88–9, 94, 95
  as birthplace of United King-
  dom, 82–3
  Festival, 8, 209
  history of, 94–6
  lake villages of, 3, 6, 40–41
  monastery, 95
  monks at, 19, 82
  Old Church, 95

Glastonbury Tor, 1, 3, 19, 61
  citadel on, 95
Glooskap, 50
Goddess, the Great, 26, 33–4, 138, 139, 211, 215
Godney lake village, 40
Godwin, William, 117, 187, 188
Golden Bough, The, 159
Gordon, Aaron David, 125
Graves, Robert, 51, 92
Gray, St George, 6
Greek revolt against Turks, 191
Greenland, 50
Grey, Lord, 104
Guardian, The, 7
Guinevere, Queen, 81, 103, 143, 167
Gwyn ap Nudd, 61, 64, 87
Gwynedd, kingdom of, 73

Hadrian's Wall, 59
Hallam, Arthur, 144
Ham, son of Noah, 36
Harfield, Mrs Mary, 6, 75
Hawkins, Dr Gerald S., 24
Hebrew patriarchs, 27
Hecataeus of Abdera, 32, 33, 44, 45, 61
Hegel, Georg W. F., 117
Hengist and Horsa, 72
Henry II, King, and legend of Arthur's immortality, 84–5, 212
Henry VII, King, 105, 106
  put forward as Arthur's heir, 103–4, 212
Henry VIII, King, 127
Hercules, 35, 36
Herzl, Theodor, 121, 124, 125, 126
Hesiod, 34, 37, 46, 53, 138, 212
  Theogony, 28
  The Works and Days, 28–9
Hess, Moses, 117
Hinduism, 136, 137, 148
  new order in, 138

Hippolytus, 45
History of the Britons, Nennius', 74
Hitler, Adolf, 115, 135, 214
  his Operation Barbarossa, 130
  his Third Reich as successor to Charlemagne's empire, 129
Hobbes, Thomas, 113
Hogg, Thomas Jefferson, 171
Holinshed, Raphael,
  his Chronicle, 36
Holy Grail, 8, 94, 96, 97, 98–101, 105
  magic cauldron as predecessor, 97
Holy Thorn, 95
Homer, 10, 47, 138
Honorius of Autun, 98
Housman, Laurence, 8, 209
Hugo, Victor, 116
Humanism, rational, 135–6, 215, 216, 217
  lack of inspiration in, 135
Humanitarian League, 200
Hume, David, 191
Huxley, Aldous, 135, 184
Hyperboreans, 32, 45
Hyperion, 26
Hyperion, Keats', 188

Iapetus, 26, 27
Iceland, 49, 50
  identified as Thule, 47
Illtud, St, 54
Illustrated London News, 205
India,
  fights for independence, 130–31, 206–9
  National Congress, 130
International Arthurian Society, 1969 Congress of, 213
Iona, 67
Isaiah, 122–3, 127
Isidore, Bishop, 47

Index

Jacobins, the, 181
James I, King, 104
Japheth, 27, 36
Jaurès, Jean, 141, 217
Jefferson, Thomas, 116, 199
Jerusalem, Blake's, 168–9, 173, 175, 178
  as Albion's consort, 188, 189
Jews, the, 120–5, 126, 216, 217–18
Jordanes, 47
Joseph of Arimathea, 94, 95, 98, 100, 157, 161, 185
Joyce, James, 151
Jung, C. G., 120, 157, 158n
Jupiter, 189, 190

Kaiser and his Times, The, Michael Balfour's, 130n
Kalischer, Zvi Hirsch, 124
Kant, Immanuel, 178
Kay, Sir, 80
Ker-Is, lost city of, 20
Kibbutzim, success of, 125, 218–19
Kingsford, Anna, 200
Koestler, Arthur, 140, 214

Labrador, 50
Lagorio, Dr Valerie, 99–100
Lancelot, Sir, 103, 143
Lao Tzu, 111
Lear, King, 13, 61, 104
Leland, John,
  Itinerary, 4
  on Cadbury Castle, 4, 104
Lenin, 119, 120, 180
  The State and Revolution, 119
Lewis, C. S., 82
  His novel That Hideous Strength, 11
Light of Asia, The, Edwin Arnold's, 199
Llantwit Major monastery, 95
Locke, John, 113, 116, 163, 165, 173, 174, 175, 176, 183, 191

London, Blake on, 185
Los, the zoa, 159–60, 172, 174, 175, 181, 191
  as Hebrew prophets, 161
'Lost World of Minnie Evans, The', Nina Howell Starr's, 182n
Lucan,
  on Druids, 45
  Pharsalia, 45n
Luther, Martin, 126, 127, 149
  The Babylonish Captivity of the Church, 127
Luvah, the zoa, 159
Lydney, temple at, 58–9
Lyonesse, 20, 87, 211

Mabinogion, the, 20, 61, 62, 65
Macbeth, Lady, 167
McLuhan, Marshall, 151
Mael Duin, 67
Maelgwn of Gwynedd, 77
Maiden Castle, 42, 58, 59
Malo, St, 68
Malory, Sir Thomas, 7, 9, 71, 86, 88, 102, 103, 181, 186, 212
  and the Holy Grail, 100
  Morte d'Arthur, 102–3, 142–3
Malthus, T. R., 150
Man,
  Blake on, 156–9, 180, 181, 186
  death and, 138, 148
  needs rituals of rebirth, 137, 138
Man, Myth and Magic, 95n
Maponus (Mabon), 64, 87
  temples of, 61
Mark, King, 70, 143
Marseilles (Massilia), founding of, 39
Marx, Karl, 117
  Das Kapital, 117
Marxism, 117–19, 138, 215
  influenced by Rousseau, 118
Masada, 125

229

Matter of Britain, 8, 10–11, 102
Maximus (Macsen), 57, 64
  in British legend, 62, 87
Meare lake village, 40
Merlin, 22, 23, 86, 102, 167
Messiah, doctrine of the, 138
Michael Angelo, 191
Milton, John, 105, 175, 184, 191
  Areopagitica, 155
  History of Britain, 36
  Paradise Lost, 54
Minos of Crete, 28
Mithras, 57
Modred, 5, 73, 82, 91, 103, 105, 212
Moloch, 27
More, Sir Thomas, 126, 128, 204
Morgan, Lewis H., 118
Moses, 122
Mount's Bay, 20, 32
Müller, Max, 207
Mycenae, 26
  trades with Britain, 24

Napoleon, 116, 129, 165
Navigatio Sancti Brendani, 67
Nebuchadnezzar, 122
Nelson, Horatio, Viscount, 176
Nennius, 74
Neptune, 27, 36
Newfoundland, 50
New Harmony, Indiana, model community at, 197–8
News from Nowhere, William Morris's, 200
Newton, Isaac, 163, 165, 173, 174, 175, 176, 179, 183
Ninian, St, 54
Nodens, the god, 59, 61
North European coast, early geography of, 20
Nuadu of the Silver Hand, 59
Nudism, 171

Ocean, the Titan, 26

Ogygia, island of, 47, 48, 50
Once and Future King, The, T. H. White's, 71
Orwell, George, 140, 214, 216
  Nineteen Eighty-Four, 164, 219
  'Wells, Hitler and the World State', 135
Osiris, 57
Owen, Robert, 195–9, 218, 219
  as workers' leader, 198
  belief in 'co-operation', 196
  forms model community, 197–8
  New Lanark mill and, 196, 197
  A New View of Society, 196
  philosophy of, 197
  pioneer of Spiritualism, 199

Paine, Tom, 179
Palamedes, 70
Pandora, 29
Paracelsus, 153
Paris Commune, 118
Patrick, St, 59, 64, 95, 96
Perlesvaus, 101
Peterloo Massacre, 193
Petrarch, 191
Phoenicians, the, 39
Picts, the, 59, 72
Piggott, Prof. Stuart, 49
Pilgrim's Progress, The, John Bunyan's, 156, 158
Pinsker, Leo, 124
Plato,
  as Urizen, 162
  on Atlantis, 30–31, 32, 33, 34
  on islands beyond Atlantis, 46, 49–50
  Republic, 31
  Timaeus and *Critias,* 30, 31, 160
Pliny, 47
  Natural History, 90
Plutarch, 48, 50, 51, 54, 92
  'The Face in the Moon', 47
  'The Silence of Oracles', 48

Polyhistor, 45
Poseidon, 27
Procopius, 63, 89
Progress, Man's disbelief in, 137
Prometheus, 26
    Aeschylus on, 35, 188
    myth of, 29, 105
    Shelley's, 188–90
Protestantism, Arthur legend and,
    127–8
Pythagoras, 45
Pytheas, 25, 49
    voyages to Britain, 46–7

Queen Camel, 4
Quest for Arthur's Britain, The, 12
Questions of Bartholomew, The, 99
Quetzalcoatl, 92n

Radford, Dr C. A. Ralegh, 7, 84
Raphael, 191
Rashi, 121
Realm of the Great Goddess, The, S.
    von Cles-Reden's, 139n
Rebel, The, Albert Camus', 139
Reed, Trelawney Dayrell, 9
    *The Battle for Britain in the Fifth
    Century*, 9
Reformation, the, 126–8
Rerum Novarum, Leo XIII's, 203
Rhadamanthus, 28
Rhea, 26
    the Mother Goddess, 33–4
Richard III, King, 103
Risorgimento, the, 132
Robert de Borron, 98
Robespierre, M. M. J., 115
Roman Antiquities, Dionysius of
    Halicarnassus', 132n
Roman Church, 203
    Blake on, 178
    pre-Reformation corruption of,
    126–7
Rousseau, Jean-Jacques, 116, 120,

148, 179, 180, 188, 191, 212,
    215
    character of, 112–13
    Discourse on Inequality, 114
    philosophy of, 112–15
    The Social Contract, 114, 115
Russell, Bertrand, 114, 192

Saints – *see under proper names*
St Lawrence, Gulf of, 50
Salt, Henry Stephens, 200, 206
Samson, St, 64
Saturn, 26
    the planet, 35, 49
    Virgil on, 52–4, 211
Satyagraha, 207, 208, 216
Saxons, the, 59, 71, 72
    conquer Britain, 82, 105
Schliemann, Heinrich, 9–10
Scilly Isles, 20, 87
Shakespeare, William, 103, 104,
    175, 191
Shaw, George Bernard, 8, 140, 199,
    209
Shelley, Percy Bysshe, 187–95, 199
    concerned with Liberty, 187,
    188, 193, 195
    Defence of Poetry, 190–91
    Hellas, 191–2, 195
    Hymn to Intellectual Beauty, 190
    The Mask of Anarchy, 193–4, 207
    The Necessity of Atheism, 187
    Prometheus Unbound, 35, 188–9,
    191, 192, 207
    Queen Mab, 187–8
    stirred by Greek revolt, 191
Sidney, Sir Henry, 104
Sidney, Sir Philip, 104
Sinn Fein movement, 132
Socialism, 195
Solomon, King, 122
Solon, 30, 31
Solway Firth circle, 61
Somerset, origin of name, 19

South Cadbury, 3, 4
Spenser, Edmund, 92, 104, 134, 212
  Faerie Queene, 36, 128, 143
  portrays Tudors as Arthur's
    successors, 104, 143
Spoils of Annwn, The, 87, 90, 97
Stalin, Joseph, as Urizen, 162
Stoics, the, 53
Stonehenge, 22–4, 37, 154, 173
  not a Druid temple, 45
Strathclyde, kingdom of, 73
Stukeley, William, 4, 24, 45
Suetonius, 41
Sutton Montis, 3, 5
Swedenborg, Emanuel, 153
Sylla, Sextius, voyages described
  by, 47–9

Tagore, Rabindranath, 131
Taliesin, 62, 90
Talus, 49
Taoism, 111
Tennyson, Alfred, Lord, 9, 88,
  213
  Idylls of the King, 71, 144
  In Memoriam, 144
Tharmas, the zoa, 159
Theodosius, Emperor, 60
Theosophy, 199, 219
Thera, 31
Thorpe, Prof. W. H., F.R.S., 74
Thule, 47
Tilak, 131
Timbuktu, 133
Times, The, 74
Tir-nan-Og, 63
Titans, the, 24, 211
  Blake on, 154, 155
  Greek myth of, 26–9, 34, 35
  Keats on, 188
  no fear of death in period of, 138,
    215
  Shelley on, 188, 192
  world of the, 27

Transfiguration, Mystique of, 134–
  5
  anthropology and, 136–41
Triads, 83, 154
Trioedd Ynys Prydein, Rachel
  Bromwich's, 65n
Tristram, Sir, 87, 143
Troy, 10, 35
Tudor, Owen, 103
Tyndale, William, 127

Ulro, Blake's, 158, 162, 166, 180,
  183, 201, 214
Urizen, the zoa, 159, 160–5, 168,
  172, 177, 185, 197
  as Satan, 162
  as Zeus, 161
  Shelley's, 189
Uther Pendragon, King, 23, 72, 73
Utopias, failure of, 125, 197–8

Vespasian, Emperor, 41, 42
Villa, the Roman, 57–8
Virgil, 102, 105, 134, 150
  Aeneid, 53, 53n
  Eclogues, 53n
  legend of Saturn (Cronus) from,
    52–4, 109
Voltaire, 110, 112, 113, 179, 191,
  215
Vortigern, 71–2
Voyage of Bran, The, 65, 67

Waite, A. E., 101
Wales, 60
  Welsh triads, 83, 87, 88, 95
Wars of the Roses, 103, 142, 212
Waste Land, The, T. S. Eliot's, 99
Waterloo, battle of, 116
*Way to be Rich and Respectable,
  The*, Rev. John Trusler's, 151
Webb, Sidney and Beatrice, 140,
  175, 199
Weizmann, Chaim, 125, 126

Wells, H. G., 10, 135, 192
Weston, Jessie, 99
Wheeler, Sir Mortimer, 7, 159
Whitby, Synod of, 97
Whitman, Walt, 201
Wilhelm II, Kaiser, 130
William of Malmesbury, 85
Williams, Charles, 11, 99, 106, 109
Wordsworth, William, 116, 151, 183
   The Prelude, 116

Zen Buddhism, 148
Zeus, 26, 28, 29, 34, 35, 37
   advent of, 27
   equated with Indra, 37
   ousts Cronus, 27, 105
Zionism, 120–5, 126, 148
   promised land and, 120–1,
   122
Zoas, Blake's, 157, 158, 159,
   175